SCOTT FORESMAN · ADDISON WESLEY

Mathematics

Math Diagnosis and Intervention System

Booklet B

Basic Facts and Algebra Concepts in Grades K-3

Overview of Math Diagnosis and Intervention System

The system can be used in a variety of situations:

- **During school** Use the system for intervention on prerequisite skills at the beginning of the year, the beginning of a chapter, or the beginning of a lesson. Use for intervention during the chapter when more is needed beyond the resources already provided for the lesson.

- **After-school, Saturday-school, summer-school (intersession) programs** Use the system for intervention offered in special programs. The booklets are also available as workbooks.

The system provides resources for:

- **Assessment** For each of Grades K–6, a Diagnostic Test is provided that assesses that grade. Use a test at the start of the year for entry-level assessment or anytime during the year as a summative evaluation.

- **Diagnosis** An item analysis identifies areas where intervention is needed.

- **Intervention** Booklets A–M identify specific topics and assign a number to each topic, for example, A12 or E10. For each topic, there is a page of Intervention Practice and a two-page Intervention Lesson that cover the same content taught in a lesson of the program.

- **Monitoring** The Teaching Guide provides both Individual Record Forms and Class Record Forms to monitor student progress.

Editorial Offices: Glenview, Illinois • Parsippany, New Jersey • New York, New York

Sales Offices: Parsippany, New Jersey • Duluth, Georgia • Glenview, Illinois
Coppell, Texas • Ontario, California • Mesa, Arizona

ISBN: 0-328-07645-7

Table of Contents

		Intervention Lesson Pages	Intervention Practice Pages	The same content is taught in the Scott Foresman-Addison Wesley Mathematics Program			
Booklet B				Gr. K	Gr. 1	Gr. 2	Gr. 3
Addition and Subtraction: Basic Facts to 12							
B1	Readiness for Addition and Subtraction	1	183	Ch. 9			
B2	Understanding Addition	3	184	Ch. 10			
B3	Understanding Subtraction	5	185	Ch. 11			
B4	Joining Stories	7	186		2-1		
B5	Using Pictures to Add	9	187		2-2		
B6	Using Symbols to Add	11	188		2-3		
B7	Ways to Add	13	189		2-3		
B8	Adding with Zero	15	190		2-4		
B9	Adding Across and Down	17	191		2-5		
B10	Missing Parts	19	192		2-7		
B11	Using Pictures to Subtract	21	193		2-8		
B12	Using Symbols to Subtract	23	194		2-9		
B13	Zero in Subtraction	25	195		2-10		
B14	Subtracting Across and Down	27	196		2-11		
B15	Subtracting to Find How Many More	29	197		2-13, 2-14		
B16	Counting On 1 and 2	31	198		3-1		
B17	Counting On 1, 2, and 3	33	199		3-1		
B18	Adding in Any Order	35	200		3-2		
B19	Adding 1, 2, or 3	37	201		3-3		
B20	Counting On from the Greater Number	39	202		3-4		
B21	Adding Doubles	41	203		3-6		
B22	Using Doubles to Add	43	204		3-7		
B23	Sums of 10	45	205		3-8		
B24	Counting Back 1, 2, and 3	47	206		4-1		
B25	Counting Back	49	207		4-2		
B26	Using Doubles to Subtract	51	208		4-3		
B27	Relating Addition and Subtraction	53	209		4-5		
B28	Fact Families	55	210		4-6		
B29	Using Addition to Subtract	57	211		4-7		
Addition and Subtraction: Basic Facts to 20							
B30	Doubles to 20	59	212		11-1	2-2	
B31	Using Doubles to Add	61	213		11-2	2-3	
B32	Adding 10	63	214		11-3		
B33	Making 10 to Add 7, 8, and 9	65	215		11-4	2-6	
B34	Using Addition Strategies	67	216		11-5		
B35	Adding Three Numbers	69	217		11-6	1-8, 2-4	
B36	Relating Addition and Subtraction	71	218		11-8		
B37	Fact Families	73	219		11-9	1-10	
B38	Using Addition to Subtract	75	220		11-10		
B39	Using 10 to Subtract	77	221		11-11		
B40	Using Subtraction Strategies	79	222		11-12		
B41	Joining Groups to Add	81	223			1-1	
B42	Writing Addition Sentences	83	224			1-2	
B43	Taking Away to Subtract	85	225			1-4	
B44	Comparing to Find How Many More	87	226			1-5	
B45	Writing Subtraction Sentences	89	227			1-6	

Table of Contents continued

		Intervention Lesson Pages	Intervention Practice Pages	The same content is taught in the Scott Foresman-Addison Wesley Mathematics Program			
				Gr. K	Gr. 1	Gr. 2	Gr. 3
Booklet B							
B46	Ways to Make Ten	91	228			1-9	
B47	Missing Addends	93	229			1-11	
B48	Counting On	95	230			2-1	
B49	Making 10 to Add 9	97	231			2-5	
B50	Counting Back	99	232			2-8	
B51	Addition Properties	101	233			2-9, 2-10	2-1
B52	Relating Addition and Subtraction	103	234				2-2
B53	Find a Rule	105	235				2-3
Multiplication and Division Facts and Properties							
B54	Skip Counting Equal Groups	107	236			12-1	
B55	Addition and Multiplication	109	237			12-2	5-1
B56	Using Arrays	111	238			12-3	
B57	Multiplying in Any Order	113	239			12-4	
B58	Multiplying Across and Down	115	240			12-5	
B59	Modeling Division	117	241			12-7	
B60	Division with Remainders	119	242			12-7	
B61	Writing Division Sentences	121	243			12-8	
B62	Using Arrays	123	244				5-2
B63	Writing Multiplication Stories	125	245				5-3
B64	Multiplying by 2	127	246				5-5
B65	Multiplying by 5	129	247				5-6
B66	Multiplying by 10	131	248				5-7
B67	Multiplying by 1 or 0	133	249				5-9
B68	Multiplying by 9	135	250				5-10
B69	Practicing Multiplication Facts	137	251				5-11
B70	Multiplying by 3	139	252				6-1
B71	Multiplying by 4	141	253				6-2
B72	Multiplying by 6 or 7	143	254				6-3
B73	Multiplying by 8	145	255				6-4
B74	Practicing Multiplication Facts	147	256				6-5
B75	Using Multiplication to Compare	149	257				6-7
B76	Patterns on a Multiplication Table	151	258				6-8
B77	Multiplying Three Numbers	153	259				6-9
B78	Input/Output Tables	155	260				6-10
B79	Division as Sharing	157	261				7-1
B80	Division as Repeated Subtraction	159	262				7-2
B81	Writing Division Stories	161	263				7-3
B82	Relating Multiplication and Division	163	264				7-5
B83	Dividing by 2 and 5	165	265				7-6
B84	Dividing by 3 and 4	167	266				7-7
B85	Dividing by 2 Through 5	169	267				7-7
B86	Dividing by 6 and 7	171	268				7-8
B87	Dividing by 8 and 9	173	269				7-9
B88	Dividing by 6 Through 9	175	270				7-9
B89	0 and 1 in Division	177	271				7-10
B90	Dividing with Remainders	179	272				7-11
B91	Division Patterns with 10, 11, 12	181	273				7-12

Name _______________________________

Readiness for Addition and Subtraction

Example

Look at the picture. Tell a
joining story about the groups.

There are 3 frogs on the log.
Two frogs join them.
Now there are 5 frogs on the log.

Look at the picture. Tell a separating story about the groups.

There are 4 ducks in the pond.
Two ducks swim away.
Now there are 2 ducks in the pond.

---

1. Draw a picture that
    shows a separating story
    about 4 frogs and 1 frog.

2. Draw a picture that shows
    a joining story about 3
    ducks and 1 duck.

Name ______________________________

Readiness for Addition and Subtraction (continued)

3. Which tells a joining story about the shells?

   A 1 shell and 2 shells   **C** 3 shells and 1 shell

   B 2 shells and 3 shells   **D** 4 shells and 2 shells

---

4. Which tells a separating story about the fish?

   A 4 fish in all.   **C** 6 fish in all.
       2 fish swim away.   3 fish swim away.

   B 4 fish in all.   **D** 6 fish in all.
       4 fish swim away.   4 fish swim away.

Understanding Addition

Activity A

Ways to Make Butterflies and Birds

 WHOLE CLASS   VISUAL/AUDITORY    15 MIN.

Materials
plain paper (2 sheets per child), crayons

- Ask children to draw 5 butterflies, making some butterflies one color and the rest another color. Ask volunteers to describe the different parts in their pictures. For example: There are 5 butterflies. Two are red and 3 are yellow. If necessary, ask children how many butterflies there are altogether.

- Write the corresponding addition number sentence on a volunteer's picture. Read the number sentence aloud, pointing to the symbols as you read. Ask the children to write number sentences for their own pictures.

- Repeat the activity with 6 birds.

Understanding Addition (continued)

Activity B

Flying Kites

 PAIRS   VISUAL/SPATIAL    20 MIN.

Materials
plain paper, crayons, scissors (one pair per child)

- Divide a sheet of plain paper into 6 equal areas as shown on the right. Draw a kite in each area. Give each child a copy.

- Have each child color all 6 kites the same color, but make them a different color from their partner's kites. Ask the children to cut the 6 kites apart, on the lines.

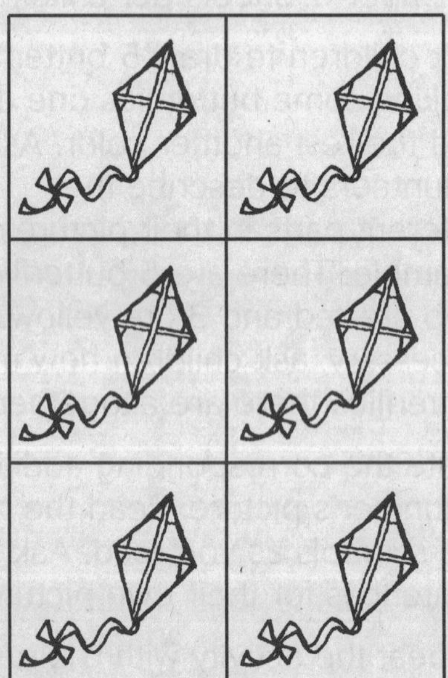

- Ask pairs to turn their kites face down and mix all 12 of the kites together. Then have them turn 6 of the kites up. Have them draw and color the kites on a sheet of paper and then write a number sentence for their pictures.

- Have the children repeat the activity until they find at least 3 different ways to make 6.

- Extend the activity by asking children to turn up 5 cards and find at least two different ways to make 5.

Understanding Subtraction

Activity A

Sitting Down

 WHOLE CLASS   KINESTHETIC    10 MIN.

Materials
writing paper

- Ask 5 volunteers to come to the front of the class. Ask: How many children are there in all? Ask two children to sit down where they are. Ask: How many children sat down? How many children are left?

- Write $5 - 2 = 3$. Point to each symbol as you read: Five minus 2 equals 3.

- Repeat the activity to show $5 - 1 = 4$, $5 - 3 = 2$, and $5 - 4 = 1$ but ask children to write the number sentences on the writing paper.

- Repeat the activity, showing $6 - 1 = 5$, $6 - 2 = 4$, $6 - 3 = 3$, $6 - 4 = 2$, and $6 - 5 = 1$.

- Ask 4 volunteers to come to the front of the class. Write $4 - 1 = 3$. Ask a volunteer to explain how to show the number sentence with the 4 students that are in front of the class. Ask: How many children are there in all? How many children sat down? How many children are left?

Understanding Subtraction (continued)

Activity B

Now You See It, Now You Don't

 INDIVIDUAL   VISUAL/TACTILE   15 MIN.

Materials
several sheets of construction paper, plain white paper, writing
paper, glue

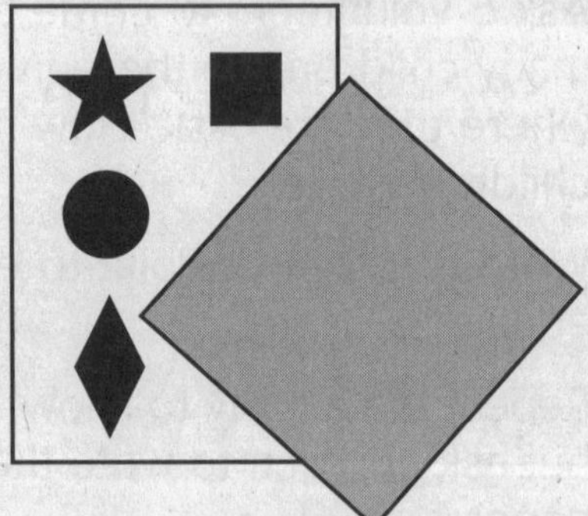

- Ask children to cut out 6 small shapes from the construction paper and glue them on the white paper. Have them cut a large square from a different color of construction paper. Ask them to use their squares to cover some of the shapes. Have the children count how many shapes are covered, how many shapes are uncovered, and how many there are in all.

- Ask children to write a subtraction number sentence for their pictures on the writing paper.

- Have children cover a different number of shapes and write a number sentence for the resulting picture. Ask them to find at least 4 ways to make 6.

Name ___________________________

Joining Stories

Example

Count how many are in each group.
Write the numbers.

How many cubes
are there in all?

   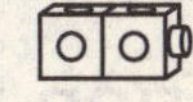   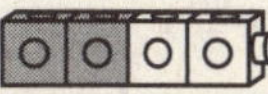

__2__   __2__   __4__ cubes

---

1. Count how many in each group. Then tell how many in all.

There are ____ cubes in all.

____   ____

---

2. Count how many in each group. Then tell how many in all.

There are ____ cubes in all.

____   ____

---

3. Count how many in each group. Then tell how many in all.

There are ____ cubes in all.

____   ____

Name _______________________________

Joining Stories (continued)

4. Count how many in each group. Then tell how many in all.

   _____   _____

   How many cubes are there in all? _____ cubes

---

5. Count how many in each group. Then tell how many in all.

   _____   _____

   How many cubes are there in all? _____ cubes

---

6. Count how many in each group. Then tell how many in all.

   _____   _____

   How many cubes are there in all? _____ cubes

---

7. **Number Sense**   Draw a picture of 3 apples and
   5 bananas.

   Tell how many fruits there are in all. _____

Name _______________________________

Using Pictures to Add

Example

Write the numbers.

3 **2** **5**

__3__ and __2__ are __5__ in all

Write the numbers.

1.   

________ and ________ are ________ in all

---

2.  

________ and ________ are ________ in all

---

3.  

________ and ________ are ________ in all

Name ____

Using Pictures to Add (continued)

Draw to show each number.
Write how many.

4.

2 and 2 are _______ in all

5.

I and 3 are _______ in all

6.

4 and I are _______ in all

10

Name _______________________________

Using Symbols to Add

Example

Write the numbers. Add.

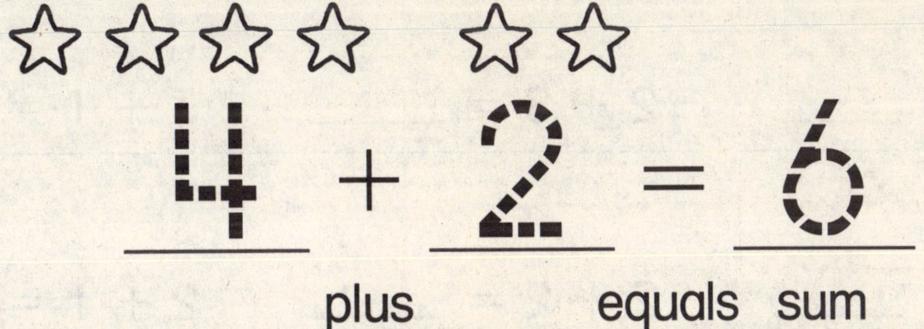

$$4 + 2 = 6$$

plus   equals sum

Write the numbers. Add.

I.  

_____ + _____ = _____

2. 

_____ + _____ = _____

3.  

_____ + _____ = _____

4.  

_____ + _____ = _____

5.  

_____ + _____ = _____

6.  

_____ + _____ = _____

7. 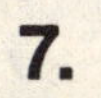  

_____ + _____ = _____

8.  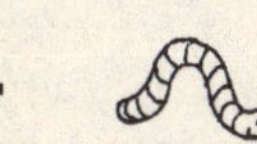 

_____ + _____ = _____

Using Symbols to Add (continued)

Find each sum.
Use counters if you like.

9.

$1 + 1 =$ _______ $2 + 3 =$ _______ $5 + 1 =$ _______

10.

$4 + 2 =$ _______ $2 + 2 =$ _______ $2 + 1 =$ _______

11.

$3 + 3 =$ _______ $4 + 1 =$ _______ $1 + 3 =$ _______

12.

$3 + 1 =$ _______ $2 + 4 =$ _______ $1 + 2 =$ _______

13.

$1 + 5 =$ _______ $3 + 2 =$ _______ $1 + 4 =$ _______

Reasoning Write a number sentence for each picture.

14.  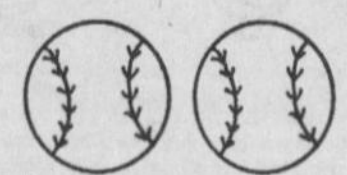 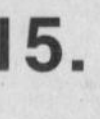

_______ + _______ = _______

15.  

_______ + _______ = _______

Name ____

Ways to Add

Example

3 birds are in a tree. 2 more join them.

How many birds are there in all?

You may use counters, pictures, or numbers.

Solve. Draw a picture or write an addition sentence.

1. 3 dogs are in the box.
   4 more jump in.
   How many dogs are there in all? ______

2. I rabbit hops into a hole.
   3 more hop by.
   How many rabbits are there in all? ______

3. 3 fish are in the bowl.
   3 more join them.
   How many fish are there in all? ______

4. 4 bugs are on the leaf.
   I more lands.
   How many bugs are there in all? ______

Ways to Add (continued)

5. Ask 3 classmates how they like to add. Color a
    box to show each classmate's choice.

Our Favorite Way to Add

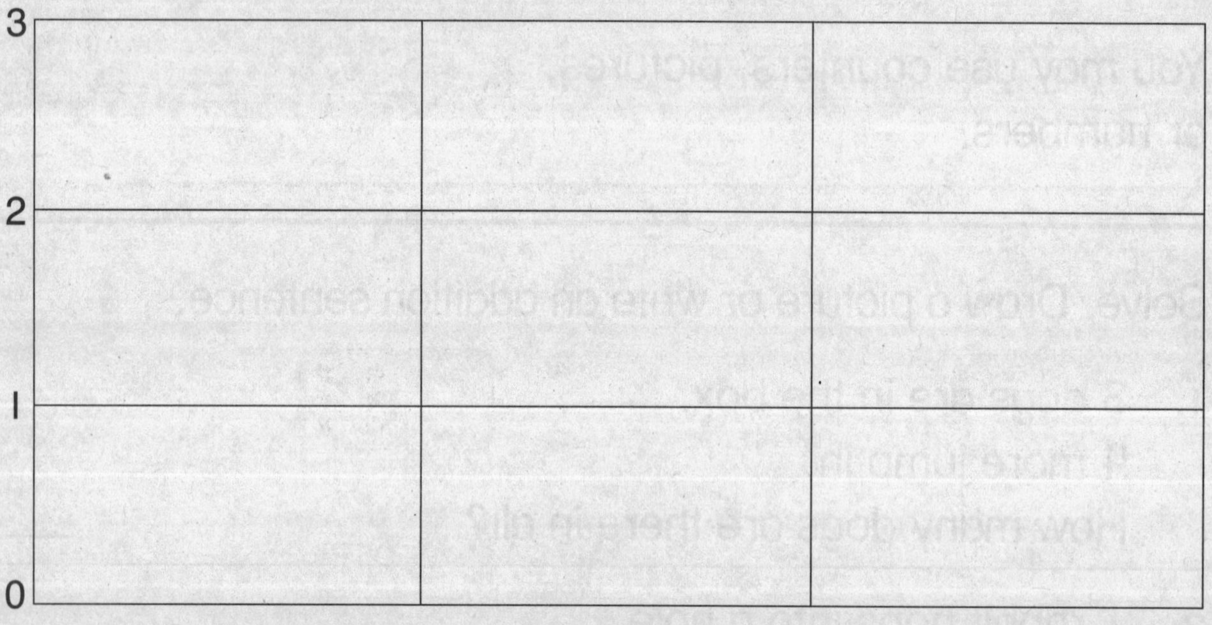

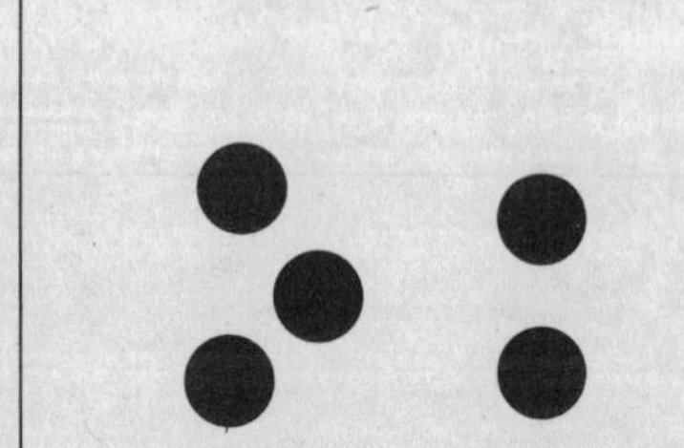

$3 + 2 = 5$

6. **Reasoning** Share your graph with a classmate. Tell how
    your graphs are the same. Tell how they are different.

Name _______________________

Adding with Zero

Example What is your sum when you add zero?

   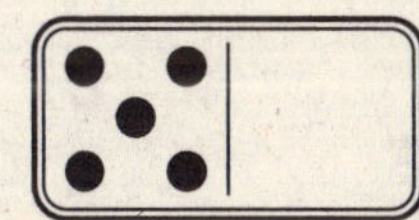

$5 + 2 = \underline{}7$ $5 + 0 = \underline{}5$

Add.

1. 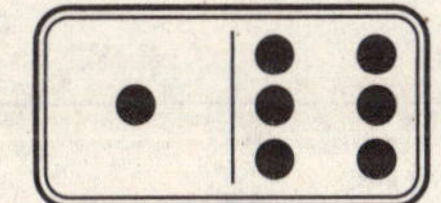

$1 + 6 = \underline{}$

2. 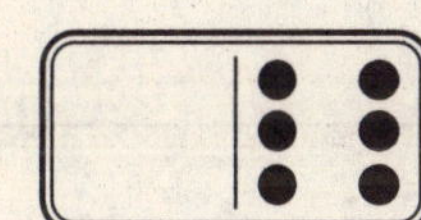

$0 + 6 = \underline{}$

3. 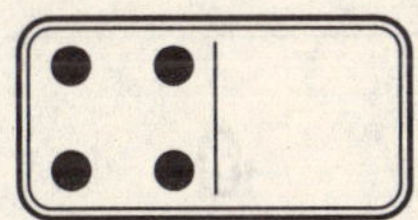

$4 + 0 = \underline{}$

4. 

$4 + 3 = \underline{}$

5. 

$3 + 3 = \underline{}$

6. 

$3 + 0 = \underline{}$

Adding with Zero (continued)

Add. Use counters if you like. Look for facts
with zero.

7.

$0 + 7 =$ __7__ $3 + 2 =$ ____ $0 + 2 =$ ____

8.

$2 + 5 =$ ____ $0 + 4 =$ ____ $1 + 0 =$ ____

9.

$$\begin{array}{cccccc} 4 & 0 & 0 & 3 & 7 & 5 \\ +4 & +8 & +0 & +1 & +1 & +0 \end{array}$$

10.

$$\begin{array}{cccccc} 0 & 6 & 0 & 7 & 3 & 4 \\ +1 & +2 & +3 & +0 & +3 & +1 \end{array}$$

11.

$$\begin{array}{cccccc} 2 & 6 & 8 & 1 & 4 & 0 \\ +2 & +0 & +0 & +6 & +3 & +3 \end{array}$$

12. Reasoning When you add any number to
zero what is your sum?

____

Name ______________________________

Adding Across and Down

Example

Write the numbers. Add.

2 + 5 = 7

+ 7

Write the numbers. Add.

1.  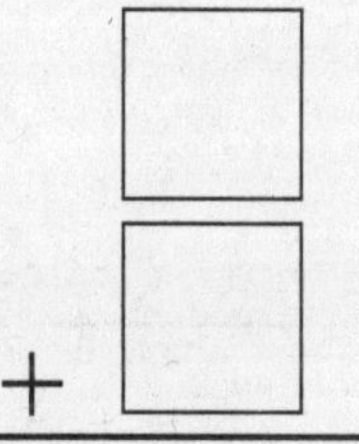 

______ + ______ = ______

2.  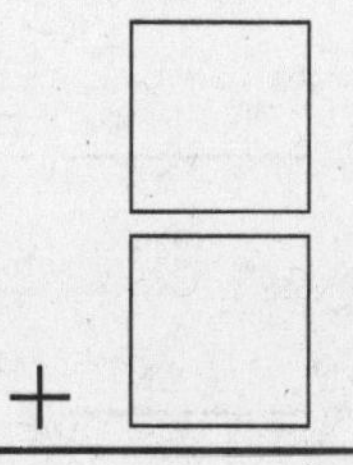 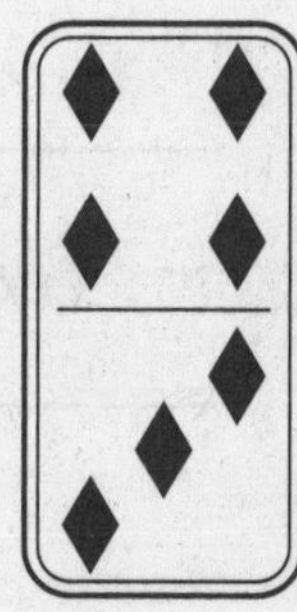

______ + ______ = ______

Name ________________________

Adding Across and Down (continued)

Add. Use counters if you like.

3.

$4 + 3 = \underline{7}$ $\qquad$ $2 + 3 = \underline{\hspace{1cm}}$ $\qquad$ $5 + 3 = \underline{\hspace{1cm}}$

4.

$3 + 3 = \underline{\hspace{1cm}}$ $\qquad$ $7 + 1 = \underline{\hspace{1cm}}$ $\qquad$ $1 + 3 = \underline{\hspace{1cm}}$

5.

$$\begin{array}{cccccc} 2 & 5 & 2 & 1 & 5 & 3 \\ +5 & +1 & +2 & +2 & +3 & +2 \\ \hline \end{array}$$

6. Reasoning Use only odd numbers: 1, 3, 5, and 7. Write as many addition sentences as you can.

____ + ____ = ____ $\qquad$ ____ + ____ = ____

____ + ____ = ____ $\qquad$ ____ + ____ = ____

____ + ____ = ____ $\qquad$ ____ + ____ = ____

____ + ____ = ____ $\qquad$ ____ + ____ = ____

Name ____

Missing Parts

Example

Draw how many are missing.

6 in all

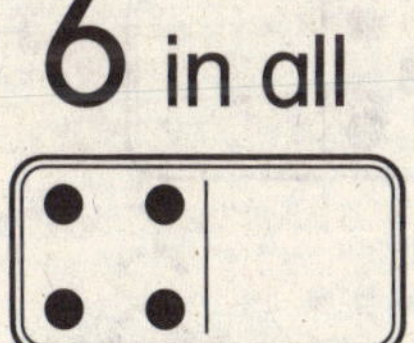

What number
is missing?

5 in all

$$4 + \underline{2} = 6 \qquad 5 = \underline{3} + 2$$

Draw how many are missing.
Write the number.
Use counters if you like.

1.   7 in all

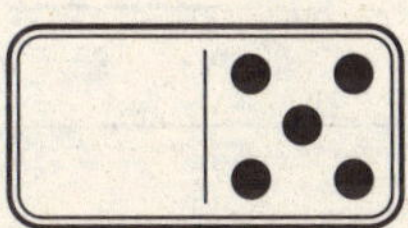

$$\underline{} + 5 = 7$$

2.   4 in all

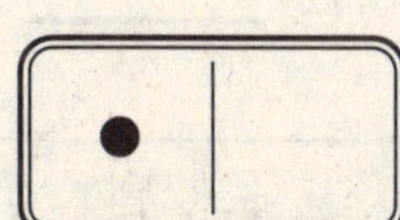

$$4 = 1 + \underline{}$$

3.   8 in all

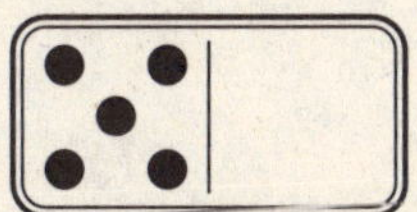

$$8 = 5 + \underline{}$$

4.   6 in all

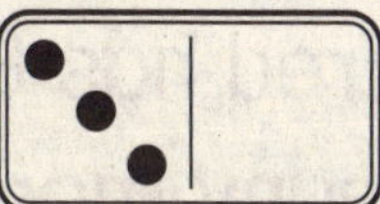

$$3 + \underline{} = 6$$

Name ______________________________

Missing Parts (continued)

Write the missing numbers.
Use counters if you like.

5.   6 in all

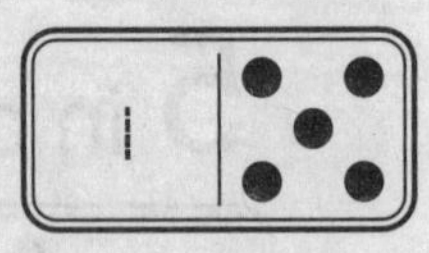

_____ + 5 = 6

6.   8 in all

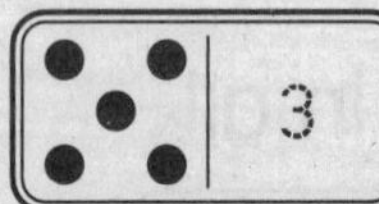

8 = 5 + _____

7.

4 + _____ = 8

8.

7 = _____ + 4

9.

5 = _____ + 5

10.

6 = 3 + _____

11.

1 + _____ = 7

12.

4 = _____ + 2

Reasoning Write the number sentence.
Solve.

13. Fred bought 5 cookies.
His mother gave him some more.
Now Fred has 8 cookies.
How many more did she
give him?

8 in all

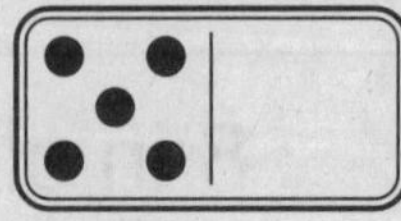

_____ + _____ = _____

20

Name ___________________________

Using Pictures to Subtract

Example

Write how many are left.

6 minus 4

2 left

Write how many are left.

1. 

5 minus 1 ______ left

2. 

3 minus 2 ______ left

3. 

6 minus 3 ______ left

4. 

6 minus 1 ______ left

Name _______________________________

Using Pictures to Subtract (continued)

Write the numbers.

5. 

4 minus 3 ____ left

6. 

____ minus ____ ____ left

7. 

____ minus ____ ____ left

Reasoning

Solve. Use counters if you like.

8. You have 6 granola bars.
   You eat 2 of them.
   How many granola bars
   are left?

   ______

9. I saw 5 bikes.
   4 bikes went away.
   How many bikes are left?

   ______

Name _______________________

Using Symbols to Subtract

Example

Cross out to subtract.

$$7 \underset{\text{minus}}{-} 3 = \underline{\quad 4 \quad}_{\text{difference}}$$

Cross out to subtract.

1. 

$8 - 6 = \underline{\quad}$

2.

$5 - 2 = \underline{\quad}$

3. 

$5 - 4 = \underline{\quad}$

4. 

$8 - 4 = \underline{\quad}$

5. 

$7 - 2 = \underline{\quad}$

6. 

$6 - 5 = \underline{\quad}$

Name ___________________________________

Using Symbols to Subtract (continued)

Cross out to subtract.

7. 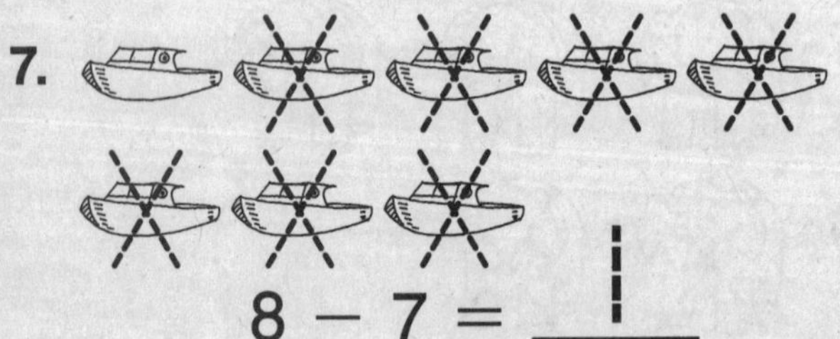

$8 - 7 =$ _____

8. 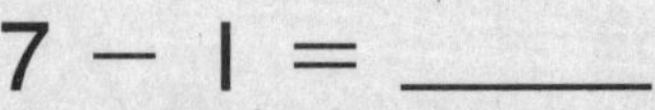

$7 - 1 =$ _____

9. 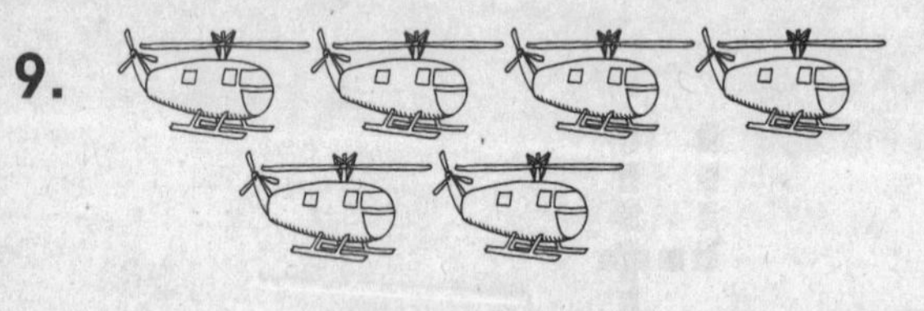

$6 - 2 =$ _____

10. 

$6 - 4 =$ _____

11. 

$5 - 2 =$ _____

12. 

$7 - 2 =$ _____

13. 

$4 - 2 =$ _____

14. 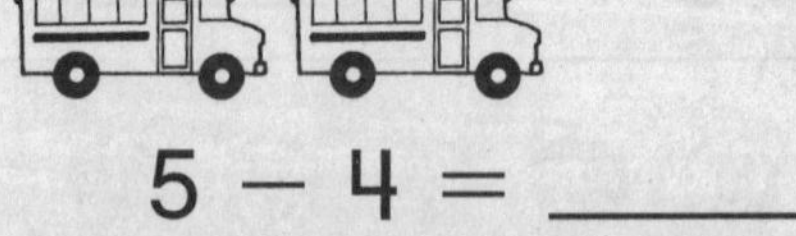

$5 - 4 =$ _____

15. **Writing in Math** Look at Questions 9 and 10 above.
How are they alike? How are they different?

____

____

24

Name ___________________

Zero in Subtraction

Example

Subtract.

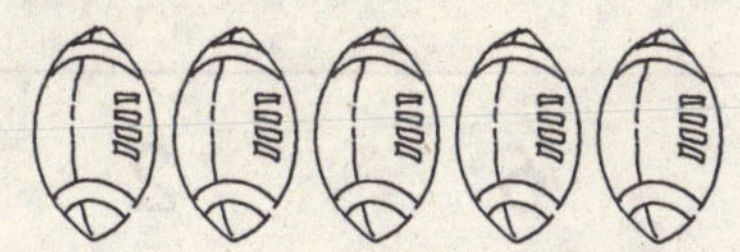

$5 - 0 = \underline{5}$

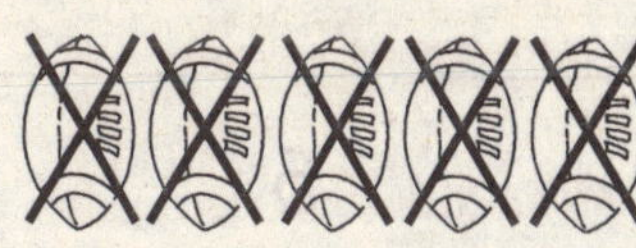

$5 - 5 = \underline{0}$

Subtract.

1.

$7 - 3 = \underline{\hphantom{00}}$

2.

$7 - 0 = \underline{\hphantom{00}}$

3.

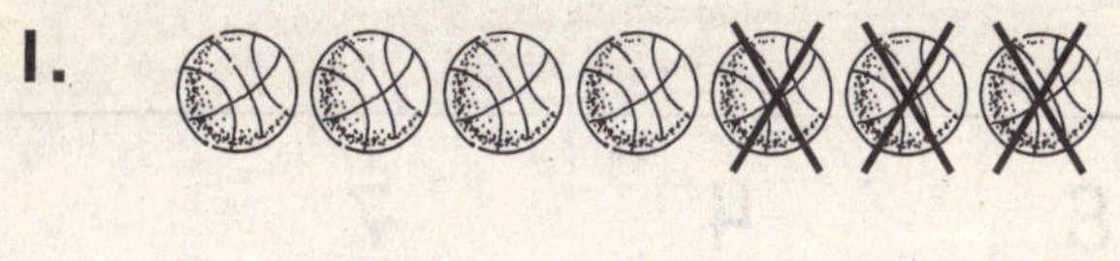

$4 - 2 = \underline{\hphantom{00}}$

4.

$4 - 4 = \underline{\hphantom{00}}$

5.

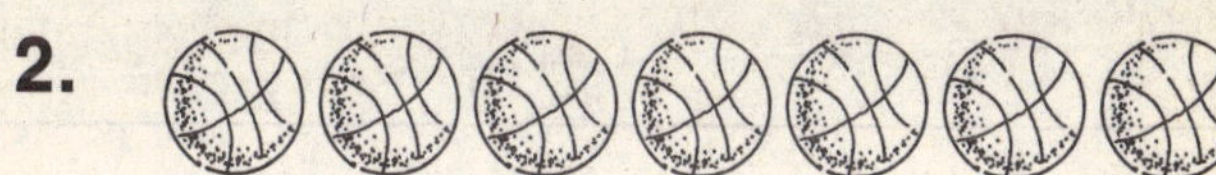

$6 - 5 = \underline{\hphantom{00}}$

6.

$6 - 0 = \underline{\hphantom{00}}$

7.

$8 - 2 = \underline{\hphantom{00}}$

8.

$8 - 8 = \underline{\hphantom{00}}$

Name _______________________________________

Zero in Subtraction (continued)

9.
$$\begin{array}{cccccc} 8 & 7 & 5 & 8 & 0 & 3 \\ -3 & -3 & -0 & -7 & -0 & -0 \\ \hline 5 \end{array}$$

10.
$$\begin{array}{cccccc} 6 & 5 & 2 & 7 & 6 & 2 \\ -4 & -5 & -0 & -0 & -5 & -2 \\ \hline \end{array}$$

11.
$$\begin{array}{cccccc} 8 & 1 & 4 & 3 & 7 & 6 \\ -0 & -1 & -2 & -3 & -1 & -6 \\ \hline \end{array}$$

12.
$$\begin{array}{cccccc} 4 & 8 & 5 & 8 & 4 & 7 \\ -4 & -6 & -4 & -8 & -0 & -6 \\ \hline \end{array}$$

13. **Writing in Math** When you subtract or add 0, do you end up with the same sum?

____

____

____

26

Name _______________________

Subtracting Across and Down

Example

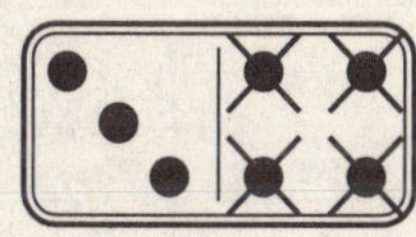

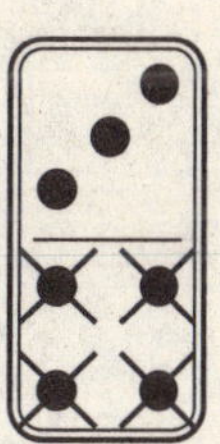

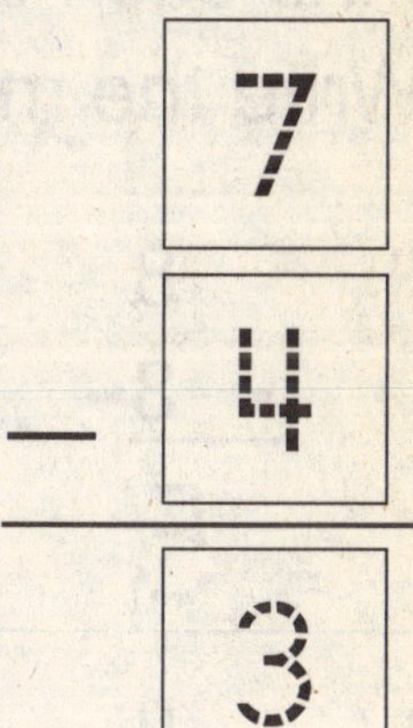

7 – 4 = 3

Write the numbers. Subtract.

1.

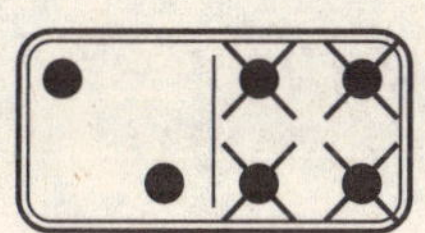

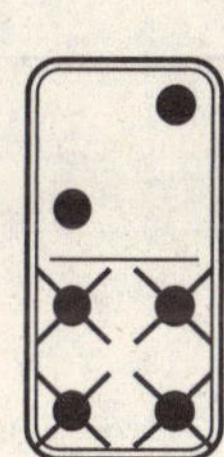

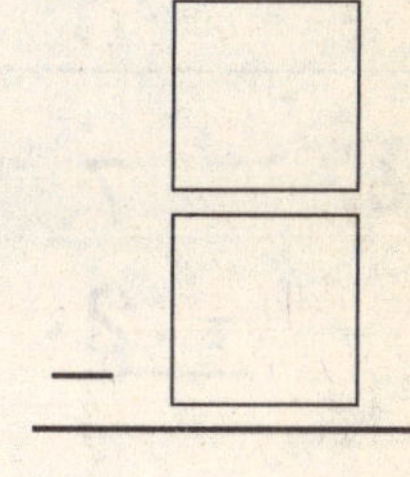

_____ – _____ = _____

2.

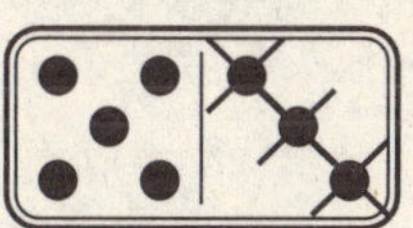

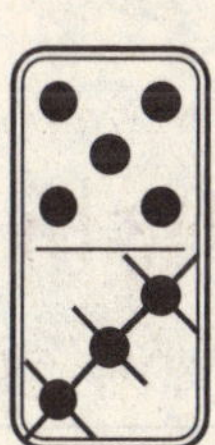

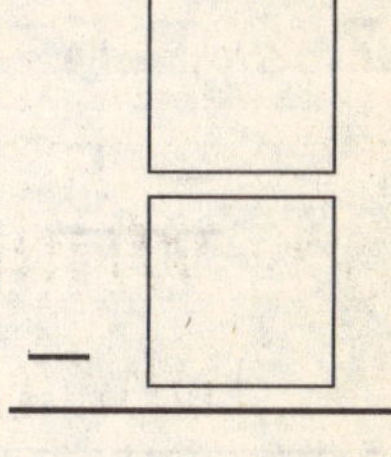

_____ – _____ = _____

3.

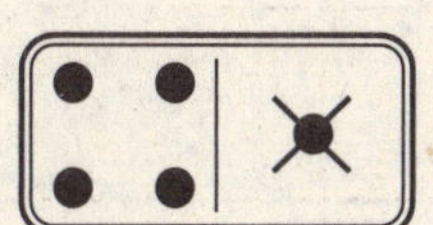

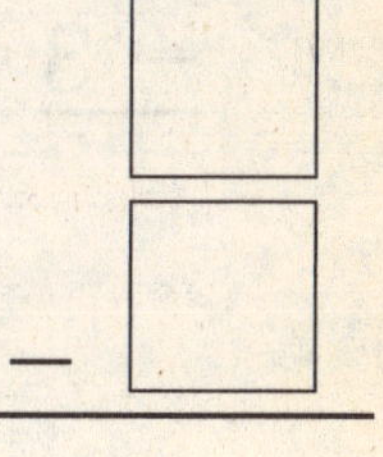

_____ – _____ = _____

Name ___________________________________

Subtracting Across and Down (continued)

Find each difference.
Write the matching subtraction sentence.

4.
$$\begin{array}{r} 8 \\ -\ 3 \\ \hline 5 \end{array}$$
$8 - 3 = 5$

5.
$$\begin{array}{r} 4 \\ -\ 3 \\ \hline \end{array}$$
____ − ____ = ____

6.
$$\begin{array}{r} 7 \\ -\ 2 \\ \hline \end{array}$$
____ − ____ = ____

7.
$$\begin{array}{r} 5 \\ -\ 5 \\ \hline \end{array}$$
____ − ____ = ____

8.
$$\begin{array}{r} 6 \\ -\ 3 \\ \hline \end{array}$$
____ − ____ = ____

Name _______________________

Subtracting to Find How Many More

Example

How many more gray cubes than white cubes?

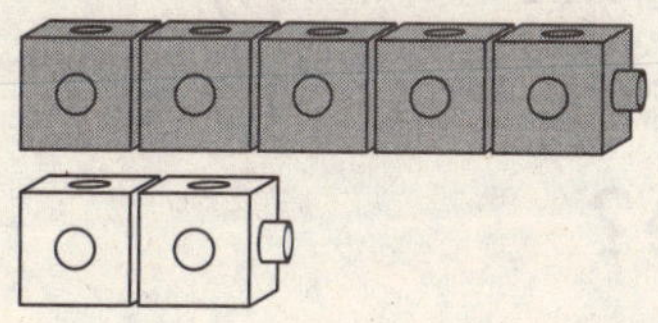   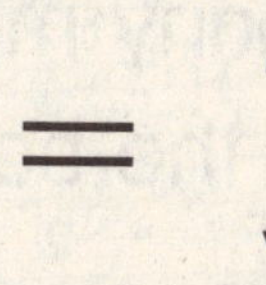 

$5 - 2 = 3$ more

How many more gray cubes than white cubes are there?
Write a number sentence. Use cubes if you like.

1. 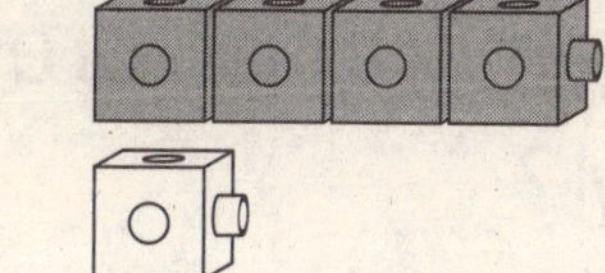

_____ − _____ = _____ more

2. 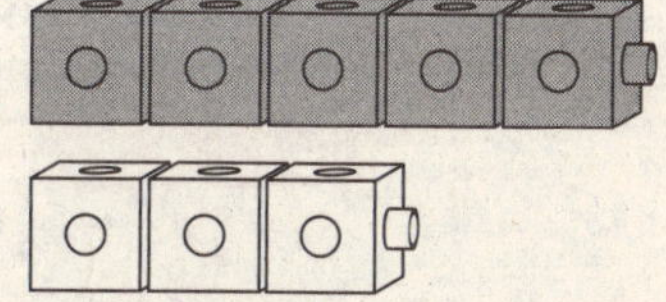

_____ − _____ = _____ more

3. 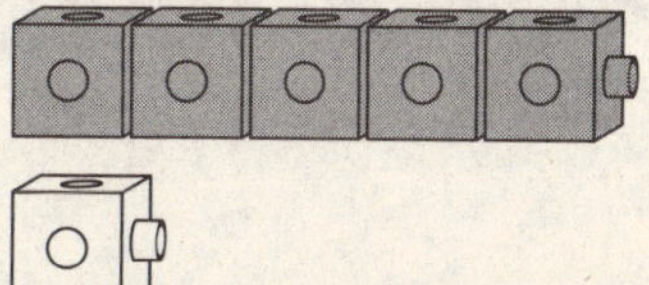

_____ − _____ = _____ more

4. 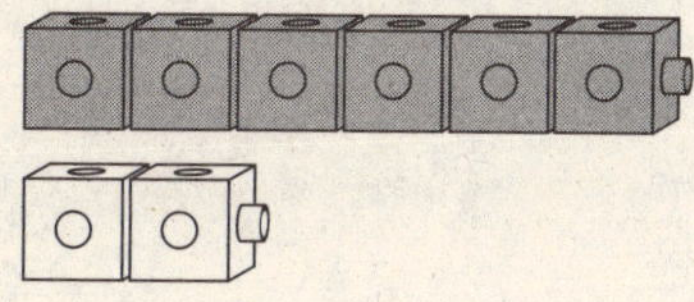

_____ − _____ = _____ more

Name _______________________________

Subtracting to Find How Many More (continued)

Write the number sentence. Solve.
You can use cubes if you like.

5. 7 dogs are in a box.
2 dogs are chasing a
cat. How many more
dogs are in the box?

____ − ____ = ____ more

6. Paul has 5 dimes. Sue has
3 dimes. How many more
dimes does Paul have
than Sue?

____ − ____ = ____ more

7. 6 apples are in a basket.
3 apples are on the
ground. How many more
apples are in the basket?

____ − ____ = ____ more

8. We have 8 fish in a bowl.
We saw 7 in the creek.
How many more fish are
in the bowl?

____ − ____ = ____ more

Problem Solving

9. Draw 5 frogs on a log.
Draw 3 frogs on the other log.
How many more frogs are on one
log than the other?
Write a number sentence.

____ − ____ = ____ more

Name ___________________________

Counting On 1 and 2

Example

There are 4 cars in the box.
Count on to find the sum.

_____5____ , _____6____

4 + 2 = _____6____

Count on to find each sum.

1.

7 + 1 = _______

2.

5 + 2 = _______

Counting On 1 and 2 (continued)

3.

$$8 \quad + \quad 2 \quad = \; \underline{\quad}$$

4.

6	5	4	7	1	8
+ 1	+ 1	+ 2	+ 2	+ 2	+ 1

5.

4	6	9	2	3	3
+ 1	+ 2	+ 2	+ 2	+ 2	+ 1

6. You started at 6.
You counted on 2.
Write the addition
sentence.

____

7. You started at 9.
You ended at 10.
Write the addition
sentence.

____

Name ___________________________

Counting On 1, 2, and 3

Example

There are 4 birds in the house.
3 birds fly into the house.
Count on to find the sum.

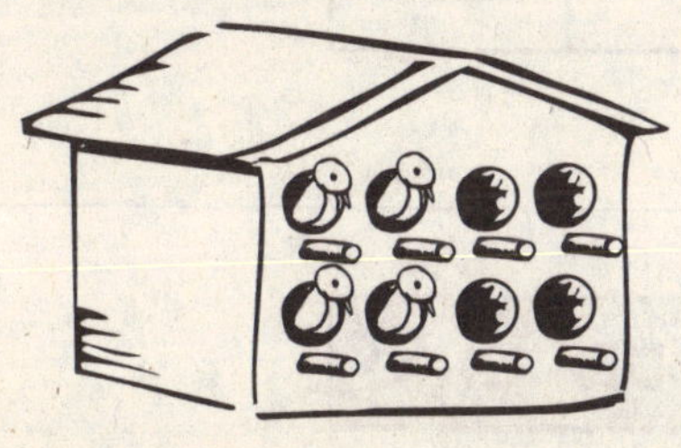

5, 6, 7
___ ___ ___

$$4 + 3 = \underline{7}$$

Count on to find each sum.

1.

$$\begin{array}{r} 4 \\ + 2 \\ \hline \end{array}$$

2.

$$7 + 1 = \underline{}$$

$$5 + 3 = \underline{}$$

$$9 + 2 = \underline{}$$

3.

$$\begin{array}{r} 8 \\ + 1 \\ \hline \end{array} \qquad \begin{array}{r} 7 \\ + 3 \\ \hline \end{array} \qquad \begin{array}{r} 5 \\ + 2 \\ \hline \end{array} \qquad \begin{array}{r} 9 \\ + 1 \\ \hline \end{array} \qquad \begin{array}{r} 6 \\ + 2 \\ \hline \end{array} \qquad \begin{array}{r} 8 \\ + 3 \\ \hline \end{array}$$

Name ___________________________

Counting On 1, 2, and 3 (continued)

4.

Count on 1	
5	
6	
7	
8	

Count on 2	
9	
8	
7	
6	

Count on 3	
3	
4	
5	
6	

5.

Count on 1	
6	
5	
4	
3	

Count on 2	
4	
5	
6	
7	

Count on 3	
3	
5	
7	
9	

6. There are 6 bees.

3 bees join them.

How many bees are there in all? _______ bees

7. There are 7 cats.

3 cats join them.

How many cats are there in all? _______ cats

Adding in Any Order

Example

Write each sum.

I can add either way.

$3 + 2 = \underline{5}$ $2 + 3 = \underline{5}$

Use counters. Write each sum.

1.

$2 + 4 = \underline{\hspace{1cm}}$

$4 + 2 = \underline{\hspace{1cm}}$

2.

$0 + 8 = \underline{\hspace{1cm}}$

$8 + 0 = \underline{\hspace{1cm}}$

3.

$3 + 4 = \underline{\hspace{1cm}}$

$4 + 3 = \underline{\hspace{1cm}}$

4.

$1 + 4 = \underline{\hspace{1cm}}$

$4 + 1 = \underline{\hspace{1cm}}$

Name ________________________

Adding in Any Order (continued)

Add. Then change the order.
Use counters if you like.

5.

$$\begin{array}{r} 3 \\ +\ 4 \\ \hline 7 \end{array} \qquad \begin{array}{r} 4 \\ +\ 3 \\ \hline 7 \end{array}$$

6.

$$\begin{array}{r} 5 \\ +\ 0 \\ \hline \end{array} \qquad \begin{array}{r} \square \\ +\ \square \\ \hline \end{array}$$

7.

$$\begin{array}{r} 7 \\ +\ 1 \\ \hline \end{array} \qquad \begin{array}{r} \square \\ +\ \square \\ \hline \end{array}$$

8.

$$\begin{array}{r} 1 \\ +\ 3 \\ \hline \end{array} \qquad \begin{array}{r} \square \\ +\ \square \\ \hline \end{array}$$

9. **Reasoning** Look at the picture. How many
butterflies are there in all? Write two addition
sentences.

_____ + _____ = _____

_____ + _____ = _____

Name ________________________

Adding 1, 2, or 3

Example

Find the sum.
Start with the greater number.
Count on.

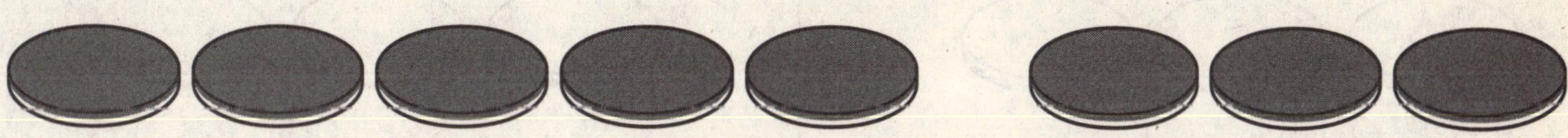

$$5 + 3 = \underline{8}$$

5 is the greater number. Count on.

$$5 \quad + \quad \text{count on 3}$$
$$5 \quad \underline{6}, \underline{7}, \underline{8}$$

Circle the greater number.
Then count on to add.

I. 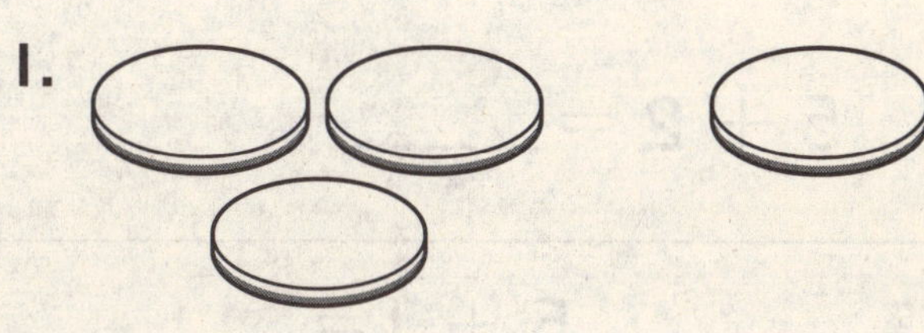

$$3 + 1 = \underline{}$$

2. 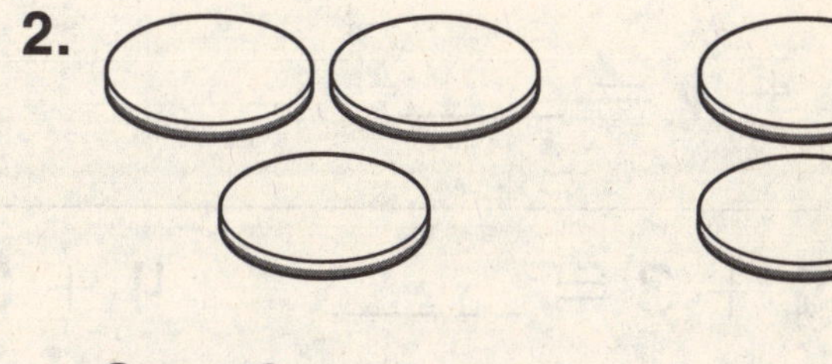

$$3 + 2 = \underline{}$$

Name ___________________________

Adding 1, 2, or 3 (continued)

Count on to find each sum. Start with the greater number.
Use counters if you like.

3. 

$9 + 2 =$ _____

4. 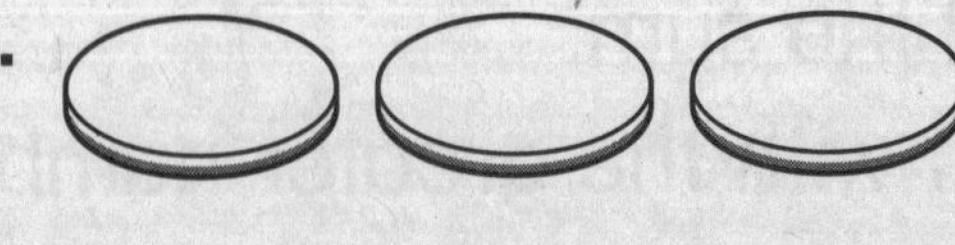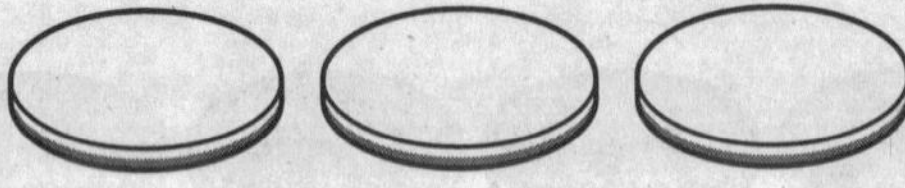

$3 + 3 =$ _____

5. 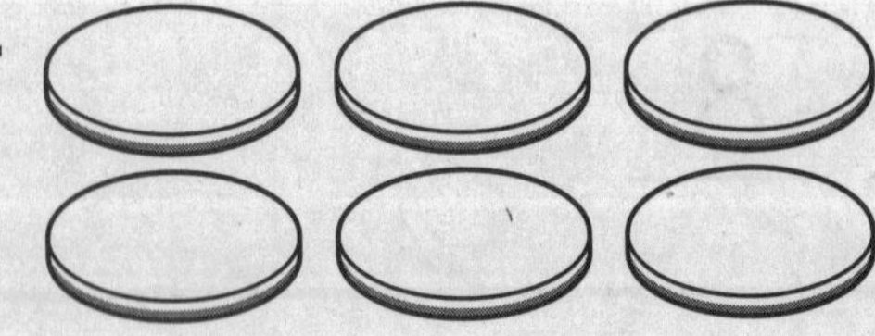

$6 + 1 =$ _____

6. 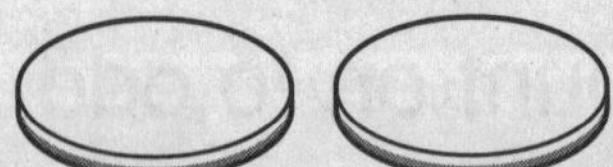

$5 + 2 =$ _____

7. $9 + 3 =$ _____ $4 + 3 =$ _____ $5 + 1 =$ _____

8. **Reasoning** Andy had 8¢. He found 3¢ more.
How much money did Andy have? _____

Counting On from the Greater Number

Example

$2 + 8 = \underline{10}$

Start with the greater number, 8.

0 1 2 3 4 5 6 7 8 9 10 11 12

Circle the greater number.
Use the number line to count on.
Write each sum.

1. $1 + 9 = \underline{}$

0 1 2 3 4 5 6 7 8 9 10 11 12

---

2. $7 + 2 = \underline{}$

0 1 2 3 4 5 6 7 8 9 10 11 12

---

3. $3 + 8 = \underline{}$

0 1 2 3 4 5 6 7 8 9 10 11 12

---

4. $2 + 9 = \underline{}$

0 1 2 3 4 5 6 7 8 9 10 11 12

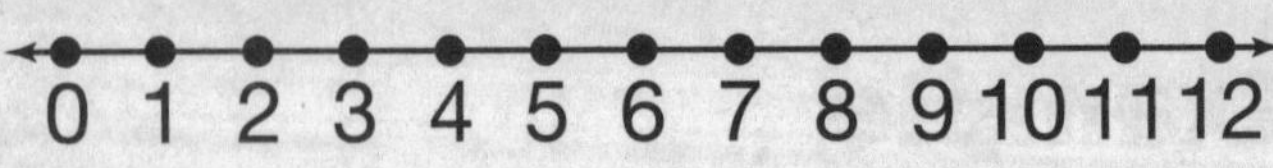

Counting On from the Greater Number (continued)

Circle the greater number.
Count on to add.
Use the number line if you like.

0 1 2 3 4 5 6 7 8 9 10 11 12

5. $1 + 5 =$ _____ $3 + 4 =$ _____ $6 + 2 =$ _____

6.

   $9 + 1 =$ _____ $2 + 5 =$ _____ $5 + 3 =$ _____

7.

2	7	1	8	3	9
+ 4	+ 3	+ 7	+ 1	+ 9	+ 2

Solve.

8. Thomas has 4 basketballs
and 3 baseballs.
How many balls does
he have altogether?

_______ balls

9. Marianna has 2 cats.
They have 8 kittens.
How many cats does
she have now?

_______ cats

Name ______________________________

Adding Doubles

Example

Add to find the double.

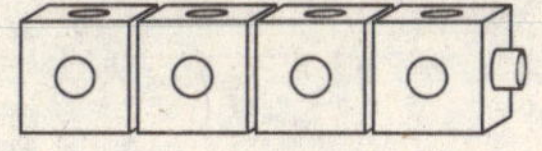 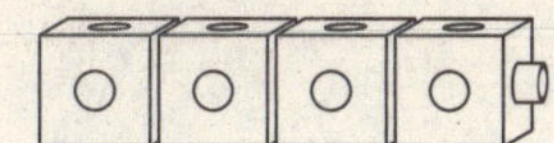

4 + 4 = 8

___ + ___ = ___

---

1. 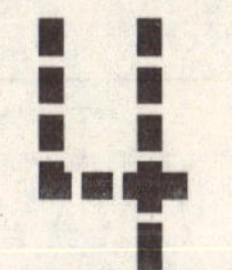

___ + ___ = ___

2. 

___ + ___ = ___

---

3. 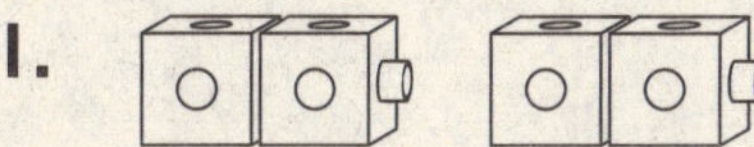

___ + ___ = ___

4. 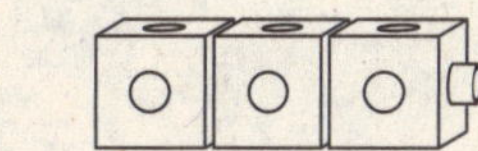

___ + ___ = ___

---

5. 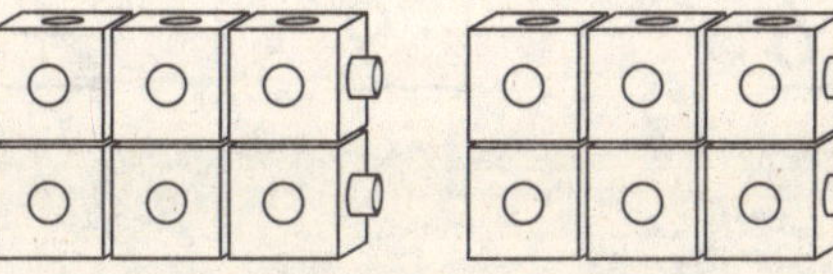

___ + ___ = ___

6. 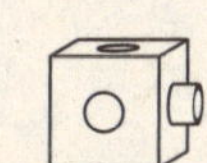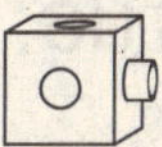

___ + ___ = ___

Adding Doubles (continued)

Add. Circle the doubles facts.

7.

5	4	3	2	1	3
+ 2	+ 4	+ 7	+ 6	+ 8	+ 3

8.

9	3	1	4	1	5	7
+ 2	+ 4	+ 6	+ 4	+ 9	+ 5	+ 1

9.

1	2	7	6	3	2
+ 1	+ 8	+ 2	+ 6	+ 9	+ 2

Write the missing number that makes
each sentence true.

10.

_____ + 5 = 10

11.

3 + _____ = 6

Name ___________________________

Using Doubles to Add

Example

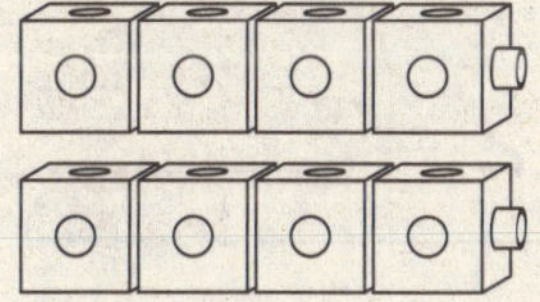

Think 4 + 4 and 1 more.

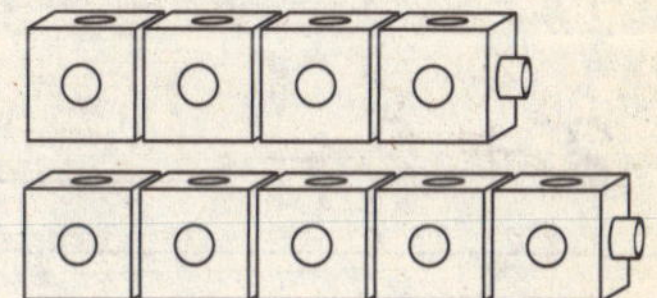

$4 + 4 = \underline{8}$ 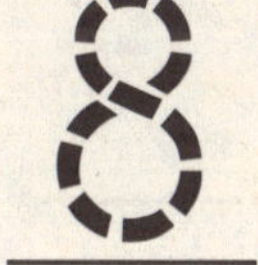 $\qquad 4 + 5 = \underline{9}$ 

Find each sum.
Use cubes if you like.

1.

$1 + 1 = \underline{\qquad}$

$1 + 2 = \underline{\qquad}$

2.

$3 + 3 = \underline{\qquad}$

$3 + 4 = \underline{\qquad}$

3.

$5 + 5 = \underline{\qquad}$

$5 + 6 = \underline{\qquad}$

4.

$2 + 2 = \underline{\qquad}$

$2 + 3 = \underline{\qquad}$

5.

$6 + 6 = \underline{\qquad}$

$6 + 7 = \underline{\qquad}$

6.

$4 + 4 = \underline{\qquad}$

$4 + 5 = \underline{\qquad}$

Math Diagnosis and
Intervention System

Name ____

Using Doubles to Add (continued)

Find each sum. Think of a double to help you.

7.

$2 + 2 =$ _______ $2 + 3 =$ _______ $3 + 2 =$ _______

8.

$3 + 3 =$ _______ $3 + 4 =$ _______ $4 + 3 =$ _______

9.

$5 + 5 =$ _______ $5 + 6 =$ _______ $6 + 5 =$ _______

10.

4	4	0	6	1	5
$+4$	$+5$	$+0$	$+6$	$+2$	$+4$

11.

1	3	6	0	7	4
$+1$	$+2$	$+7$	$+1$	$+6$	$+3$

Solve.

12. There are 4 birds in a tree.
There are double that many
and one more flying. How   _______ birds
many birds are flying away?

Name _______________________

Sums of 10

Example

You can use the ten-frame to learn sums of 10.
Write the addition sentence for the sum.

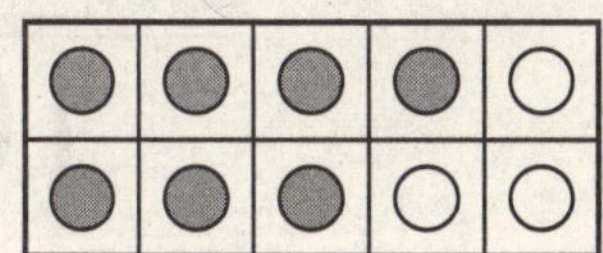

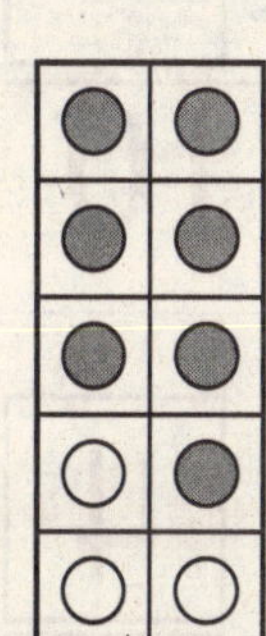

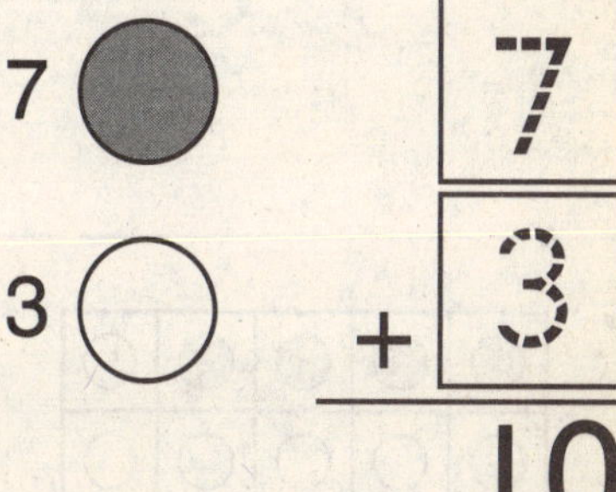

$$7 + 3 = 10$$

Write the addition sentence for each sum.
Use the ten-frame to help you.

1.

$$8 + 2 = 10$$

2.

____ + ____ = 10

3.

____ + ____ = 10

4.

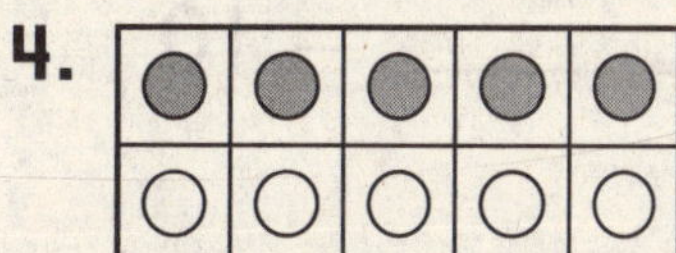

____ + ____ = 10

Sums of 10 (continued)

Fill in the missing numbers to find each sum of 10.

5. 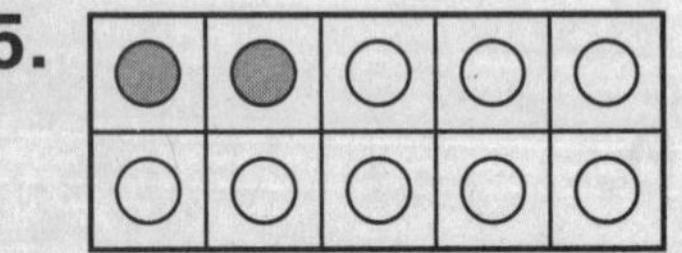

$$2 + \boxed{} = 10$$

6. 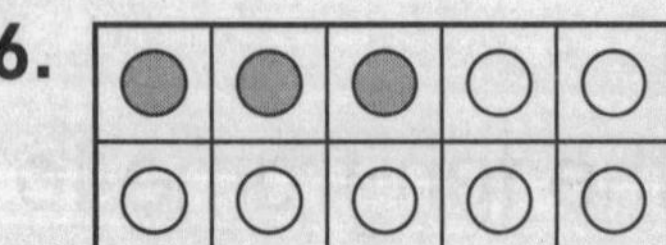

$$3 + \boxed{} = 10$$

7. 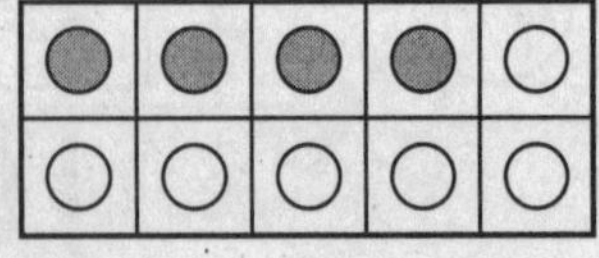

$$4 + \boxed{} = 10$$

8. 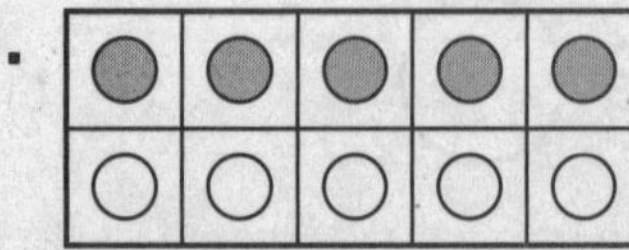

$$5 + \boxed{} = 10$$

9. 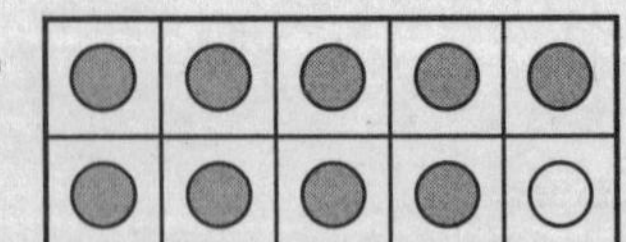

$$9 + \boxed{} = 10$$

______ + ______ = 10

10. 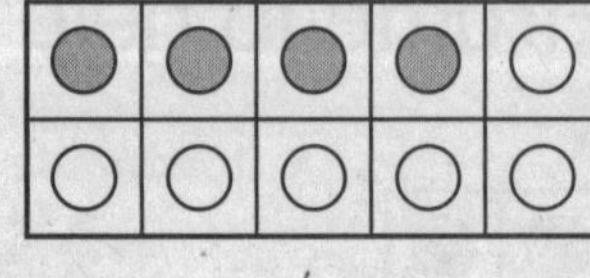

$$4 + \boxed{} = 10$$

______ + ______ = 10

Name ___________________________________

Counting Back 1, 2, and 3

Example

Use the number line to count back.
Circle the number where you start.
Write the difference.

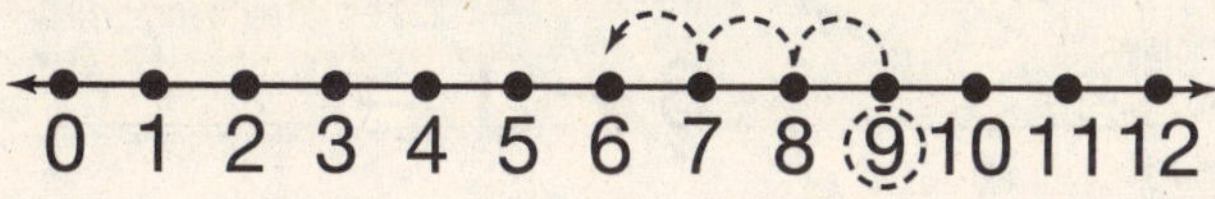

$$9 - 3 = 6$$

Use the number line to count back.
Circle the number where you start.
Write the difference.

1.
$6 - 1 = $ _______

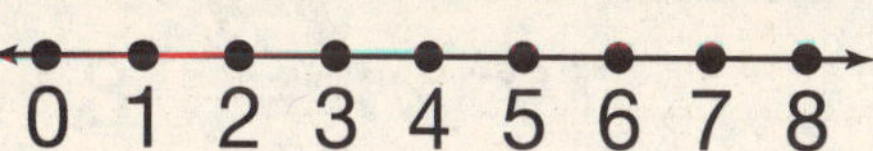

2.
$7 - 3 = $ _______

0 1 2 3 4 5 6 7 8

3.
$6 - 2 = $ _______

0 1 2 3 4 5 6 7 8

4.
$8 - 3 = $ _______

0 1 2 3 4 5 6 7 8

Name ___________________________________

Counting Back 1, 2, and 3 (continued)

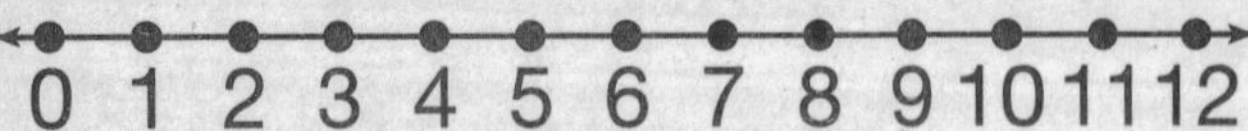

Count back to subtract.
Use the number line to help you.

5.

$9 - 2 =$ _______ $5 - 3 =$ _______ $8 - 1 =$ _______

6.

$10 - 3 =$ _______ $7 - 2 =$ _______ $9 - 1 =$ _______

7.

4	5	8	10	6	3
$-\ 1$	$-\ 2$	$-\ 3$	$-\ 2$	$-\ 2$	$-\ 1$

8.

6	9	8	6	9	10
$-\ 3$	$-\ 2$	$-\ 2$	$-\ 1$	$-\ 3$	$-\ 1$

Solve.

9. Shauna has 7 hats and
3 scarves. How many more
hats than scarves does she have?   _______ more hats

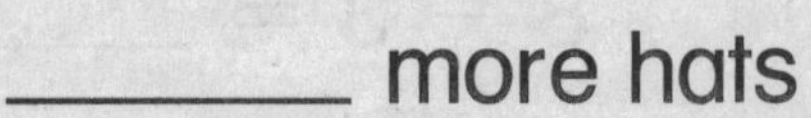

Name ___________________________

Counting Back

Example

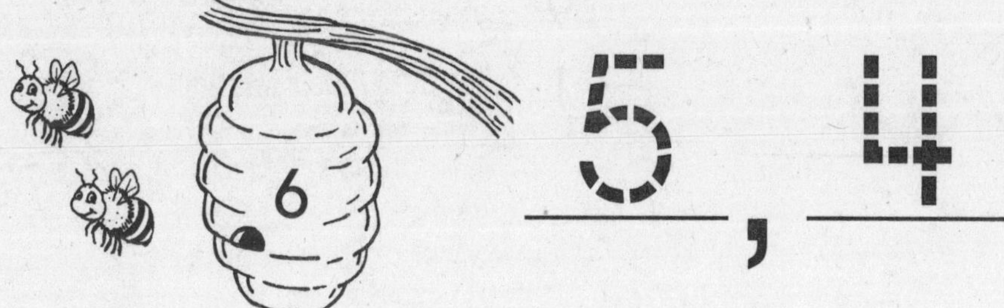

$$5, \ 4$$

| Start at 6 | Count back 2 |

$$6 - 2 = 4$$

Count back to subtract.

1.

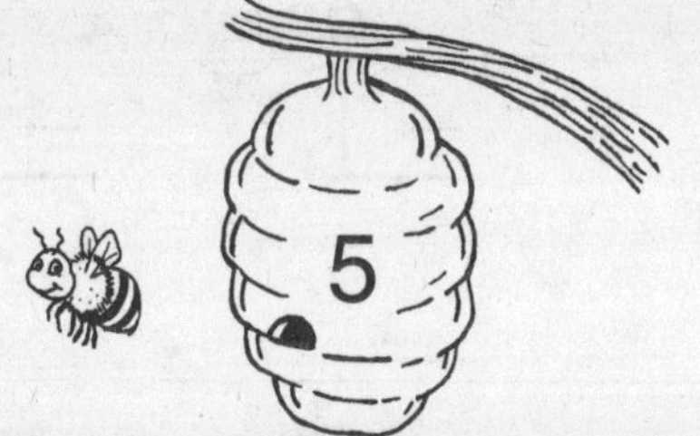

_____ $5 - 1 =$ _____

2.

_____ , _____ $7 - 2 =$ _____

3.

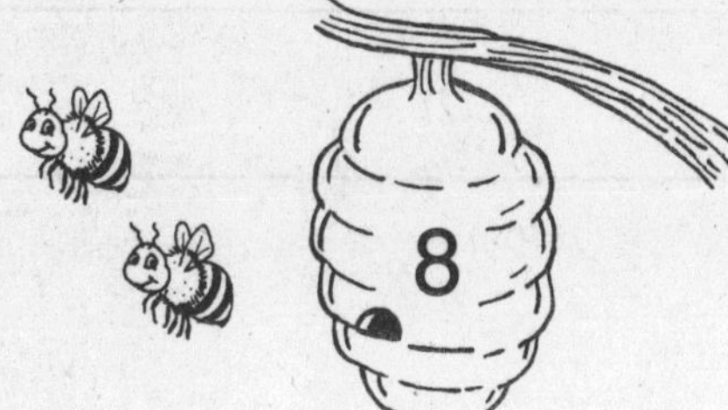

_____ , _____ $8 - 2 =$ _____

Counting Back (continued)

Count back to subtract.

4.

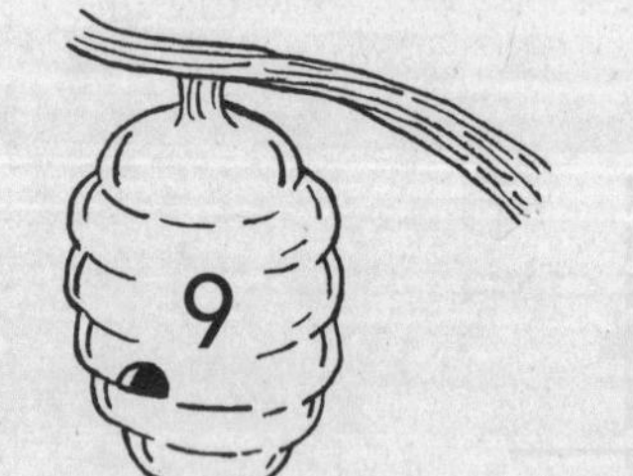

$$\begin{array}{r} 9 \\ -\ 1 \\ \hline \end{array}$$

______

5.

$$\begin{array}{r} 4 \\ -\ 1 \\ \hline \end{array}\qquad \begin{array}{r} 8 \\ -\ 1 \\ \hline \end{array}\qquad \begin{array}{r} 5 \\ -\ 2 \\ \hline \end{array}\qquad \begin{array}{r} 2 \\ -\ 1 \\ \hline \end{array}\qquad \begin{array}{r} 4 \\ -\ 2 \\ \hline \end{array}\qquad \begin{array}{r} 9 \\ -\ 2 \\ \hline \end{array}$$

6.

$$\begin{array}{r} 3 \\ -\ 1 \\ \hline \end{array}\qquad \begin{array}{r} 6 \\ -\ 2 \\ \hline \end{array}\qquad \begin{array}{r} 7 \\ -\ 1 \\ \hline \end{array}\qquad \begin{array}{r} 3 \\ -\ 2 \\ \hline \end{array}\qquad \begin{array}{r} 6 \\ -\ 1 \\ \hline \end{array}\qquad \begin{array}{r} 10 \\ -\ 1 \\ \hline \end{array}$$

7. Writing in Math Lisa had 5 apples.
Karl gave her 2 more.
Would you <u>count on</u> or <u>count back</u> to find out
how many apples Lisa has now? Why?

____

____

Name _______________________

Using Doubles to Subtract

Example

Find the double. Then subtract.

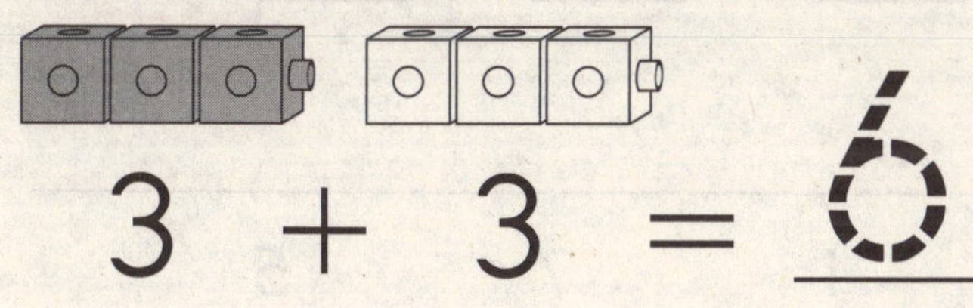

$3 + 3 = \underline{6}$ so $6 - 3 = \underline{3}$

Find the double. Then subtract.
Use cubes if you like.

1. 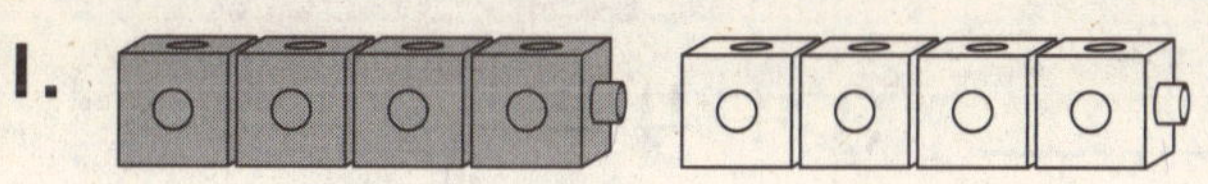

$4 + 4 = \underline{}$

so $8 - 4 = \underline{}$

2.

$2 + 2 = \underline{}$

so $4 - 2 = \underline{}$

3.

$6 + 6 = \underline{}$

so $12 - 6 = \underline{}$

4. 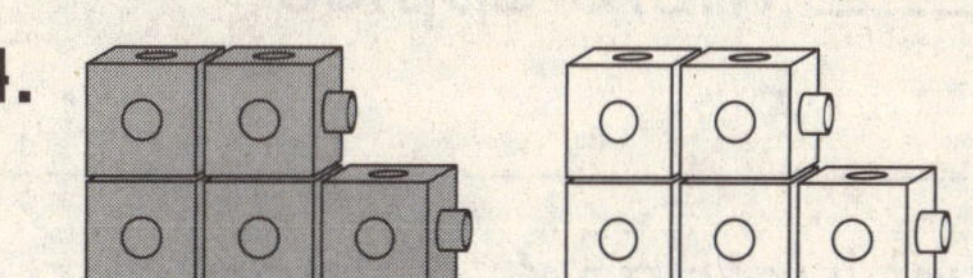

$5 + 5 = \underline{}$

so $10 - 5 = \underline{}$

Name ___________________________________

Using Doubles to Subtract (continued)

Add or subtract.

5.
$$\begin{array}{cccccc}
3 & 8 & 10 & 2 & 12 & 6 \\
+3 & -4 & -5 & +2 & -6 & -3 \\
\end{array}$$

6.
$$\begin{array}{cccccc}
4 & 2 & 4 & 1 & 7 & 5 \\
-2 & -1 & +4 & +1 & -0 & +5 \\
\end{array}$$

7.

$6 + 6 =$ _____ $9 - 1 =$ _____ $3 + 4 =$ _____

8. Carolyn has 6 apples and 3 oranges.
   How many more apples does she have?

   _____ more apples

9. Carolyn has 6 apples and 3 oranges.
   How many pieces of fruit does she have in all?

   _____ pieces of fruit

Name ______________________________

Relating Addition and Subtraction

Example

Write an addition sentence.
Write a subtraction sentence.

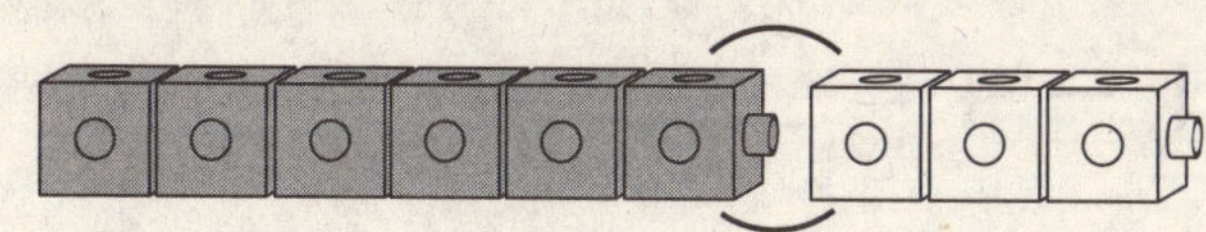 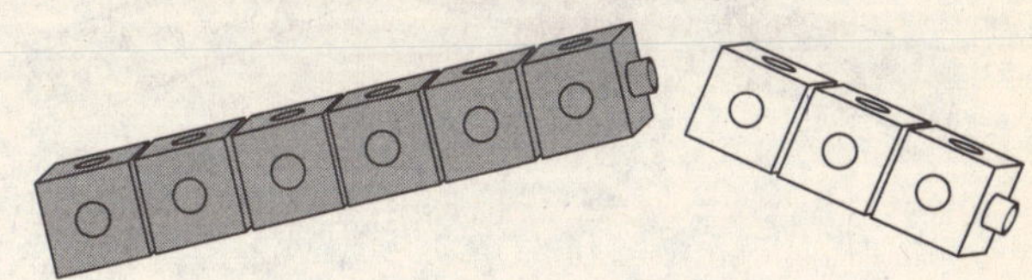

$$6 + 3 = 9 \qquad 9 - 3 = 6$$

Use two colors of cubes.
Show each number.
Write an addition sentence.
Write a subtraction sentence.

1. 3 and 5

    ___ + ___ = ___   ___ − ___ = ___

2. 5 and 4

    ___ + ___ = ___   ___ − ___ = ___

Name ____________________________________

Relating Addition and Subtraction (continued)

Add and subtract.

3.

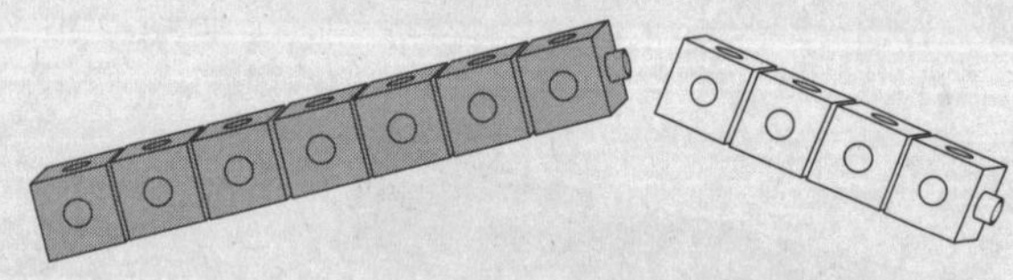

$7 + 4 =$ _____

$11 - 4 =$ _____

4.

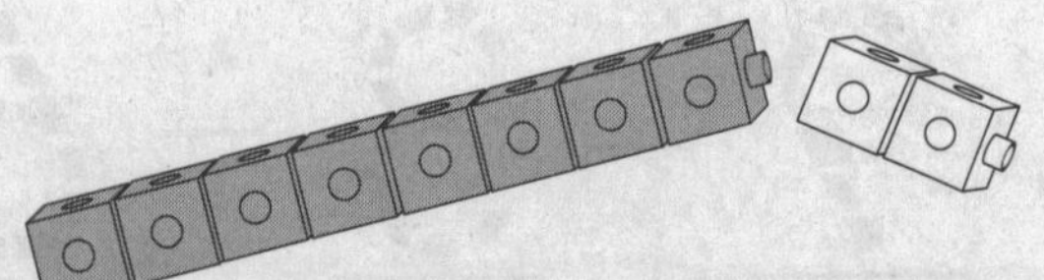

$8 + 2 =$ _____

$10 - 2 =$ _____

5.

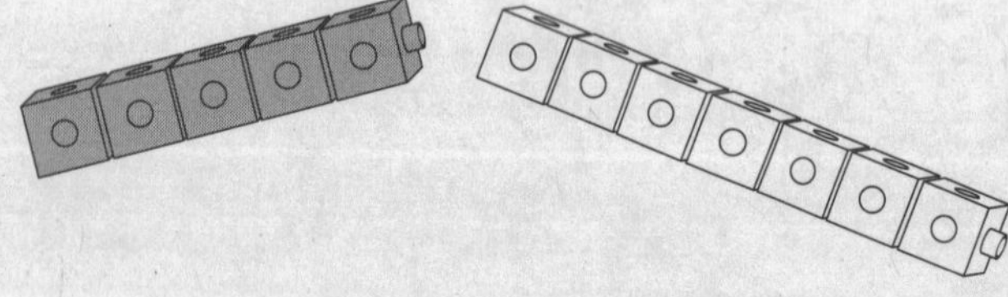

$5 + 7 =$ _____

$12 - 7 =$ _____

6. Tonya saw 8 butterflies. 3 flew away. How many butterflies are left?

____ − ____ = ____

7. Jerome found 5 fossils. Kobe found 3 fossils. How many fossils did they find in all?

____ + ____ = ____

Name ______________________________

Fact Families

Example

Write the fact family.

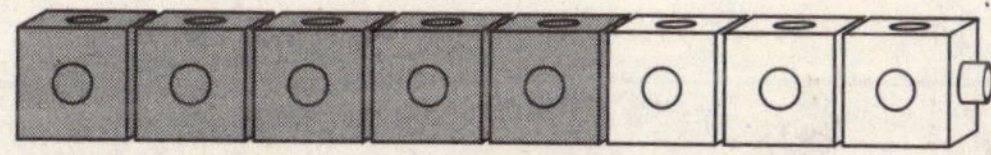

$$5 + 3 = 8 \qquad 8 - 3 = 5$$

$$3 + 5 = 8 \qquad 8 - 5 = 3$$

Write each fact family. Use cubes if you like.

1.

___ + ___ = ___   ___ − ___ = ___

___ + ___ = ___   ___ − ___ = ___

2.

___ + ___ = ___   ___ − ___ = ___

___ + ___ = ___   ___ − ___ = ___

Name ___________________________

Fact Families (continued)

Use the pictures.
Write each fact family.

3.

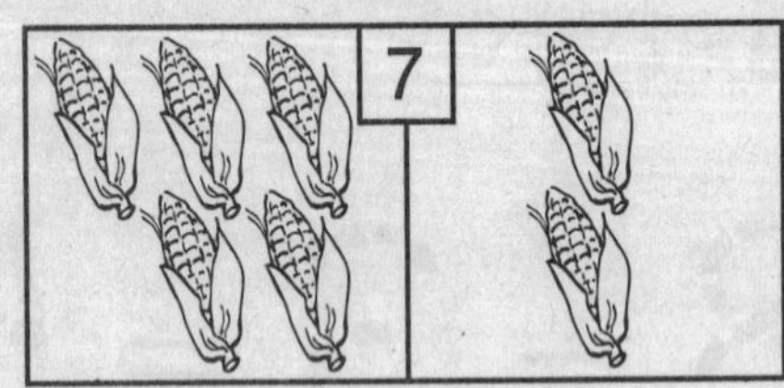

___ + ___ = ___

___ + ___ = ___

___ − ___ = ___

___ − ___ = ___

4.

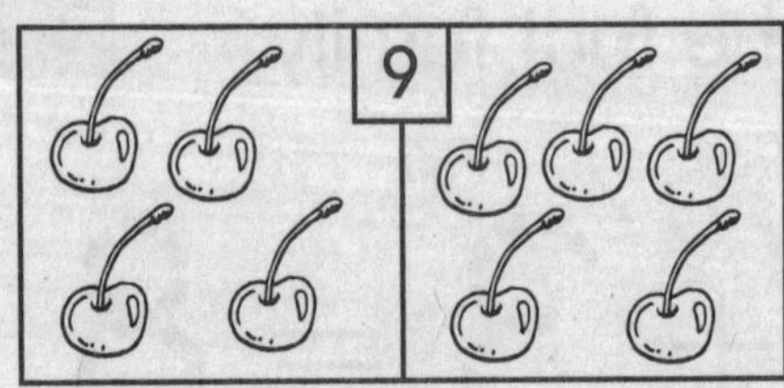

___ + ___ = ___

___ + ___ = ___

___ − ___ = ___

___ − ___ = ___

5.

___ + ___ = ___   ___ − ___ = ___

___ + ___ = ___   ___ − ___ = ___

56

Name ______________________________

Using Addition to Subtract

Example

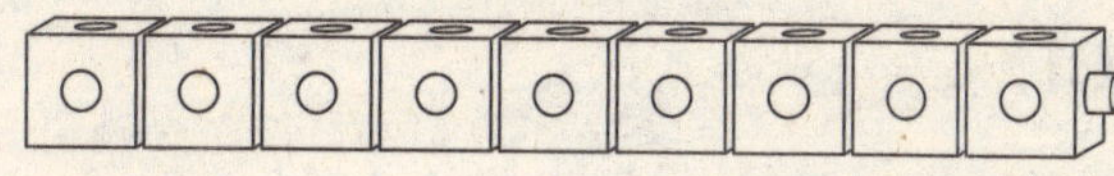

What addition fact
can help you find
12 − 3?

$$12 - 3 = 9$$

$$3 + 9 = 12$$
so $12 - 3 = 9$

Circle the related addition fact.
Then subtract.

1.   9
  − 2

$2 + 5 = 7$

$2 + 6 = 8$

$2 + 7 = 9$

2.   10
  − 8

$8 + 2 = 10$

$8 + 3 = 11$

$8 + 4 = 12$

3.   11
  − 3

$3 + 8 = 11$

$3 + 7 = 10$

$3 + 6 = 9$

4.   14
  − 6

$6 + 7 = 13$

$6 + 8 = 14$

$6 + 9 = 15$

Name ______________________________

Using Addition to Subtract (continued)

Write a related addition fact.
Then subtract.

5.

$7 - 2 =$ _____   _____ $+$ _____ $=$ _____

6.

$8 - 5 =$ _____   _____ $+$ _____ $=$ _____

7.

$10 - 6 =$ _____   _____ $+$ _____ $=$ _____

8.

$12 - 5 =$ _____   _____ $+$ _____ $=$ _____

9.

$13 - 9 =$ _____   _____ $+$ _____ $=$ _____

Solve.

10. Michael saw 8 bees by a hive.
2 bees went in the hive.
Then, 3 more bees went in the hive.
Next, 5 bees came out of the hive.
How many bees are by the hive now?   _____ bees

Doubles to 20

Example

Complete each addition sentence to make a double.

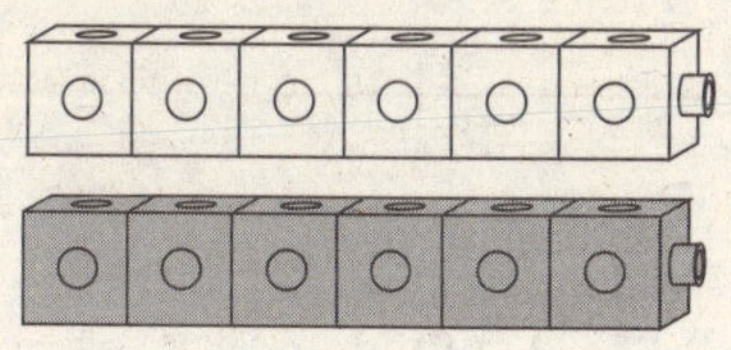

$$6 + \underline{6} = \underline{12}$$

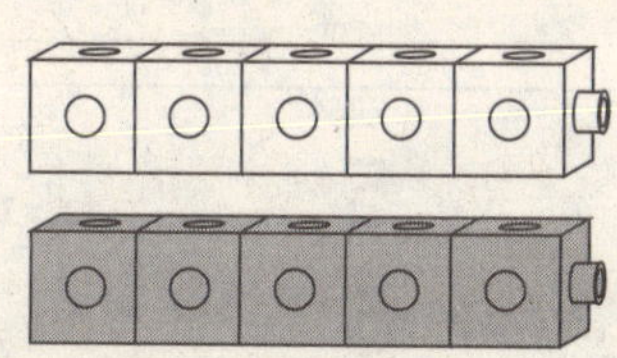

$$5 + \underline{5} = \underline{10}$$

Use two colors of cubes. Show each number. Then show the double. Complete the addition sentence.

1. Show 2.

   2 + _____ = _____

2. Show 7.

   7 + _____ = _____

3. Show 9.

   9 + _____ = _____

4. Show 4.

   4 + _____ = _____

5. Show 10.

   10 + _____ = _____

6. Show 8.

   8 + _____ = _____

Doubles to 20 (continued)

Add. Circle the doubles. Use cubes if you like.

7.

$3 + 3 =$ _____ $\qquad$ $8 + 2 =$ _____ $\qquad$ $9 + 9 =$ _____

8.

$2 + 9 =$ _____ $\qquad$ $10 + 10 =$ _____ $\qquad$ $7 + 3 =$ _____

9.
$$\begin{array}{cccccc} 6 & 1 & 4 & 3 & 4 & 5 \\ +3 & +1 & +4 & +5 & +9 & +5 \end{array}$$

Solve.

10. Thomas picked 12 flowers. He picked the same number of yellow flowers as red flowers. How many flowers of each color does he have?

_____ yellow _____ red

11. Rhonda has 16 flowers altogether. She has 2 more yellow flowers than blue flowers. How many flowers of each color does she have?

_____ yellow _____ blue

Name ______________________________

Using Doubles to Add

Example

How can you use doubles to add 6 + 7?

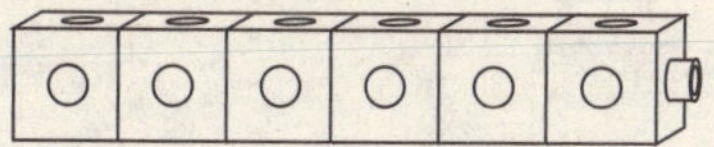

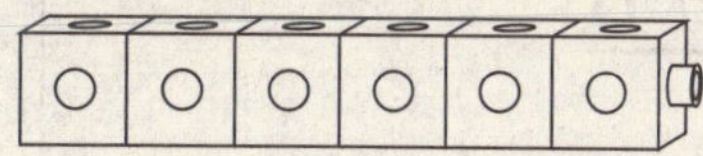

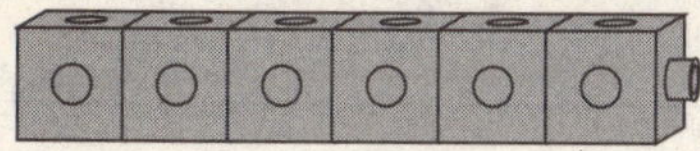

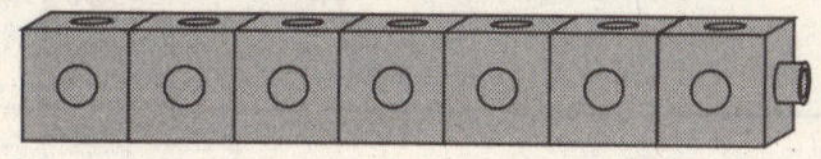

$6 + 6 = \underline{12}$ $6 + 7 = \underline{13}$

Think 6 + 6 = 12 and 1 more is 13.

Use cubes. Write each sum.

1.

$2 + 2 = \underline{\hspace{1.5cm}}$

$2 + 3 = \underline{\hspace{1.5cm}}$

2.

$5 + 5 = \underline{\hspace{1.5cm}}$

$5 + 6 = \underline{\hspace{1.5cm}}$

3.

$8 + 8 = \underline{\hspace{1.5cm}}$

$8 + 9 = \underline{\hspace{1.5cm}}$

4. $4 + 4 = \underline{\hspace{1.5cm}}$

$4 + 5 = \underline{\hspace{1.5cm}}$

Name ______________________________

Using Doubles to Add (continued)

Write each sum.
Use cubes if you like.

5. $\begin{array}{r} 7 \\ +7 \\ \hline \end{array}$ $\begin{array}{r} 7 \\ +8 \\ \hline \end{array}$ **6.** $\begin{array}{r} 4 \\ +4 \\ \hline \end{array}$ $\begin{array}{r} 5 \\ +4 \\ \hline \end{array}$

7. $\begin{array}{r} 1 \\ +1 \\ \hline \end{array}$ $\begin{array}{r} 2 \\ +1 \\ \hline \end{array}$ **8.** $\begin{array}{r} 6 \\ +6 \\ \hline \end{array}$ $\begin{array}{r} 7 \\ +6 \\ \hline \end{array}$

9. $\begin{array}{r} 5 \\ +5 \\ \hline \end{array}$ $\begin{array}{r} 6 \\ +5 \\ \hline \end{array}$ **10.** $\begin{array}{r} 8 \\ +8 \\ \hline \end{array}$ $\begin{array}{r} 9 \\ +8 \\ \hline \end{array}$

Solve.

11. There are 9 bees near a hive. There are double
that many and one more in the hive. How many
bees are in the hive?

________ bees

Name ______________________________

Adding 10

Example

Find $10 + 3$

$10 + 3 = \underline{13}$

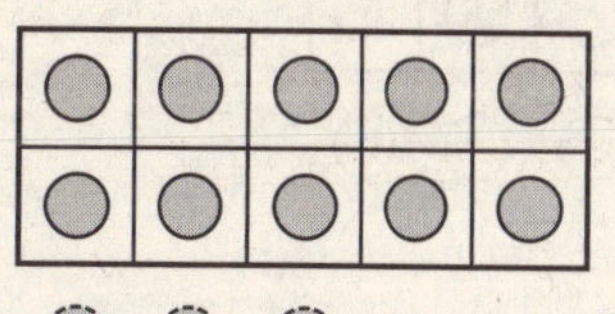

10

11 12 13

There are 10 counters
in the ten-frame. Add
3 more counters.

Draw the counters. Then find the sum.

1.

$10 + 1 = \underline{\hspace{2cm}}$

2.

$10 + 2 = \underline{\hspace{2cm}}$

3. 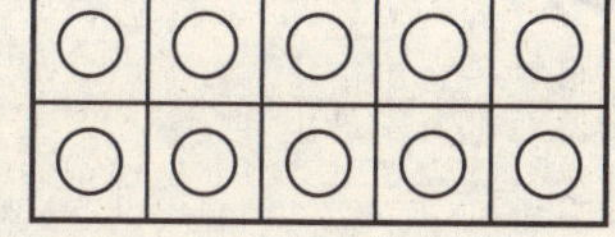

$10 + 4 = \underline{\hspace{2cm}}$

4. 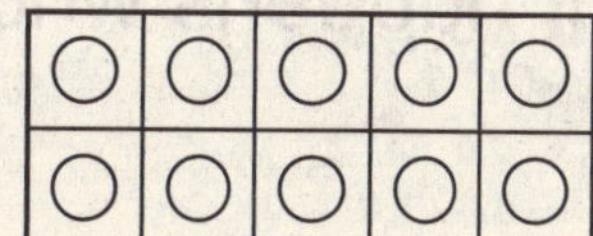

$10 + 5 = \underline{\hspace{2cm}}$

Name ___________________________

Adding 10 (continued)

Write the addition sentence for each ten-frame.

5. 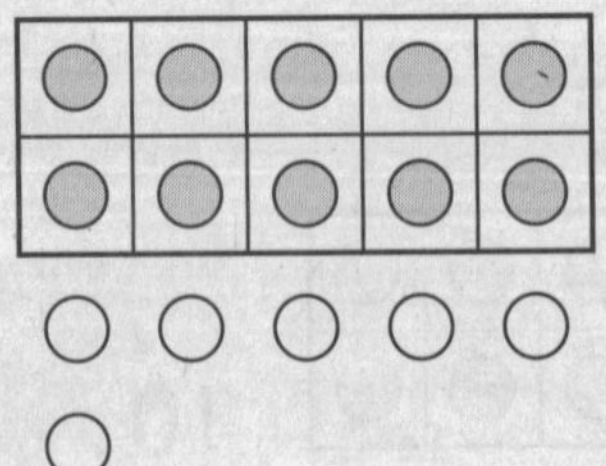

__10__ + __6__ = _____

6. 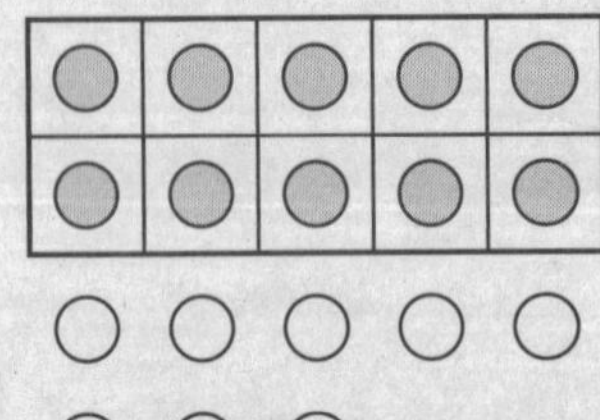

_____ + _____ = _____

7. 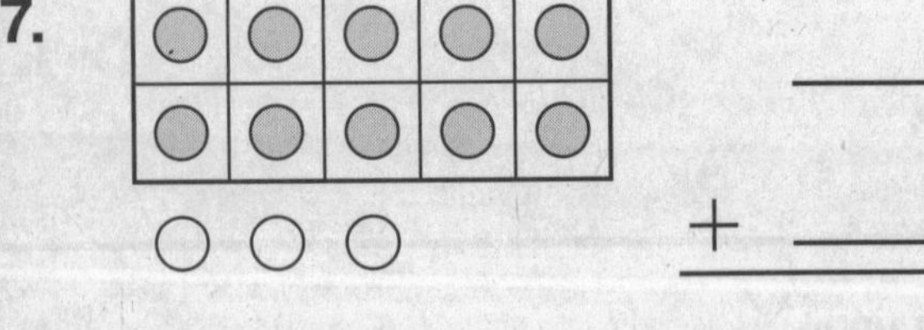

   _____
+ _____
   _____

8. 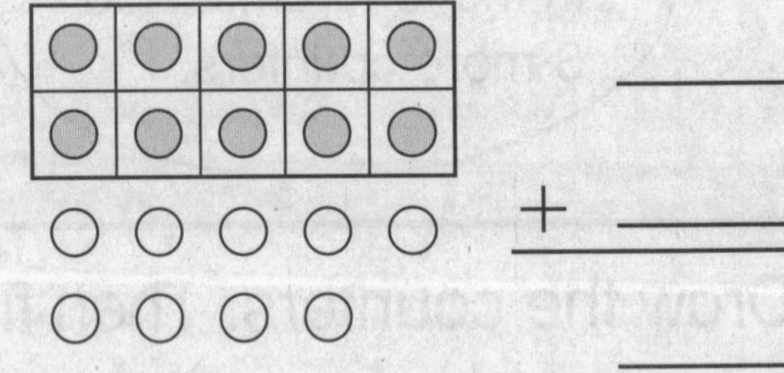

   _____
+ _____
   _____

9. **Writing in Math**   Look at the addition sentences.

$$10 + 1 = 11 \qquad 10 + 2 = 12 \qquad 10 + 3 = 13$$

$$10 + 4 = 14 \qquad 10 + 5 = 15 \qquad 10 + 6 = 16$$

Tell what happens when you add $10 + 8$.

____

____

Name ______________________

Making 10 to Add 7, 8, and 9

Example

Draw more dots to add.

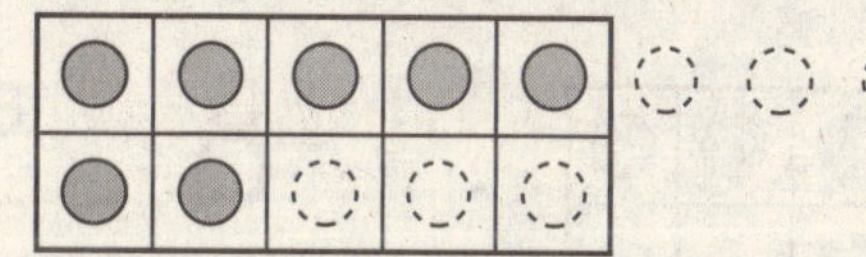

$7 + 6$ $10 + 3 = \underline{13}$

so $7 + 6 = \underline{13}$

Draw more dots to add.

1.
$\begin{array}{r} 8 \\ + 3 \\ \hline \end{array}$

2.
$\begin{array}{r} 7 \\ + 7 \\ \hline \end{array}$

3.
$\begin{array}{r} 7 \\ + 4 \\ \hline \end{array}$

4.
$\begin{array}{r} 8 \\ + 7 \\ \hline \end{array}$

5.
$\begin{array}{r} 8 \\ + 8 \\ \hline \end{array}$

6.
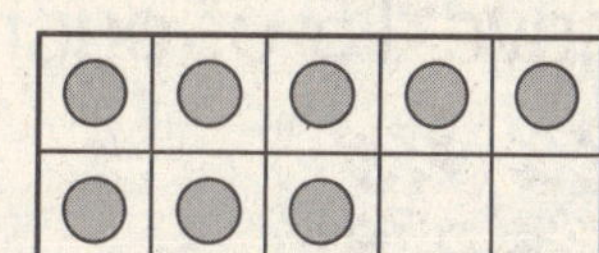
$\begin{array}{r} 8 \\ + 4 \\ \hline \end{array}$

Name ____

Making 10 to Add 7, 8, and 9 (continued)

Draw more dots to add.

7. 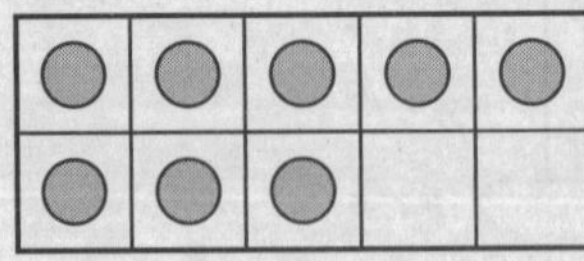
$$\begin{array}{r} 8 \\ +5 \\ \hline \end{array}$$

8. 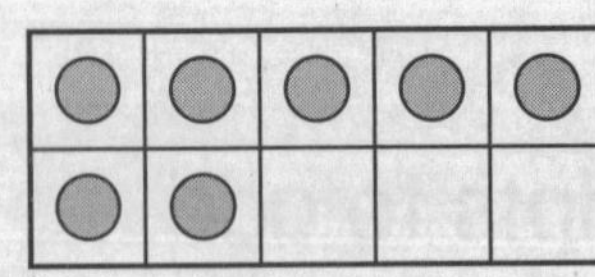
$$\begin{array}{r} 7 \\ +5 \\ \hline \end{array}$$

9. 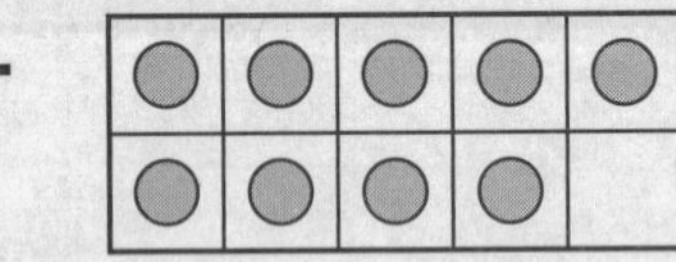
$$\begin{array}{r} 9 \\ +6 \\ \hline \end{array}$$

10. 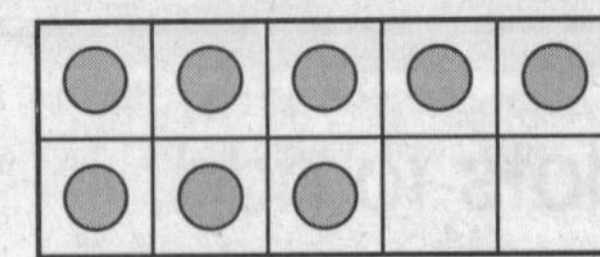
$$\begin{array}{r} 8 \\ +6 \\ \hline \end{array}$$

11. 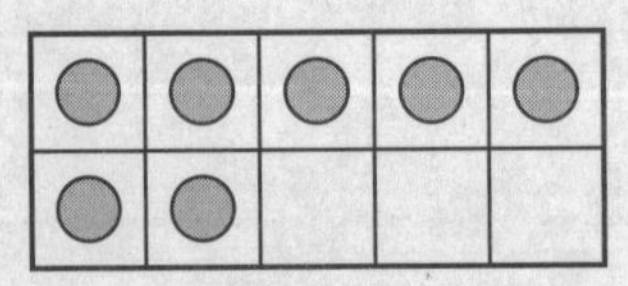
$$\begin{array}{r} 7 \\ +8 \\ \hline \end{array}$$

12. 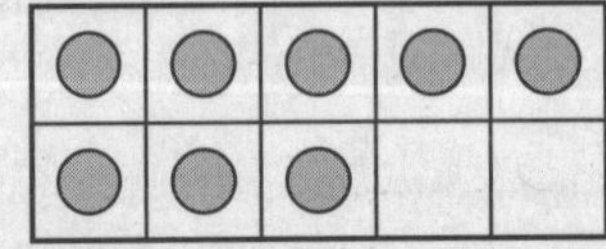
$$\begin{array}{r} 8 \\ +9 \\ \hline \end{array}$$

13. Brittany is planning a picnic for 15 people.
How many more hamburgers, buns, and
cartons of juice does Brittany need so that
she will have 15 of each?

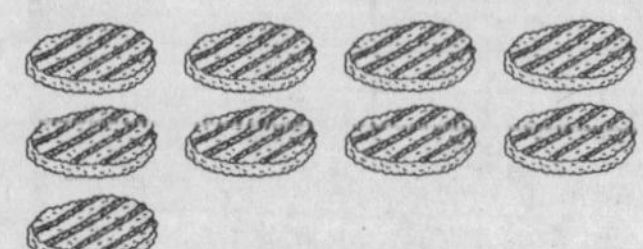

_______   _______   _______
more hamburgers   more buns   more cartons of juice

Using Addition Strategies

Examples

Use doubles to add.

$$\begin{array}{r} 5 \\ +6 \\ \hline 11 \end{array}$$

Think $5 + 5 = 10$
and 1 more is 11.

Make 10 to add.

$$\begin{array}{r} 8 \\ +4 \\ \hline 12 \end{array}$$

Think $8 + 2 = 10$
and 2 more is 12.

Count on to add.

$$3 + 9 = 12$$

$$9, 10, 11, 12$$

Add. Tell how you found each sum.

1.
$$\begin{array}{r} 7 \\ +8 \\ \hline \end{array} \qquad \begin{array}{r} 9 \\ +5 \\ \hline \end{array} \qquad \begin{array}{r} 6 \\ +3 \\ \hline \end{array} \qquad \begin{array}{r} 9 \\ +9 \\ \hline \end{array} \qquad \begin{array}{r} 4 \\ +5 \\ \hline \end{array} \qquad \begin{array}{r} 8 \\ +5 \\ \hline \end{array}$$

2.
$$\begin{array}{r} 6 \\ +4 \\ \hline \end{array} \qquad \begin{array}{r} 3 \\ +4 \\ \hline \end{array} \qquad \begin{array}{r} 9 \\ +6 \\ \hline \end{array} \qquad \begin{array}{r} 7 \\ +2 \\ \hline \end{array} \qquad \begin{array}{r} 8 \\ +1 \\ \hline \end{array} \qquad \begin{array}{r} 6 \\ +7 \\ \hline \end{array}$$

Name ____

Using Addition Strategies (continued)

Follow each rule.

3.

Double it. Then add 1.	
3	
4	
5	
6	
7	

4.

Add 9.	
2	
3	
4	
5	
6	

5.

Add 2.	
10	
9	
8	
7	
6	

6.

Add 3.	
9	
8	
7	
6	
5	

7.

Add 8.	
4	
6	
3	
7	
5	

8.

Double it.	
5	
6	
7	
8	
9	

Name ___________________________

Adding Three Numbers

Example

Find each sum.

Make 10.

5
*2 ⎤→ 10
+ 8 ⎦

5
+ 10
15

Add doubles first.

9
*3 ⎤→ 6
+ 3 ⎦

9
+ 6
15

Find each sum.

1.

7	8	2	2	9	3
5	3	9	8	6	3
+ 5	+ 7	+ 1	+ 6	+ 4	+ 7

2.

9	6	7	4	1	7
2	6	2	4	8	7
+ 2	+ 1	+ 8	+ 7	+ 8	+ 2

3.

$9 + 1 + 9 = $ _______ $4 + 8 + 2 = $ _______

Adding Three Numbers (continued)

Find each sum.

4.

$$
\begin{array}{cccccc}
4 & 7 & 2 & 5 & 1 & 3 \\
3 & 3 & 8 & 5 & 9 & 4 \\
+\,3 & +\,5 & +\,2 & +\,3 & +\,6 & +\,4 \\
\hline
\end{array}
$$

5.

$$0 + 8 + 8 = \underline{\hspace{2em}} \qquad 4 + 6 + 8 = \underline{\hspace{2em}}$$

6.

$$2 + 6 + 6 = \underline{\hspace{2em}} \qquad 6 + 7 + 3 = \underline{\hspace{2em}}$$

Add across. Add down.
The sum is the same. Complete each ⊞.

7.

1		5
	4	0
	2	

8.

		4
7	5	
	1	8

Each sum is 12.   Each sum is 15.

Name ____

Relating Addition and Subtraction

Example

Add. Then subtract.

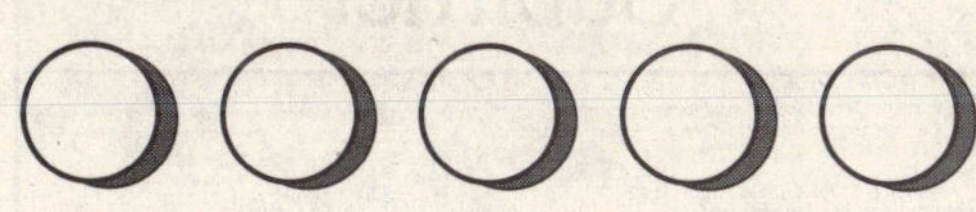 

$$5 + 6 = 11$$

$$11 - 6 = 5$$

Use two colors of counters.
Show each number. Add. Then subtract.

1.

Start with 6. Add 8. ______ + ______ = ______

Now subtract 8. ______ − ______ = ______

2.

Start with 9. Add 7. ______ + ______ = ______

Now subtract 7. ______ − ______ = ______

Name ___________________________________

Relating Addition and Subtraction (continued)

Use two colors of counters.
Show each number. Add. Then subtract.

	Add	Subtract
3. \[6\] \[7\]	___ + ___ = ___	___ − ___ = ___
4. \[7\] \[5\]	___ + ___ = ___	___ − ___ = ___
5. \[9\] \[4\]	___ + ___ = ___	___ − ___ = ___
6. \[7\] \[8\]	___ + ___ = ___	___ − ___ = ___
7. \[9\] \[6\]	___ + ___ = ___	___ − ___ = ___

Solve.

8. The sum of two numbers is 9.
    The difference of the numbers is 1.
    What are the numbers?   _______ and _______

Name _______________________________

Fact Families

Example

Add or subtract.

(17
9 8)

$9 + 8 = \underline{17}$ $17 - 8 = \underline{9}$

$8 + 9 = \underline{17}$ $17 - 9 = \underline{8}$

Add or subtract. Use the numbers to write the fact family.

1.

(10
6 4)

___ + ___ = ___   ___ − ___ = ___

___ + ___ = ___   ___ − ___ = ___

2.

(13
4 9)

___ + ___ = ___   ___ − ___ = ___

___ + ___ = ___   ___ − ___ = ___

3.

(17
9 8)

___ + ___ = ___   ___ − ___ = ___

___ + ___ = ___   ___ − ___ = ___

Fact Families (continued)

Add or subtract. Use the numbers to write the fact family.

4.

(13 / 7 6)

___ + ___ = ___   ___ − ___ = ___

___ + ___ = ___   ___ − ___ = ___

5.

(16 / 7 9)

___ + ___ = ___   ___ − ___ = ___

___ + ___ = ___   ___ − ___ = ___

6.

(12 / 5 7)

___ + ___ = ___   ___ − ___ = ___

___ + ___ = ___   ___ − ___ = ___

7.

(18 / 9 9)

___ + ___ = ___   ___ − ___ = ___

8.

(15 / 7 8)

___ + ___ = ___   ___ − ___ = ___

___ + ___ = ___   ___ − ___ = ___

Name ______________________________

Using Addition to Subtract

Example

You can use an addition fact to help you subtract.

$$7 + 4 = 11 \qquad 11 - 4 = \underline{7}$$

Add. Then use the addition fact to help you subtract.

1.

$$5 + 9 = \underline{14}$$

$$14 - 9 = \underline{}$$

2.

$$4 + 5 = \underline{}$$

$$9 - 5 = \underline{}$$

Using Addition to Subtract (continued)

Circle the addition fact that will help you subtract.
Then subtract.

3. $8 - 3 =$ ___ 5

$5 + 3 = 8$

$4 + 5 = 9$

4. $10 - 3 =$ ___

$7 + 5 = 12$

$7 + 3 = 10$

5. $16 - 9 =$ ___

$9 + 7 = 16$

$8 + 8 = 16$

6. $11 - 3 =$ ___

$3 + 9 = 12$

$8 + 3 = 11$

7. $14 - 7 =$ ___

$7 + 7 = 14$

$6 + 7 = 13$

8. $17 - 9 =$ ___

$8 + 9 = 17$

$9 + 6 = 15$

Number Sense

9. If 5¢ plus 9¢ is 14¢, 14¢ minus 9¢ is _______¢.

Using 10 to Subtract

Example

Cross out to subtract.

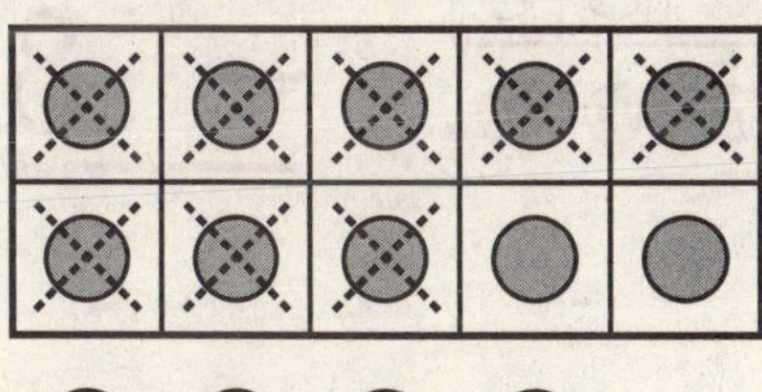

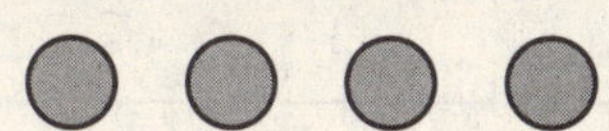

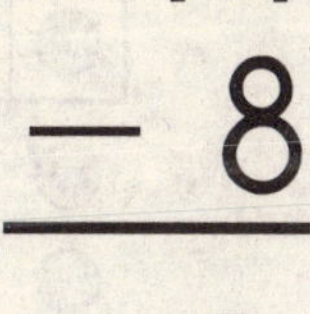

There are 2 in
the ten-frame and
4 extra.

So, $14 - 8 = 6$.

Cross out to subtract.
Use counters and Workmat 2 if you like.

1. 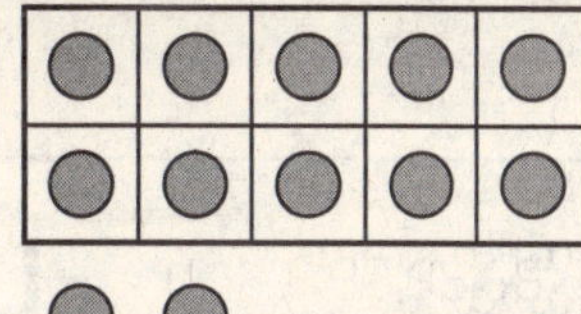

$$\begin{array}{r} 14 \\ -\ 9 \\ \hline \end{array}$$

2.

$$\begin{array}{r} 12 \\ -\ 9 \\ \hline \end{array}$$

3. 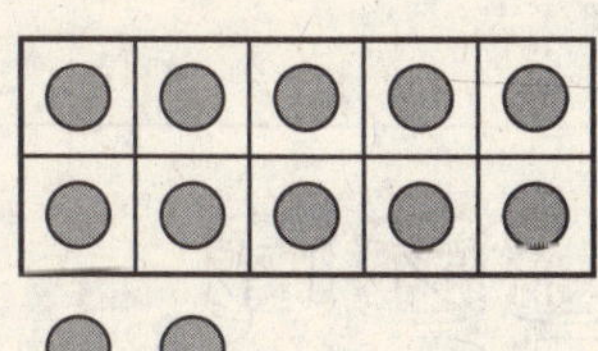

$$\begin{array}{r} 12 \\ -\ 8 \\ \hline \end{array}$$

4. 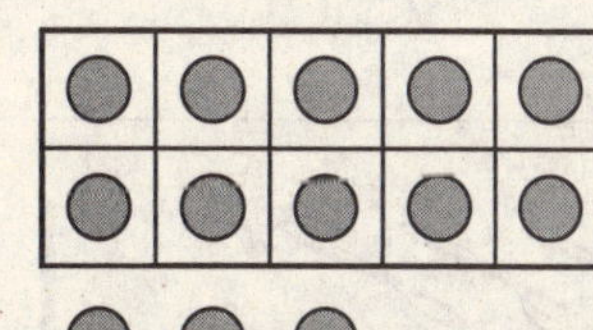

$$\begin{array}{r} 13 \\ -\ 8 \\ \hline \end{array}$$

Name ___________________________

Using 10 to Subtract (continued)

Cross out to subtract.

5. 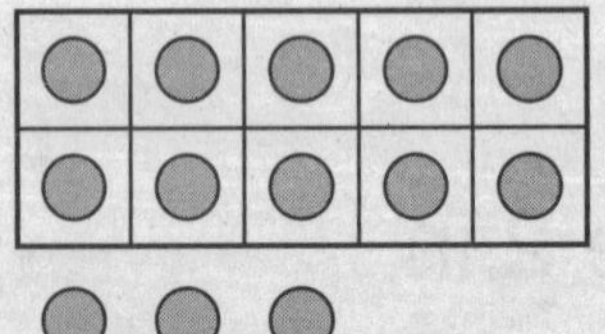

$$13 - 9$$

6. 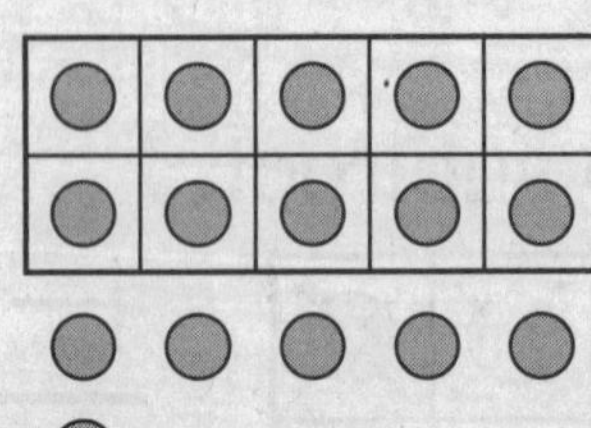

$$16 - 8$$

7. 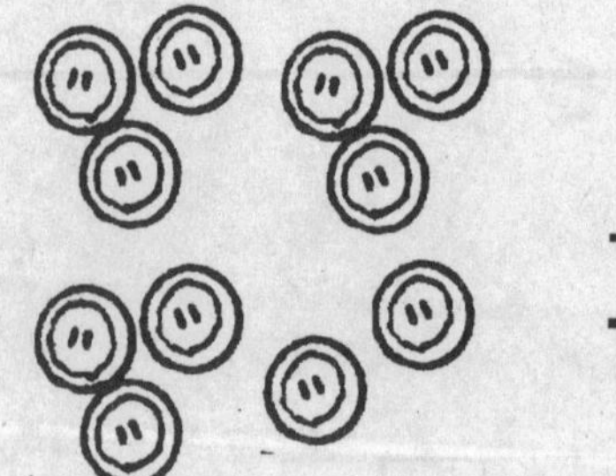

$$11 - 9$$

8. 

$$11 - 8$$

9. 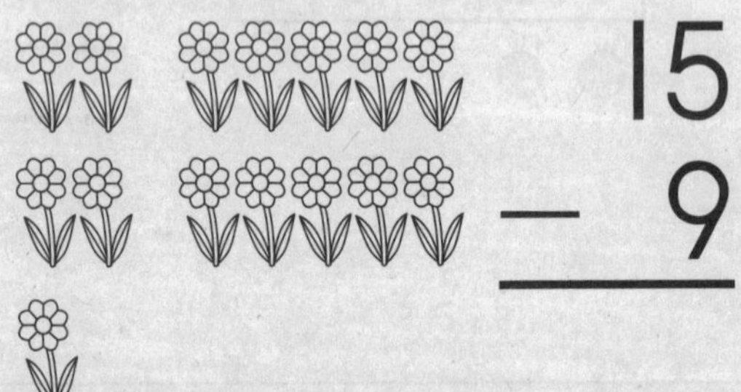

$$15 - 9$$

10. 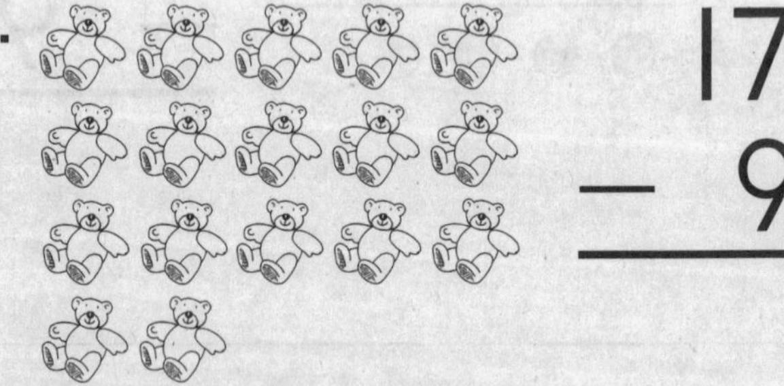

$$17 - 9$$

11. 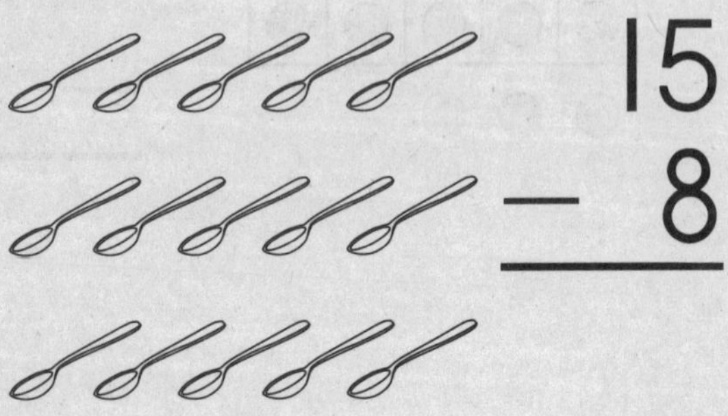

$$15 - 8$$

12. 

$$16 - 9$$

Name ______________________________

Using Subtraction Strategies

Examples

Subtract.

$$13 - 6 = 7$$

Think $6 + 7 = 13$
So, $13 - 6 = 7$.

$$14 - 9 = 5$$

Use ten. Think
$9 + 1 = 10$
$1 + 4 = 5$
So, $14 - 9 = 5$.

$$11 - 2 = \underline{9}$$ Count back. 11, 10, 9

Subtract. Tell how you found each difference.

1.

9	10	15	12	13	12
− 2	− 1	− 6	− 4	− 9	− 8

2.

16	17	12	11	15	6
− 8	− 9	− 5	− 3	− 7	− 1

Using Subtraction Strategies (continued)

Follow the path to add and subtract.

3. Write the missing numbers.

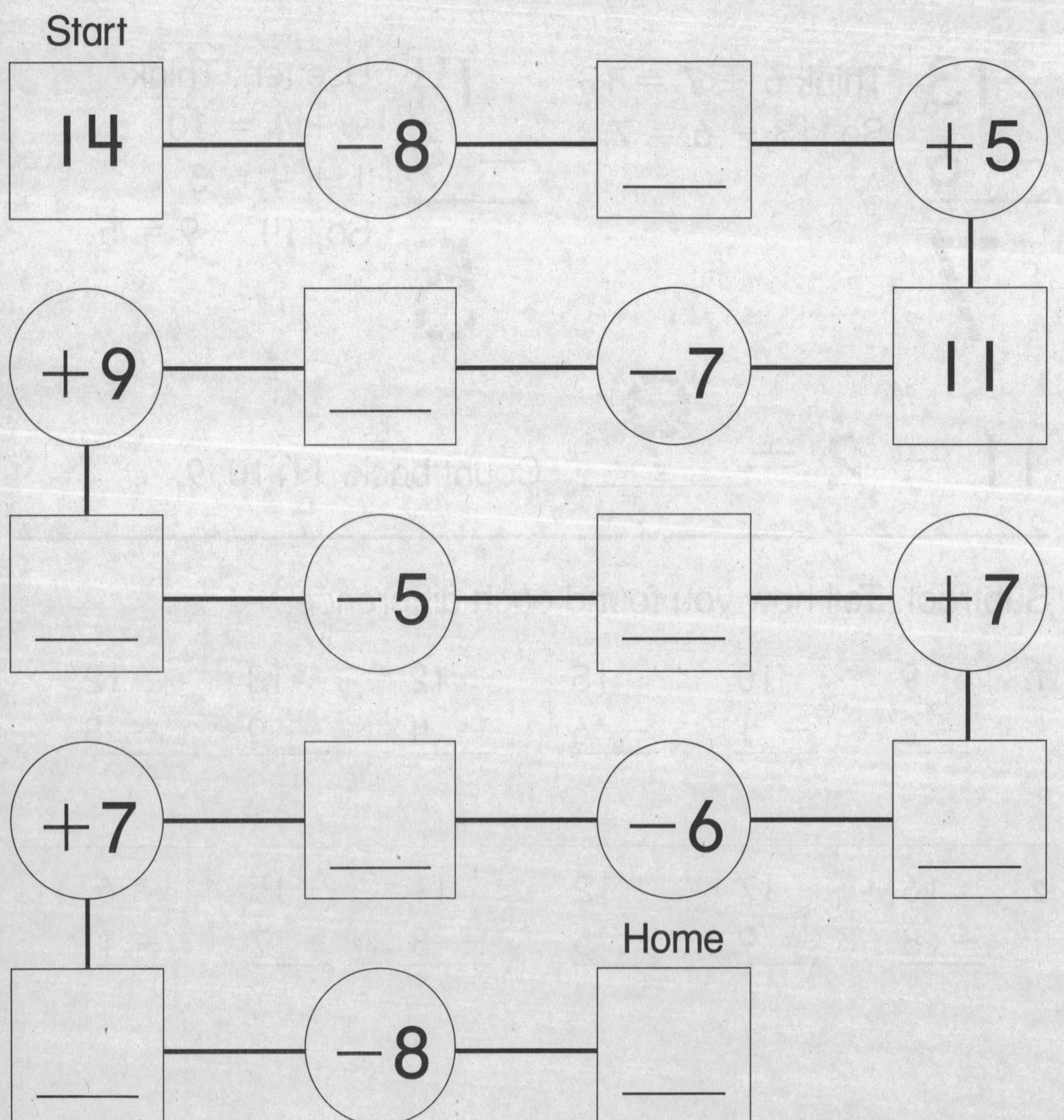

Name ___________________________

Joining Groups to Add

Example

Count the counters in each group.
Add to join the groups and show how many in all.

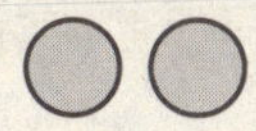 

____2____ and ____3____ is ____5____ in all.

2 gray counters and 3 white counters is 5 counters in all.

Count the counters in the two groups.
Write how many there are in all.

1. 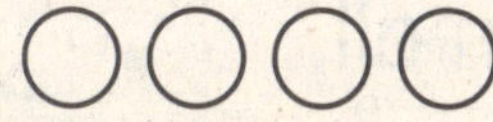

   ____2____ and ____4____ is ____ in all.

2. 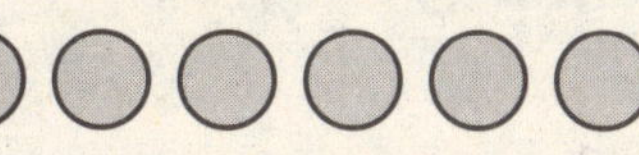 

   ____6____ and ____1____ is ____ in all.

3. 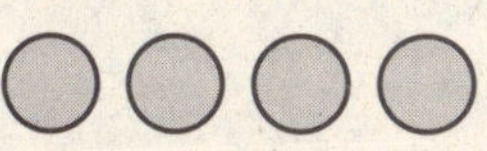 

   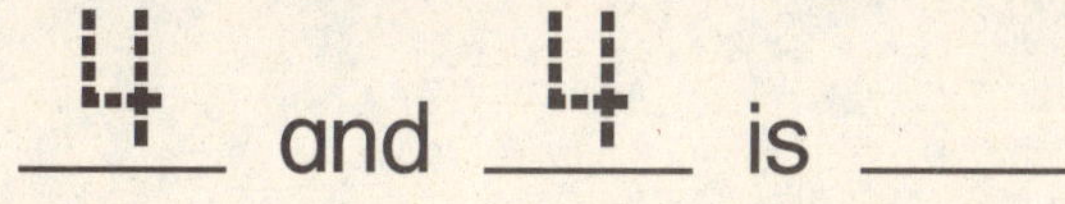
   ____4____ and ____4____ is ____ in all.

Name ____

Joining Groups to Add (continued)

Count the counters in the two groups.
Write how many there are in all.

4.  

_____ and _____ is _____ in all.

5. 

_____ and _____ is _____ in all.

6.

_____ and _____ is _____ in all.

7. Reasoning Kim cut out circles and put them
in two groups. There are 2 circles in one group.
There are 5 circles in another group.
Write how many circles in all.

_____ and _____ is _____ in all.

Name ___________________

Writing Addition Sentences

Example

Write an addition sentence.
Count the counters in each group.
How many counters in all?

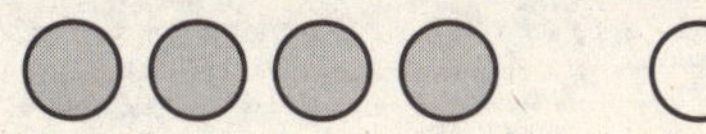

___4___ and ___2___ is ___6___.

___4___ and ___2___ equals ___6___.

___4___ + ___2___ = ___6___

Write the addition sentence.

1. 

   ______ + ______ = ______

2. ______ + ______ = ______

3. 

   ______ + ______ = ______

Name ____

Writing Addition Sentences (continued)

Add to find out how many in all.
Write the addition sentence.

4. 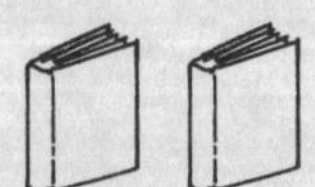   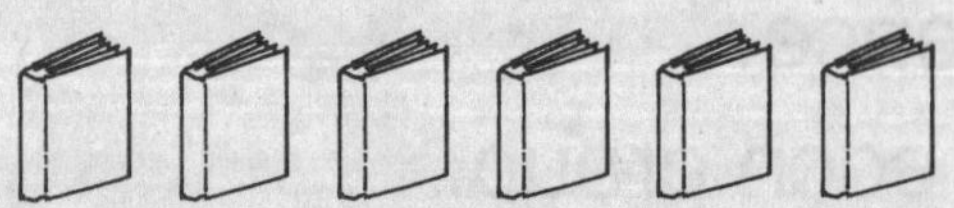

_______ + _______ = _______

5. 

_______ + _______ = _______

6. 

_______ + _______ = _______

7. 

_______ + _______ = _______

Write the number sentence.

8. Sasha has 2 books.
    Ann has 5 books.
    How many books do they have in all?

_______ + _______ = _______ books

Name ________________________

Taking Away to Subtract

Example

There are 6 hearts. Take away 3 hearts.
Count how many hearts are left.

_____ take away _____ is _____.

_____ hearts are left.

Cross out to subtract.
Write how many are left.

1. 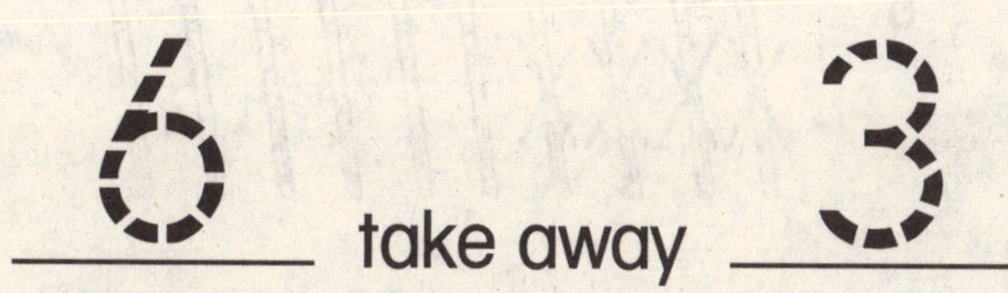

5 take away 3 is _____.

2.

7 take away 4 is _____.

3. 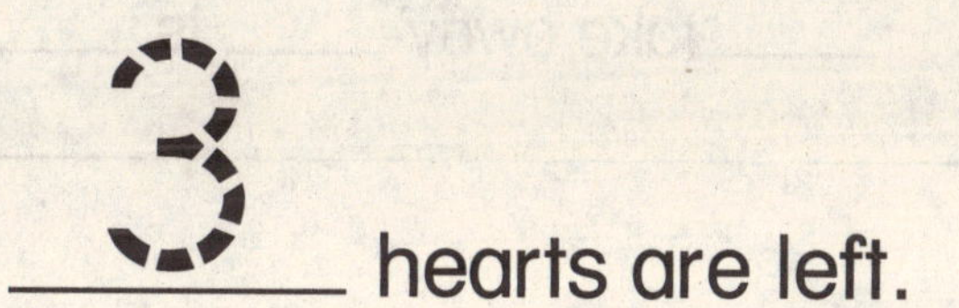

8 take away 5 = _____.

4.

9 take away 4 = _____.

Name ____

Taking Away to Subtract (continued)

Take away to subtract.
Write the numbers.

5.

_____ take away _____ is _____.

6.

_____ take away _____ is _____.

7.

_____ take away _____ is _____.

8.

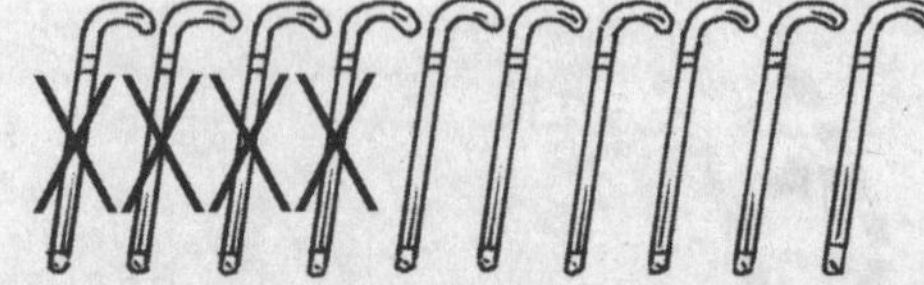

_____ take away _____ is _____.

Cross out to subtract.
Write how many are left.

9. 8 pennies take away 2 pennies.

8 take away 2 is _____

10. 10 pennies take away 8 pennies.

10 take away 8 is _____.

86

Name ______________________

Comparing to Find How Many More

Example

How many more  than  are there?

You can compare to find how many more.
Match each counter in one group to a counter in the other group. Count how many are left over.

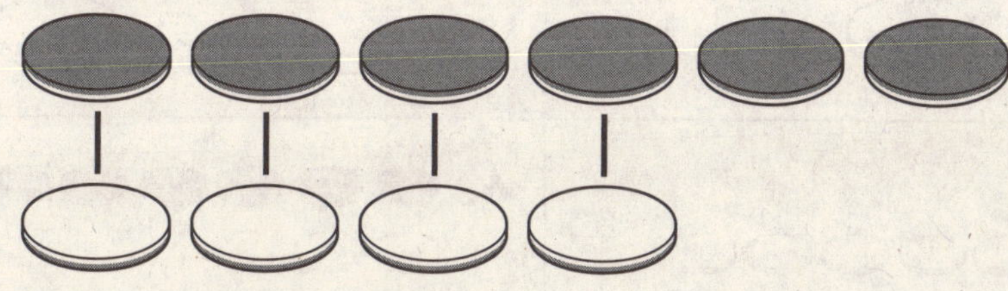

There are _____ 2 _____ left over.

There are _____ 2 _____ more than .

Compare. Write the numbers.
Use counters if you need to.

1. 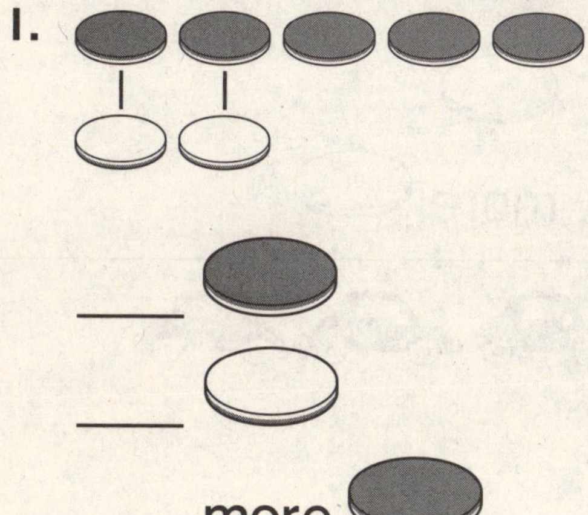

2. 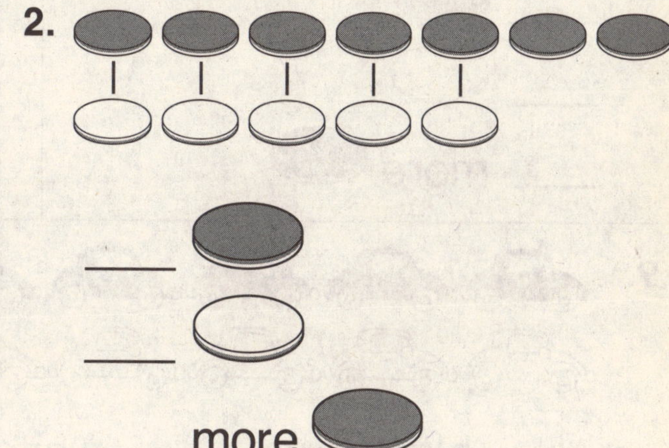

87

Name _______________________________

Comparing to Find How Many More (continued)

Compare. Write the numbers.
Use counters if you need to.

3. 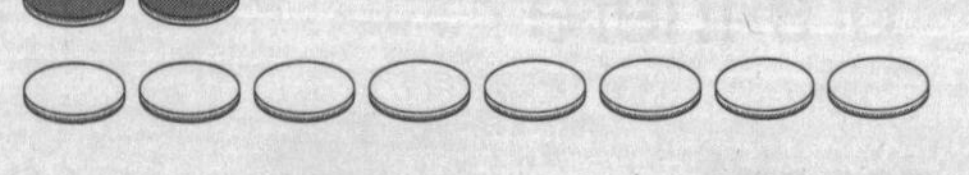

____
____
____ more

4. 

____
____
____ more

5. 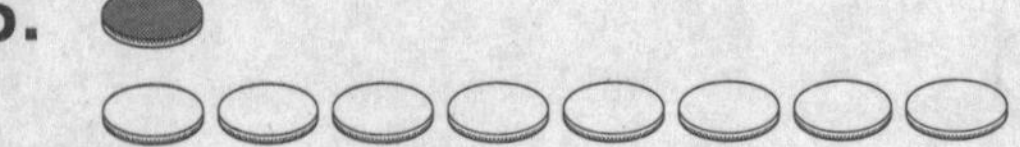

____
____
____ more

6.  

____
____
____ more

7.  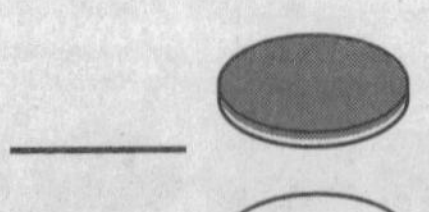

____
____
____ more

8. 

____
____
____ more

9. 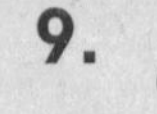 

____ black cars ____ white cars ____ more black cars

88

Name ____

Writing Subtraction Sentences

Example 1

There are 6 bees. Take away 2 bees.
How many bees are left? 

______ take away ______ is ______.

______ − ______ is ______.

______ − ______ = ______ bees left

Example 2

How many more bees are there? 
Compare 6 to 2.

______ minus ______ is ______.

______ − ______ = ______ more bees

Write the subtraction sentence.

ı. Kristen had 7 books.
    She gave 3 away.
    How many books does she have left? 

______ − ______ = ______ books

89

Name _______________________________

Writing Subtraction Sentences (continued)

Write the subtraction sentence.

2. Pedro caught 8 butterflies.
    David caught 3 butterflies.
    How many more butterflies did Pedro catch?

    ____ − ____ = ____ butterflies

3. 9 birds were sitting on a fence.
    6 birds flew away.
    How many birds were left?

    ____ − ____ = ____ birds

4. There are 2 ducks in the pond.
    There are 8 ducks out of the pond.
    How many more ducks are out of the pond?

    ____ − ____ = ____ ducks

Write the subtraction sentence. Use counters if you need to.

5. There were 9 pigs in the
    pen. 2 ran away. How
    many pigs are still in the
    pen?

    ____ − ____ = ____ pigs

6. There are 10 spotted
    cows. There are 6 white
    cows. How many more
    spotted cows are there?

    ____ − ____ = ____ cows

Ways to Make Ten

Example

Find different ways to make ten.
Complete the number sentence.

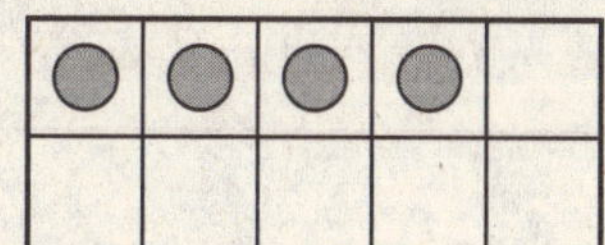

$$4 + \underline{6} = 10 \qquad 9 + \underline{1} = 10$$

Use the ten-frames to find different ways to make 10.
Complete each number sentence.

1.
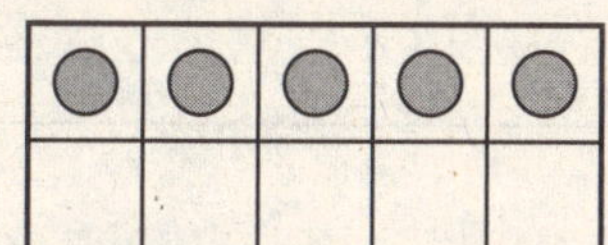

$$5 + \underline{} = 10$$

2.
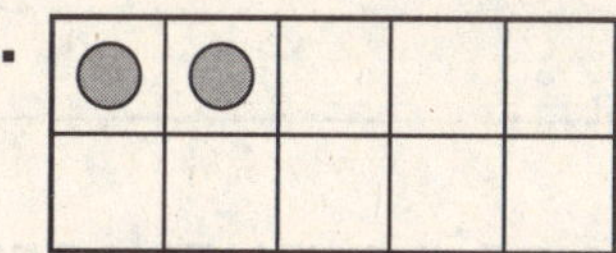

$$2 + \underline{} = 10$$

3.
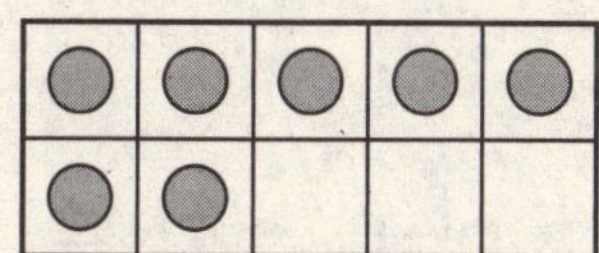

$$7 + \underline{} = 10$$

4.
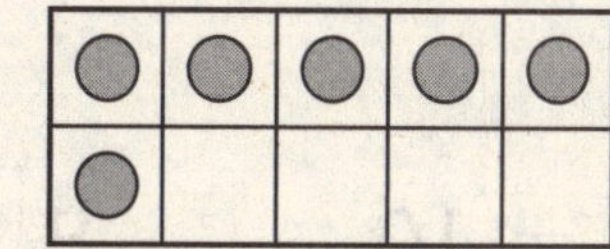

$$6 + \underline{} = 10$$

5.
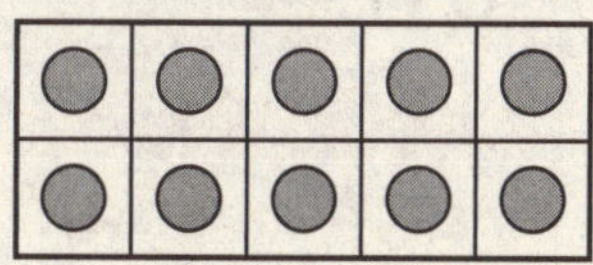

$$10 + \underline{} = 10$$

6.
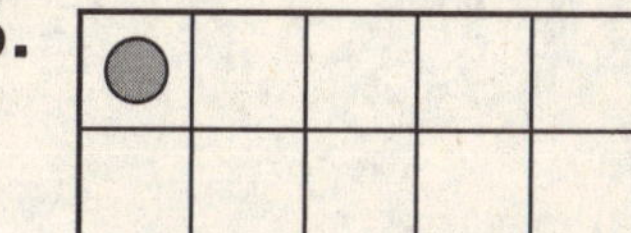

$$1 + \underline{} = 10$$

Name ______________________________

Ways to Make Ten (continued)

Find different ways to make 10.
Complete each number sentence.

7. ____ + 2 = 10

8. 0 + ____ = 10

9. 6 + 4 = ____

10. ____ + 5 = 10

11. ____ + 3 = 10

12. 1 + 9 = ____

13. Write the missing numbers.

10 + ____ = 10   4 + ____ = 10   9 + ____ = 10

3 + ____ = 10   8 + ____ = 10   2 + ____ = 10

7 + ____ = 10   1 + ____ = 10   6 + ____ = 10

0 + ____ = 10   5 + ____ = 10

Name ______________________________

Missing Addends

Use counters to find how many pieces of fruit are in the basket.

8 in all  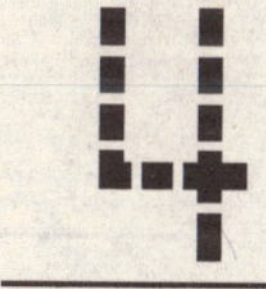   Add 4 counters to make 8 in all.

4

_______ are in the basket.

$$4 + \underline{4} = 8$$

Find how many pieces of fruit there are in each basket.
Use counters to act out the problems.

I.   16 in all

 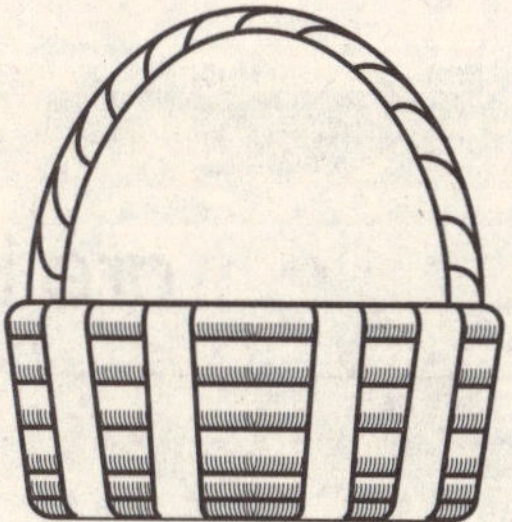

$$7 + \underline{} = 16$$

_______ are in the basket.

2.   15 in all

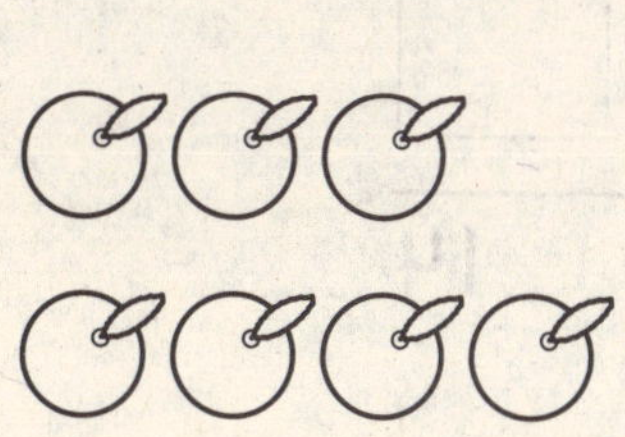 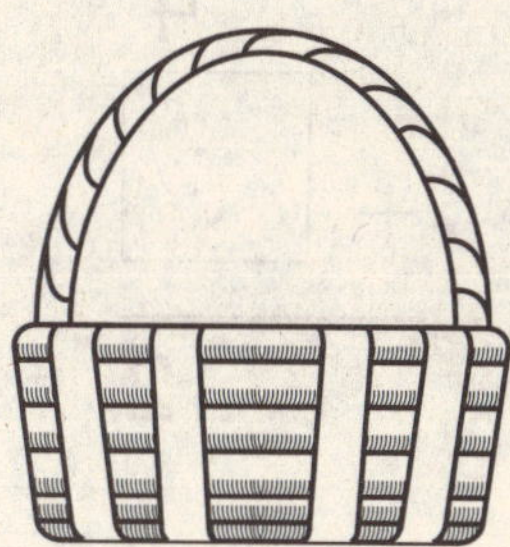

$$7 + \underline{} = 15$$

_______ are in the basket.

Missing Addends (continued)

Find how many pieces of fruit there are in each basket.
Use counters to act out the problems.

3. 14 in all

$$7 + \rule{2cm}{0.4pt} = 14$$

______ are in the basket.

4. 9 in all

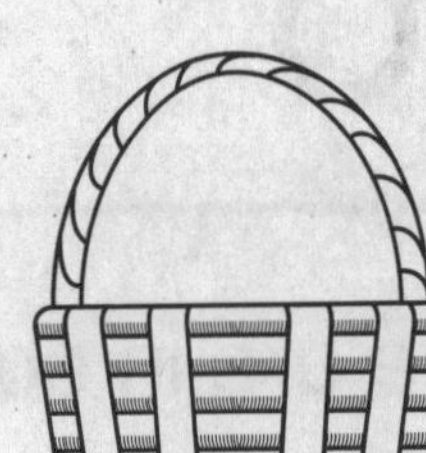

$$9 + \rule{2cm}{0.4pt} = 9$$

______ are in the basket.

5. 12 in all

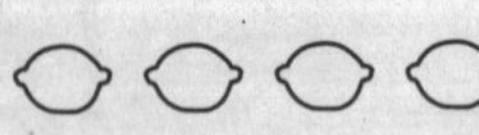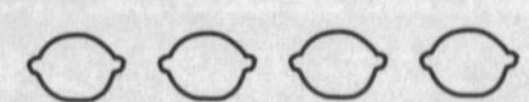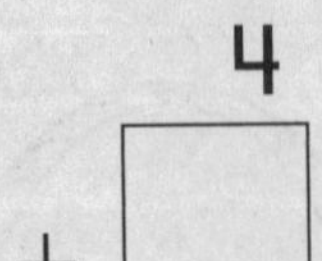

$$8 + \rule{2cm}{0.4pt} = 12$$

______ are in the basket.

Number Sense

Find the missing numbers.

6.

4	4	4	4	4
+ ☐	+ ☐	+ ☐	+ ☐	+ ☐
6	8	10	12	14

Name ___________________________________

Counting On

Example

You can **count on** to **add** 1, 2, or 3 to the greater number.

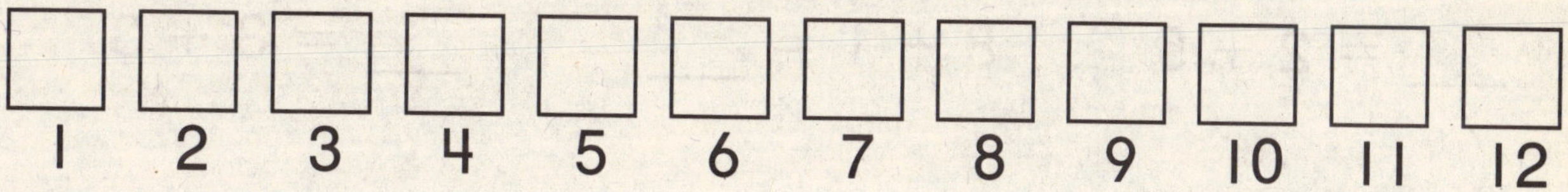

Find the sum for 6 + 2.
Start at 6.
Count on by moving ahead two boxes.

6, _7_, _8_

6 + 2 = _8_

Count on to find each sum.
Use the boxes in the Example to help you.

1. 5 + 1 = ___   2. 3 + 2 = ___

3. 4 + 3 = ___   4. 7 + 2 = ___

5. 9 + 1 = ___   6. 6 + 3 = ___

Counting On (continued)

Count on to find each sum.

7. $7 + 1 =$ ___ $4 + 3 =$ ___ $6 + 2 =$ ___

8. ___ $= 2 + 5$ $8 + 1 =$ ___   ___ $= 3 + 3$

9. $3 + 5 =$ ___   ___ $= 1 + 9$ $7 + 2 =$ ___

10. ___ $= 9 + 2$ $6 + 1 =$ ___   ___ $= 8 + 3$

11.
$$\begin{array}{ccccc} 2 & 4 & 5 & 7 & 3 \\ +\,4 & +\,3 & +\,1 & +\,1 & +\,6 \end{array}$$

12.
$$\begin{array}{ccccc} 7 & 9 & 1 & 2 & 4 \\ +\,3 & +\,1 & +\,8 & +\,1 & +\,6 \end{array}$$

Reasoning Count on to solve.
Write a number sentence.

13. Roberto had 5 dimes. His brother gave him 2 more.
How many dimes does Roberto have in all?

___ + ___ = ___

Name ___________________________________

Making 10 to Add 9

Example

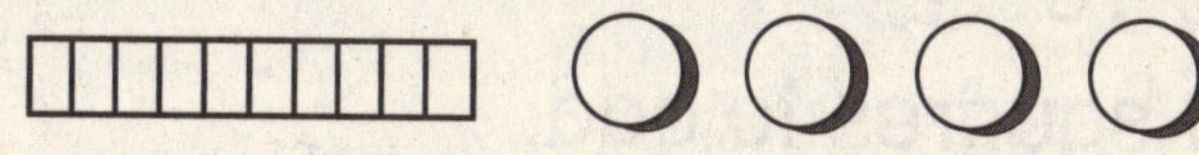

Make 10. Add.

9 + 5

$10 + 4 = \underline{14}$

so $9 + 5 = \underline{14}$

Use counters and Workmat 2.
Show 9 in the ten-frame. Make 10. Add.

1.
$$\boxed{9 + 4}$$

$10 + 3 = \underline{\hspace{2cm}}$

so $9 + 4 = \underline{\hspace{2cm}}$

2.
$$\boxed{9 + 7}$$

$10 + 6 = \underline{\hspace{2cm}}$

so $9 + 7 = \underline{\hspace{2cm}}$

3.
$$\boxed{9 + 6}$$

$10 + 5 = \underline{\hspace{2cm}}$

so $9 + 6 = \underline{\hspace{2cm}}$

4.
$$\boxed{9 + 8}$$

$10 + 7 = \underline{\hspace{2cm}}$

so $9 + 8 = \underline{\hspace{2cm}}$

Name _______________________________

Making 10 to Add 9 (continued)

Make 10.
Draw squares to add.

5. 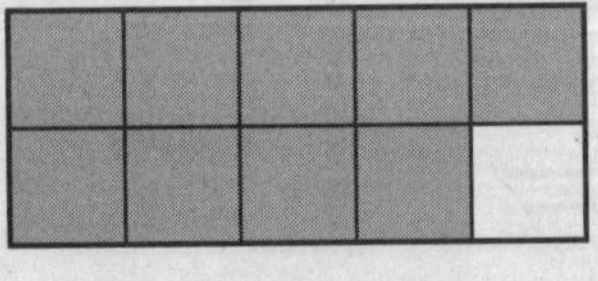
$$\begin{array}{r} 9 \\ +6 \\ \hline \end{array}$$

6. 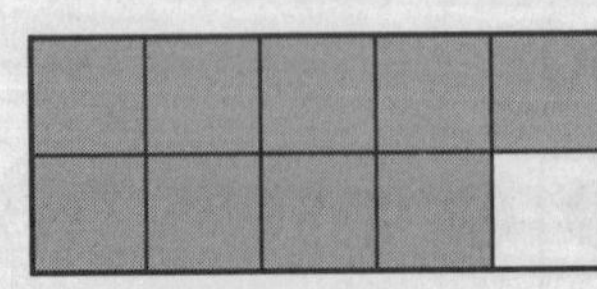
$$\begin{array}{r} 9 \\ +3 \\ \hline \end{array}$$

7. 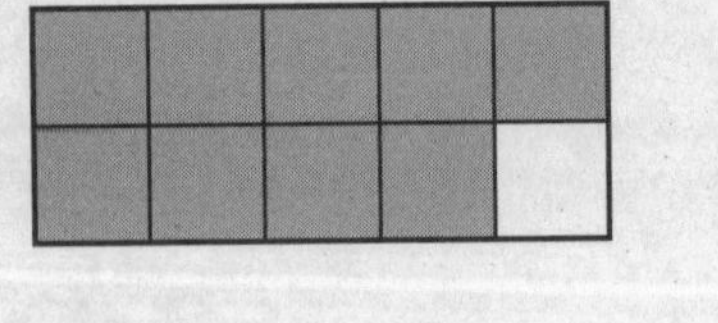
$$\begin{array}{r} 9 \\ +9 \\ \hline \end{array}$$

8. 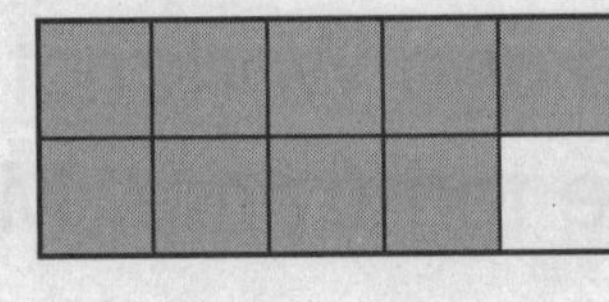
$$\begin{array}{r} 9 \\ +5 \\ \hline \end{array}$$

Solve. The sum of two numbers fits in a ten-frame
with 2 left over.

9. What two numbers could they be? ______ and ______

10. Tell other numbers that could also solve
the problem.

____

Counting Back

Example

You can **count back** to **subtract** 1 or 2.
Use a hundred chart to help you.

1	2	3	4	5	6	7	8	9	10
11	12	13	14	15←—16←—17			18	19	20

Find 17 − 2.

Start at 17 on the hundred chart.
Count back 2.

17, 16, 15

17 − 2 = 15

Subtract. Use the hundred chart to count back.

1. 5 − 1 = ___

1	2	3	4←—5		6	7	8	9	10
11	12	13	14	15	16	17	18	19	20

2. 15 − 2 = ___

1	2	3	4	5	6	7	8	9	10
11	12	13	14	15	16	17	18	19	20

3. 3 − 2 = ___

1	2	3	4	5	6	7	8	9	10
11	12	13	14	15	16	17	18	19	20

Name _______________________

Counting Back (continued)

Subtract. Use the hundred
chart to help you.

1	2	3	4	5	6	7	8	9	10
11	12	13	14	15	16	17	18	19	20

4. $8 - 1 =$ ___ $19 - 2 =$ ___ $7 - 2 =$ ___

5. $4 - 2 =$ ___ $20 - 1 =$ ___ $6 - 1 =$ ___

6. $9 - 1 =$ ___ $10 - 2 =$ ___ $11 - 1 =$ ___

7.
$$\begin{array}{r} 6 \\ -2 \\ \hline \end{array} \qquad \begin{array}{r} 15 \\ -2 \\ \hline \end{array} \qquad \begin{array}{r} 9 \\ -1 \\ \hline \end{array} \qquad \begin{array}{r} 13 \\ -1 \\ \hline \end{array} \qquad \begin{array}{r} 10 \\ -1 \\ \hline \end{array}$$

Reasoning Write a number sentence.

8. Karen had 11 kittens. She gave 2 away.
   How many kittens did she have left?

   ___ − ___ = ___

9. Ramon had 9 trading cards. He gave 2 away.
   How many cards did he have left?

   ___ − ___ = ___

Name ____

Addition Properties

Example 1

The Commutative (Order) Property says that you can change the order of the addends and the sum will be the same.

$2 + 6 = 6 + 2$.

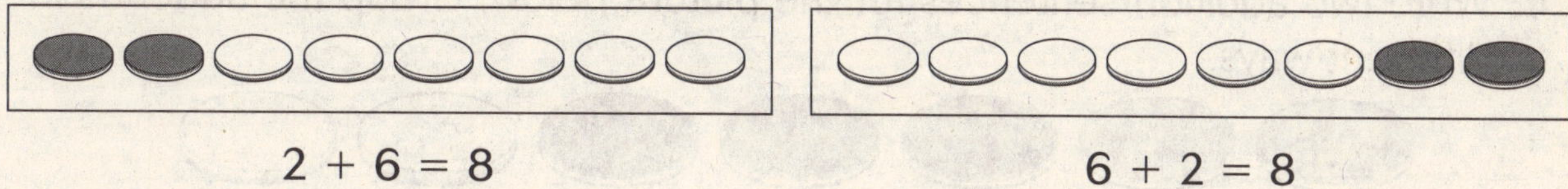

$$2 + 6 = 8 \qquad\qquad 6 + 2 = 8$$

Example 2

The Associative (Grouping) Property says that you can group addends in any way and the sum will be the same.

$(4 + 3) + 1 = 4 + (3 + 1)$.

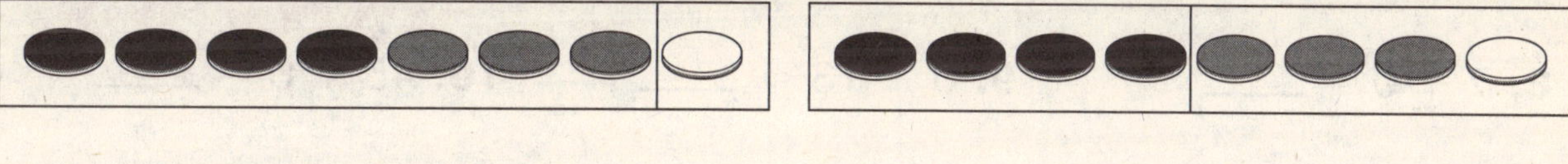

$$(4 + 3) + 1 = 8 \qquad\qquad 4 + (3 + 1) = 8$$

The parentheses show which numbers to add first.

Example 3

The Identity (Zero) Property of addition says that the sum of any number and 0 is that number.

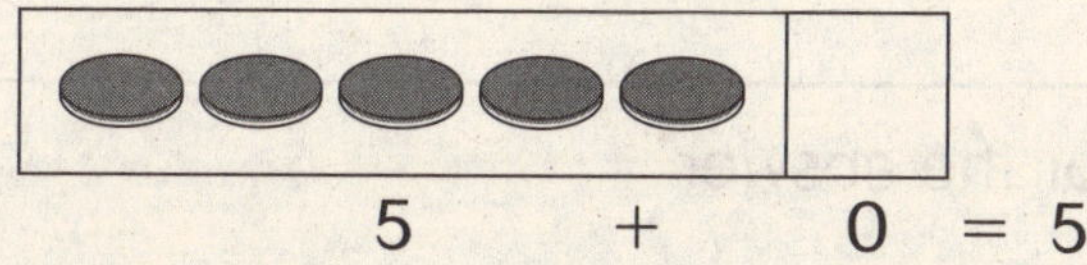

$$5 \quad + \quad 0 = 5$$

---

1. Draw a picture to show that $4 + 6 = 6 + 4$.

Name _______________________________

Addition Properties (continued)

Write the addition sentence.

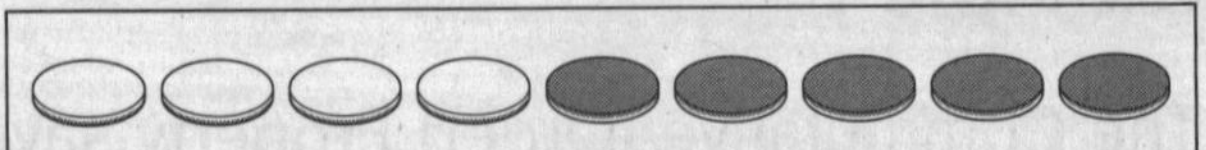

2. ____ + ____ = ____   **3.** ____ + ____ = ____

4. Write two addition sentences for the picture below. Group the addends in different ways.

____

____

Find each sum.

5. $(4 + 6) + 2 =$ ____   **6.** $7 + (1 + 2) =$ ____   **7.** $6 + 9 + 3 =$ ____

8. $7 + 0 =$ ____   **9.** $0 + 13 =$ ____   **10.** $45 + 0 =$ ____

Write each missing number.

11. $4 + 6 = 6 +$ ____   **12.** $7 + 4 =$ ____ $+ 7$ **13.** $6 + 9 = 9 +$ ____

14. Writing in Math Carla ate 2 bananas and 10 raisins. The next day she ate 10 raisins and 2 bananas. Did she eat the same number of pieces of fruit each day? Explain.

____

____

Test Prep Circle the correct letter for the answer.

15. $6 + 4 + 3$ is the same as:

   A $6 + 3 + 3$ **B** $4 + 3 + 6$ **C** $3 + 6 + 0$ **D** $4 + 3 + 0$

16. $732 + 0 =$ ____

   A 7,230   **B** 723   **C** 720   **D** 732

102

Name ________________________________

Relating Addition and Subtraction

Example

Find related addition and subtraction facts that make a fact family.
If you know one fact, you can find the other facts in the fact family.

$9 + 4 = 13$ $\qquad$ $13 - 4 = 9$

$4 + 9 = 13$ $\qquad$ $13 - 9 = 4$

Related addition and subtraction facts
have the same numbers. They are a
fact family.

$4 + 9 = 13$ $\qquad$ $13 - 4 = 9$
$9 + 4 = 13$ $\qquad$ $13 - 9 = 4$

Complete the related addition and subtraction facts.

1.

$3 + 7 = $ _____

$10 - 3 = $ _____

2.

$7 + 5 = $ _____

$12 - 5 = $ _____

3. $2 + 9 = $ _____ $11 - 2 = $ _____

$9 + 2 = $ _____ $11 - 9 = $ _____

4. $9 + 6 = $ _____ $15 - 6 = $ _____

$6 + 9 = $ _____ $15 - 9 = $ _____

Name _______________________________________

Relating Addition and Subtraction (continued)

Complete each fact family. Use cubes to help you.

5. $4 + 8 =$ _____ $12 -$ _____ $= 8$ **6.** $5 + 9 =$ _____   _____ $- 5 = 9$

_____ $+ 4 = 12$ _____ $- 8 = 4$ $9 +$ _____ $= 14$ $14 -$ _____ $= 5$

7. $8 + 3 =$ _____ $11 - 8 =$ _____   **8.** $6 +$ _____ $= 13$ $13 -$ _____ $= 7$

$3 +$ _____ $= 11$ _____ $- 3 = 8$ $7 +$ _____ $= 13$ _____ $- 7 = 6$

9. $7 + 8 =$ _____   _____ $- 8 = 7$

$7 +$ _____ $= 15$ $15 - 7 =$ _____

Find each missing number.

10. $5 + 5 =$ _____ $10 -$ _____ $= 5$ **11.** $8 +$ _____ $= 16$ _____ $- 8 = 8$

12. Reasoning John has 14 pencils. He gives some to Sonja.
He has 8 left. How many pencils did he give to Sonja?   _____

13. Write two facts that are related to the subtraction fact in Question 12.

____

____

Test Prep Circle the correct letter for the answer.

14. Find the related fact for $7 + 7 = 14$.

A $7 + 8 = 15$ **B** $15 - 8 = 7$

C $14 + 7 = 21$ **D** $14 - 7 = 7$

15. Eight frogs were in the pond. Five more frogs joined them. What number
sentence tells what happened?

A $13 - 8 = 5$ **B** $5 + 8 = 13$

C $8 + 5 = 13$ **D** $8 + 5 = 12$

104

Name _______________________________________

Find a Rule

Find a rule by looking at the table as if it is a machine.
For each number you put "In," you get "Out" a number.

Example 1

This machine makes apple pies.
Find a rule.

Apples	In	2	3	4	5
Apple pies	Out	4	5	6	7

Think: Look for the pattern in the table.

Put 2 apples in the machine.
4 apple pies come out.

Put 3 apples in the machine.
5 apple pies come out.

Put 4 apples in the machine.
6 apple pies come out.

So, the rule for this machine is Add 2.

Example 2

Find a rule for this machine.

In	9	8	5	12
Out	6	5	2	9

Think: Look for the pattern in the table.

Put 9 in the machine.
6 come out.

Put 8 in the machine.
5 come out.

Put 5 in the machine.
2 come out.

So, the rule for this machine is Subtract 3.

---

1. What is the rule for this table?

Bees	In	3	5	11	2
Honey pots	Out	7	9	15	6

Name ____

Find a Rule (continued)

Write a rule for each function machine.

2.

In	12	18	7	10
Out	5	11	0	3

Rule: ________________

3.

In	3	12	2	8
Out	8	17	7	13

Rule: ________________

4.

In	4	6	1	11
Out	10	12	7	17

Rule: ________________

5.

In	9	12	7	4
Out	7	10	5	2

Rule: ________________

Complete each table and write the rule.

6.

In	14	10	9	7	11
Out	8	4	3		

Rule: ________________

7.

In	9	4	10	3	7
Out	17	12	18		

Rule: ________________

8. Reasoning Toni uses the rule, Add 7, for her table. If she puts in 4, what should she get out? ________________

9. Paco puts 8 into his function machine and 8 comes out. What is his rule?

____

Test Prep Circle the correct letter for the answer.

10. What is the rule for this table?

In	4	5	2	0
Out	13	14	11	9

A Add 8   **B** Subtract 9   **C** Add 9   **D** Add 7

Name _______________________

Skip Counting Equal Groups

Example

Skip count equal groups to find how many apples there are in all.

I equal group

I equal group

I equal group

5   10   15

______ **3** equal groups

______ **5** apples in each **equal group**

______ **15** apples in all

Skip count to find how many there are in all.

1.

I equal group   I equal group   I equal group

______ equal groups

______ bananas in each **equal group**

______ bananas in all

107

Skip Counting Equal Groups (continued)

Draw the equal groups.
Skip count to find how many there are in all.

2. 2 groups, 2 in each
    group

    ___4___ in all

3. 3 groups, 2 in each
    group

    _______ in all

4. 2 groups, 4 in each
    group

    _______ in all

5. 4 groups, 3 in each
    group

    _______ in all

6. **Reasoning** Rosa has 4 baskets. There are 3 flowers in
    each. How many flowers does Rosa have in all?

    _______ flowers in all

Name _______________________

Addition and Multiplication

Example

Add. Then multiply. Use counters if you like.
How many apples are there in all? 3 groups of 3

$$3 + 3 + 3 = \underline{9}$$

$$3 \times 3 = \underline{9}$$

Add. Then multiply. Use counters if you like.

1. 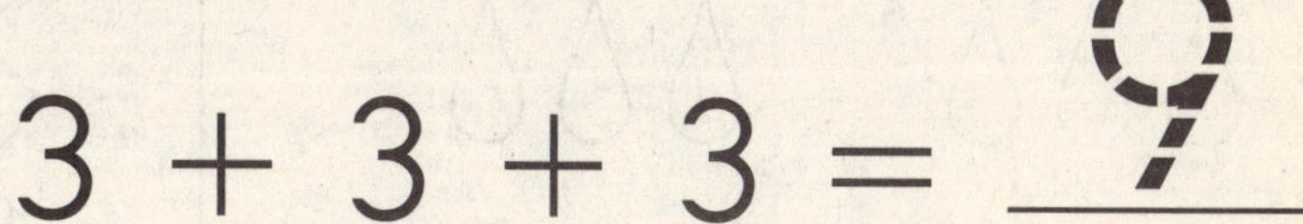

$$2 + 2 = \underline{\hspace{1.5cm}}$$

$$2 \times 2 = \underline{\hspace{1.5cm}}$$

2. 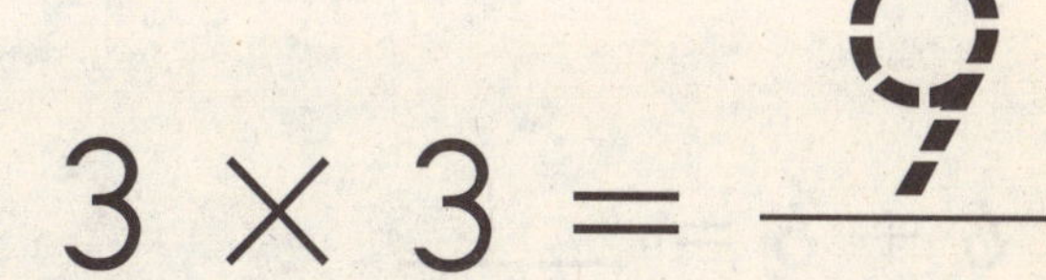

$$2 + 2 + 2 + 2 = \underline{\hspace{1.5cm}}$$

$$4 \times 2 = \underline{\hspace{1.5cm}}$$

3.

$$2 + 2 + 2 = \underline{\hspace{1.5cm}}$$

$$3 \times 2 = \underline{\hspace{1.5cm}}$$

4.

$$3 + 3 = \underline{\hspace{1.5cm}}$$

$$2 \times 3 = \underline{\hspace{1.5cm}}$$

Name _______________________________

Addition and Multiplication (continued)

Add. Then multiply.
Use counters if you like.

5. 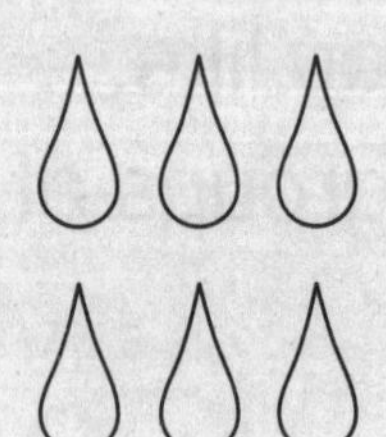

$6 + 6 = $ _____

$2 \times 6 = $ _____

6.

$4 + 4 + 4 = $ _____

$3 \times 4 = $ _____

7.

$6 + 6 + 6 = $ _____

$3 \times 6 = $ _____

8. 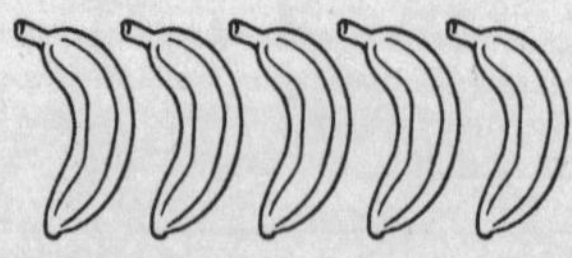

$5 + 5 = $ _____

$2 \times 5 = $ _____

Name _______________________________

Using Arrays

Use counters and the grid to show each fact.

Example

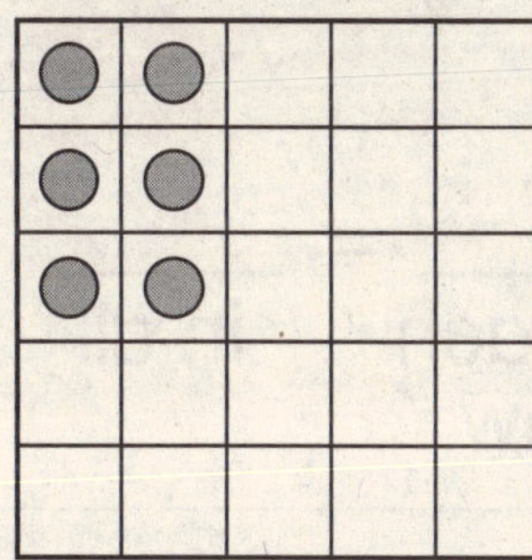

$$3 \times 2 = \underline{6}$$

rows   in each   in all
      row

1.
$$2 \times 2 = \underline{}$$
rows   in each   in all
      row

2.
$$2 \times 4 = \underline{}$$
rows   in each   in all
      row

3.
$$3 \times 5 = \underline{}$$
rows   in each   in all
      row

4.
$$3 \times 4 = \underline{}$$
rows   in each   in all
      row

Name ____

Using Arrays (continued)

Write each multiplication fact.

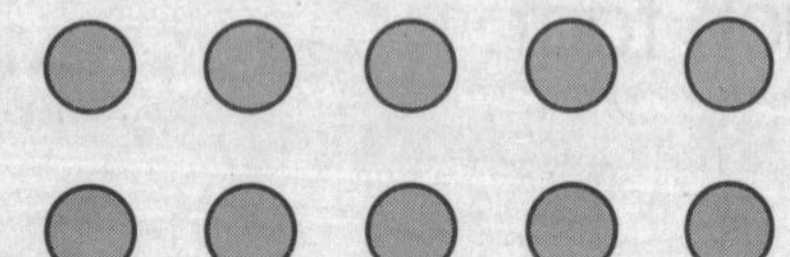

$$\underline{\quad 2 \quad} \times \underline{\quad 5 \quad} = \underline{\quad 10 \quad}$$
rows   in each   in all
      row

5.

$$\underline{\quad\quad} \times \underline{\quad\quad} = \underline{\quad\quad}$$
rows   in each   in all
      row

6. 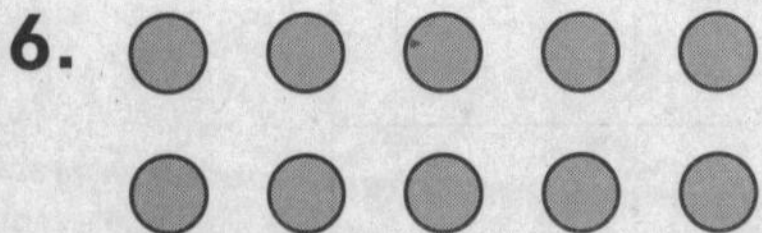

$$\underline{\quad\quad} \times \underline{\quad\quad} = \underline{\quad\quad}$$
rows   in each   in all
      row

7.

$$\underline{\quad\quad} \times \underline{\quad\quad} = \underline{\quad\quad}$$
rows   in each   in all
      row

8. 

$$\underline{\quad\quad} \times \underline{\quad\quad} = \underline{\quad\quad}$$
rows   in each   in all
      row

9.

$$\underline{\quad\quad} \times \underline{\quad\quad} = \underline{\quad\quad}$$
rows   in each   in all
      row

Name ___________________________

Multiplying in Any Order

Use grid paper. Color to show the number in each row.
Then turn the grid.
Write the multiplication sentences.

Example

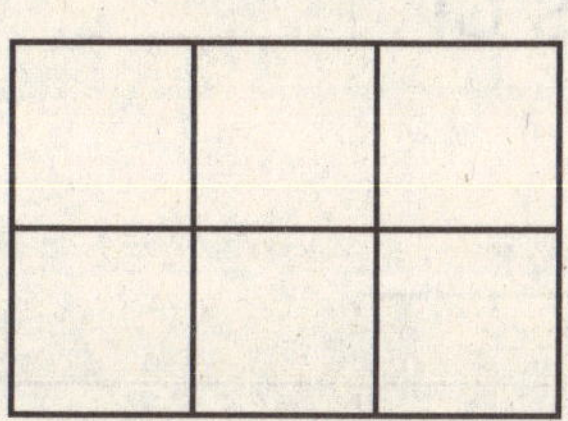

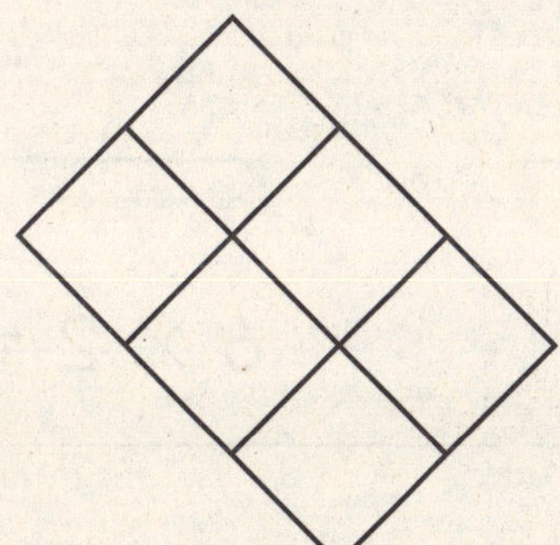

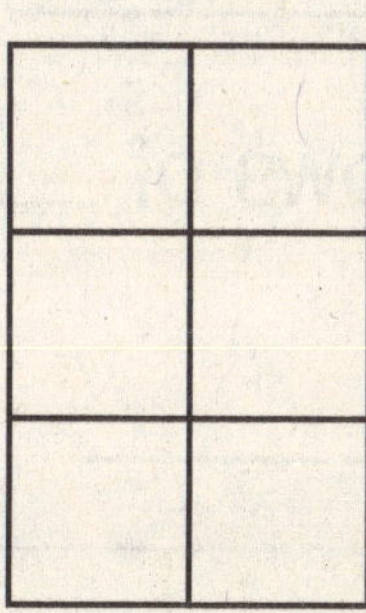

2 rows of 3   3 rows of 2

$2 \times 3 = \underline{6}$ $3 \times 2 = \underline{6}$

Use grid paper. Color to show the number in each row.
Then turn the grid.
Write the multiplication sentences.

1. 7 rows of 2   or   2 rows of 7

    ___ $\times$ ___ = ___   ___ $\times$ ___ = ___

2. 6 rows of 3   or   3 rows of 6

    ___ $\times$ ___ = ___   ___ $\times$ ___ = ___

Name ________________________________

Multiplying in Any Order (continued)

Write the missing numbers. Multiply.

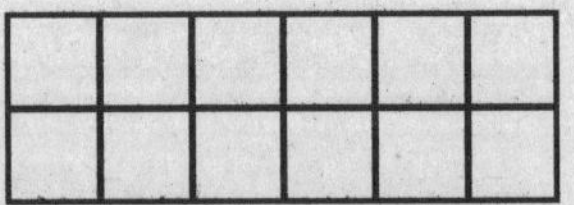

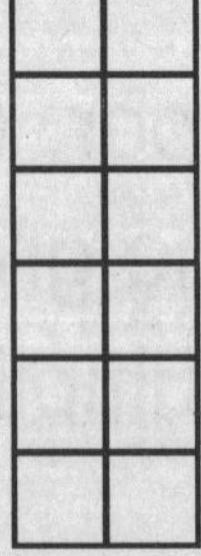

3. ______ rows of ______   ______ rows of ______

   $2 \times 6 =$ ______ $6 \times 2 =$ ______

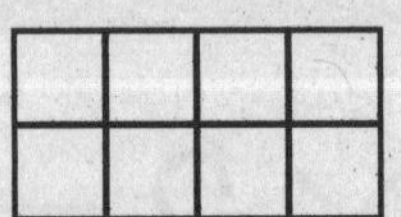

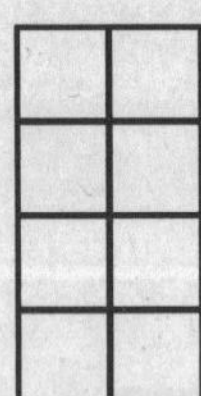

4. ______ rows of ______   ______ rows of ______

   $2 \times 4 =$ ______ $4 \times 2 =$ ______

5. ______ rows of ______   ______ rows of ______

   $5 \times 4 =$ ______ $4 \times 5 =$ ______

Name ______________________________

Multiplying Across and Down

Example

You can multiply across or down.
Find each product.

3 groups of cherries.
4 cherries in each group.

$$\begin{array}{r} 4 \\ \times\, 3 \\ \hline 12 \end{array}$$

$3 \times 4 = \underline{12}$

---

1. 3 groups of 2

$$\begin{array}{r} 2 \\ \times\, 3 \\ \hline \end{array}$$

$3 \times 2 = \underline{\hspace{2em}}$

2. 3 groups of 6

$$\begin{array}{r} 6 \\ \times\, 3 \\ \hline \end{array}$$

$3 \times 6 = \underline{\hspace{2em}}$

---

3. 3 groups of 3

$$\begin{array}{r} 3 \\ \times\, 3 \\ \hline \end{array}$$

$3 \times 3 = \underline{\hspace{2em}}$

4. 2 groups of 7

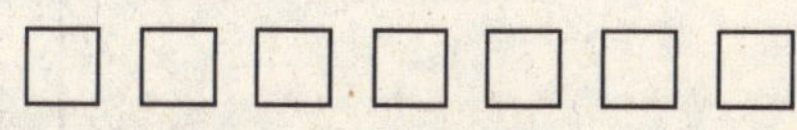
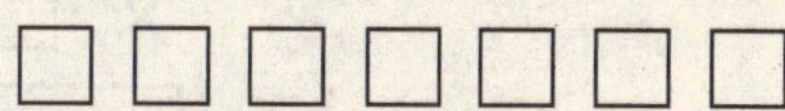
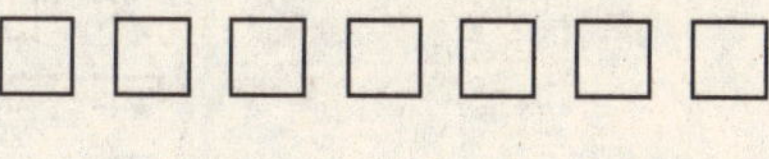

$$\begin{array}{r} 7 \\ \times\, 2 \\ \hline \end{array}$$

$2 \times 7 = \underline{\hspace{2em}}$

Multiplying Across and Down (continued)

Multiply across and down. Write the number.

$$\underline{4} \times \underline{2} = \underline{8}$$

5. 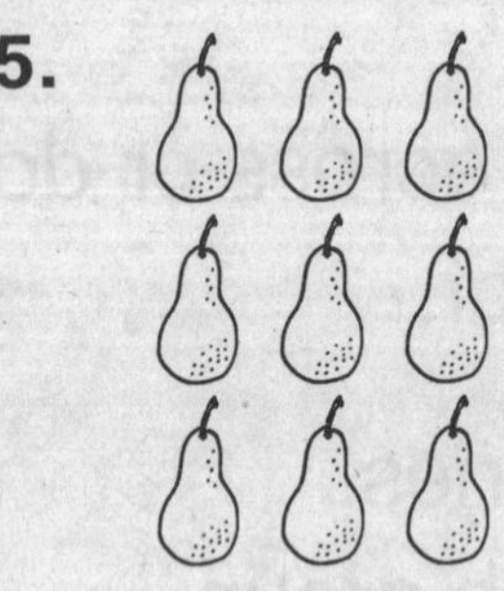 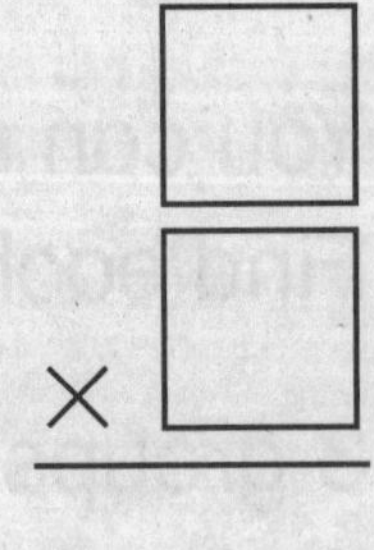

___ × ___ = ___

6.  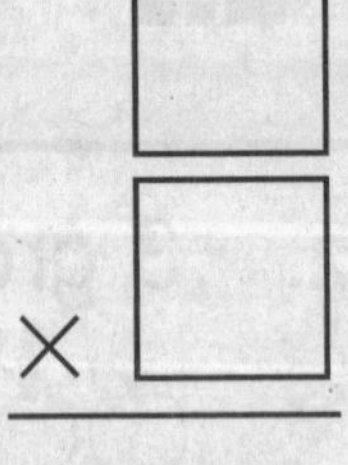

___ × ___ = ___

7. 

___ × ___ = ___

8. 

___ × ___ = ___

9. 

___ × ___ = ___

Name ___________________________

Modeling Division

Make equal groups.
Write the number in each group.

Example

Two children have 10 bananas. They want to share
the bananas equally. How many bananas should
each child get?

Each child should get **5** bananas.

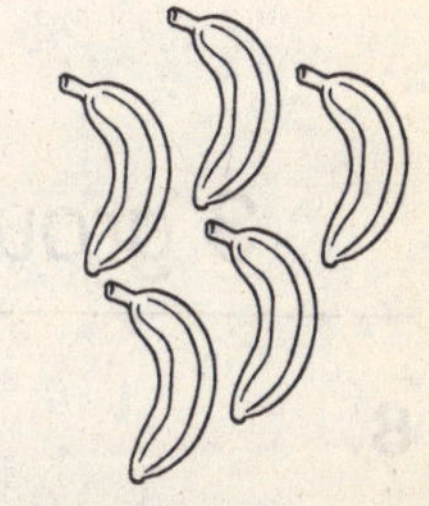

	Number in All	Number of Groups	Number in Each Group
1.	10	2	5
2.	6	3	
3.	18	6	
4.	8	2	
5.	12	3	

Name ___________________________________

Modeling Division (continued)

Circle equal groups.
Write the number in each group.

6.

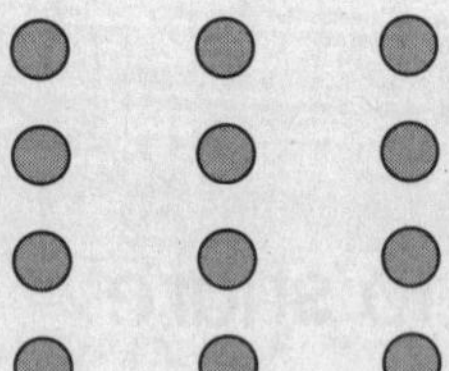

3 groups of _______

7.

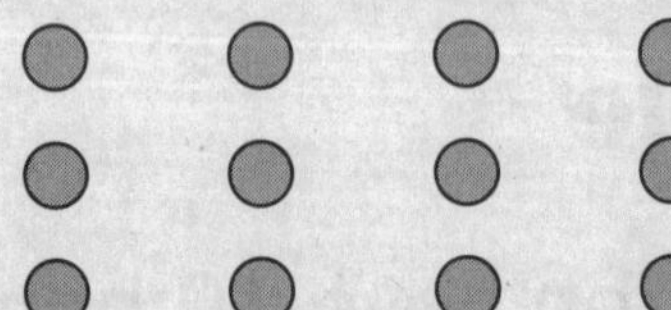

4 groups of _______

8.

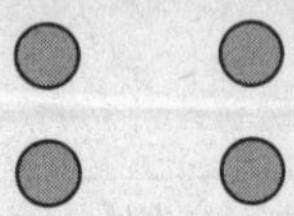

2 groups of _______

9.

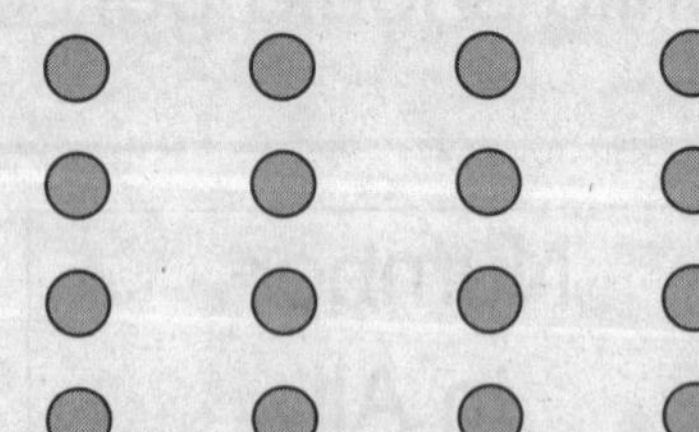

4 groups of _______

10.

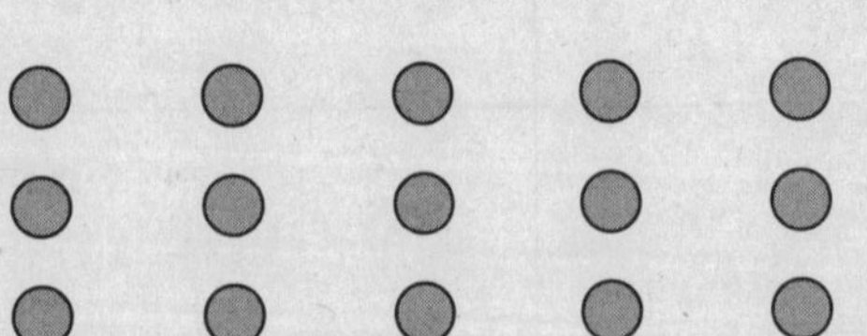

5 groups of _______

11.

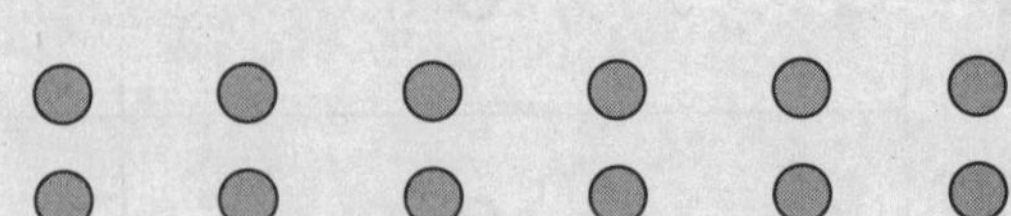

6 groups of _______

Name ___________________________________

Division with Remainders

Example

Circle groups to solve. Write how many are left over.

13 cupcakes are put on 4 plates. The same
number of cupcakes is on each plate.
How many cupcakes are on each plate?  _______

How many cupcakes are left? _______

1. Lisa has 11 eggs. It takes 2 eggs to make an
    omelet. How many omelets can Lisa make?

Lisa can make _______ omelets.

How many eggs are left over? _______ left over.

Division with Remainders (continued)

Use counters to solve.
Draw to show what you did.

2. Tom has 13 marbles. He can put 6 marbles
    in each bag. How many bags can he fill?

    Tom can fill ______ bags.

    How many marbles are left over?   ______ left over.

3. Lara has 15 beads to use for making necklaces.
    She puts 4 beads on each necklace. How
    many necklaces can she make?

    Lara can make ______ necklaces.

    How many beads are left over?   ______ left over.

4. Jay has 23 beans. He can put 7 beans in each
    bowl. How many bowls can he fill?

    Jay can fill ______ bowls.

    How many beans are left over?   ______ left over.

Name _______________________

Writing Division Sentences

Example 1

Divide.

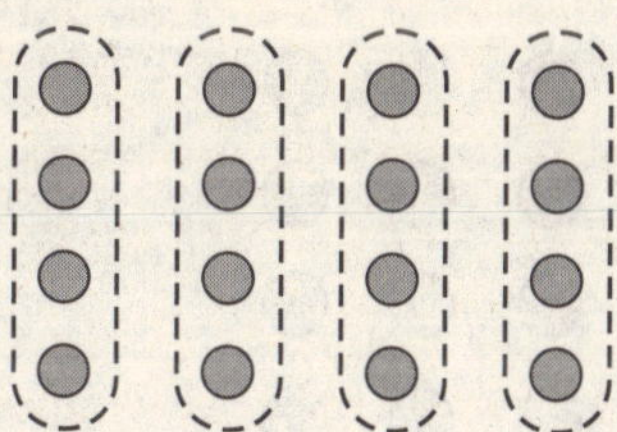

$16 \div 4 = \underline{4}$

16 divided by 4 equals 4.

Example 2

$6 \div 2 = \underline{3}$

6 divided by 2 is 3.

---

1. Circle groups of 2. Complete the division sentence.

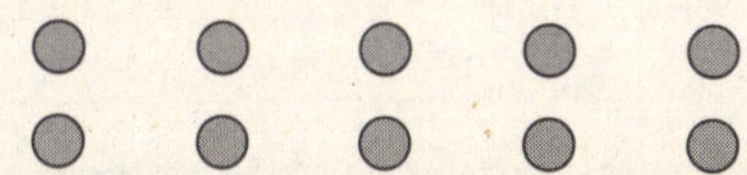

$10 \div 2 = \underline{}$

2. Circle groups of 5. Complete the division sentence.

$10 \div 5 = \underline{}$

---

3. Circle groups of 5. Complete the division sentence.

$15 \div 5 = \underline{}$

4. Circle groups of 9. Complete the division sentence.

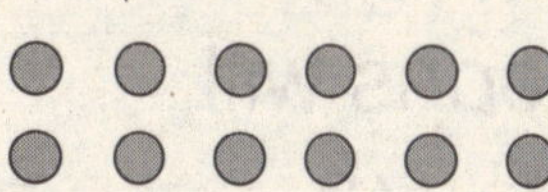

$18 \div 9 = \underline{}$

Name _______________________________

Writing Division Sentences (continued)

Circle equal groups to divide.
Complete the division sentence.

5.

$12 \div 3 = \underline{\quad}$

6.

$21 \div 7 = \underline{\quad}$

7.

$9 \div 3 = \underline{\quad}$

8.

$18 \div 2 = \underline{\quad}$

Write the division sentence.

9. 5 children share 15 balloons equally. How many balloons will each child get?

$\underline{\quad} \div \underline{\quad} = \underline{\quad}$

10. 8 children share 24 marbles equally. How many marbles will each child get?

$\underline{\quad} \div \underline{\quad} = \underline{\quad}$

122

Using Arrays

Example

How many squares are in the arrays below? The display on the right
is the array on the left turned sideways. Compare the two arrays.

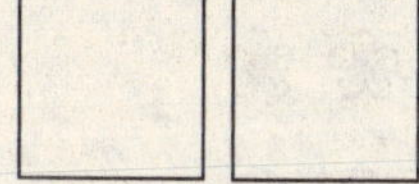

4 rows
2 squares in
each row
$4 \times 2 = 8$

There are 8
squares in the
array.

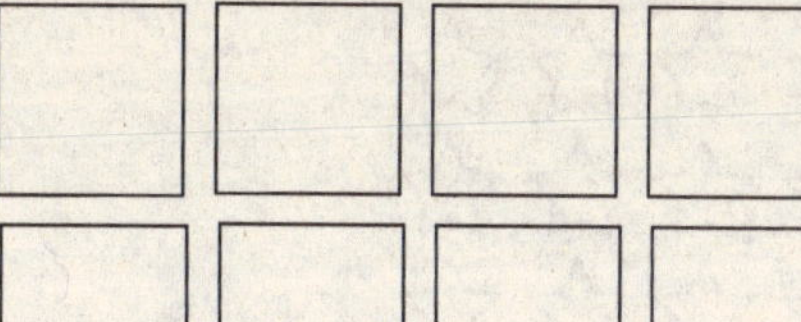

2 rows
4 squares in each row
$2 \times 4 = 8$
There are 8 squares in the array.

Both arrays have 8 squares.

Write a multiplication sentence for each array.

1. 

____

2. 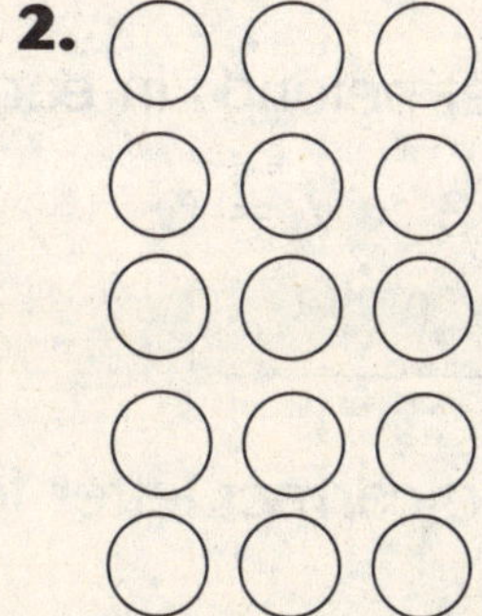

____

Write the number that belongs in each ●.

3. $4 \times 8 = 32$, so $8 \times 4 = ●$

4. $9 \times 2 = 18$, so $● \times 9 = 18$

5. $5 \times 7 = 35$, so $7 \times ● = 35$

6. $3 \times 6 = 18$, so $● \times 3 = 18$

Name ______________________________

Using Arrays (continued)

Write a multiplication sentence for each array.

7.

____

8. 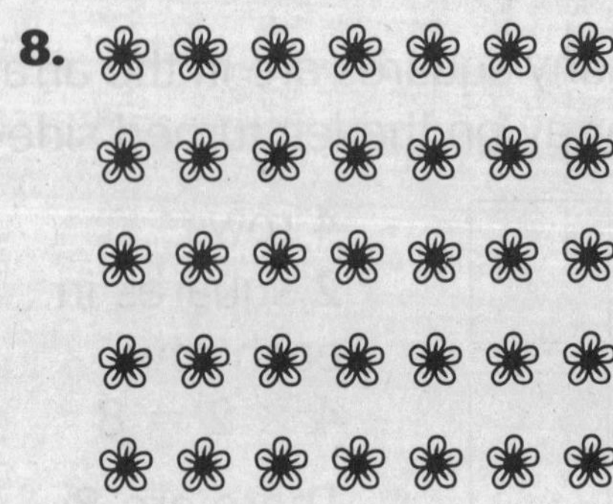

____

9. A bookstore displays books by several authors
in an array. There is 1 row of books by local writers
and there are 2 rows of books by other
authors. If there are 9 books in each
row, how many books are on display? _______________________

Write the number that belongs in each ●.

10. $7 \times 3 = 21$, so $3 \times 7 =$ ●

11. $3 \times 2 = 6$, so $2 \times$ ● $= 6$

____

____

Test Prep Circle the correct letter for the answer.

12. Which multiplication sentence
shows how many cherries are
in the array displayed at the right?

  A $3 \times 4 = 12$ **C** $3 \times 6 = 18$

  B $3 \times 5 = 15$ **D** $3 \times 7 = 21$

13. $4 \times 7 = 28$, so ● $\times 4 = 28$

  A 4   **C** 7

  B 8   **D** 28

Name ______________________________________

Writing Multiplication Stories

Example 1

You can write a multiplication story to show a multiplication problem.

Write a multiplication story for $4 \times 6 = 24$.

Beth made cookies for a bake sale. She put 4 rows of cookies on the baking sheet with 6 cookies in each row. How many cookies did she bake in all?

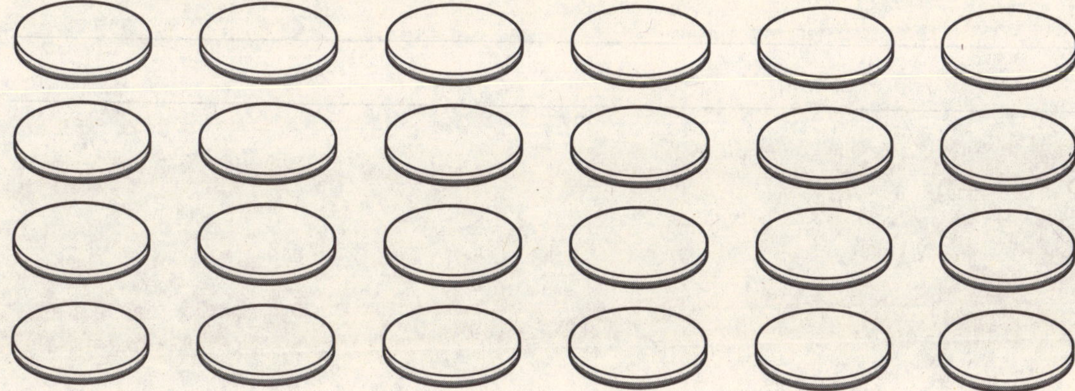

$4 \times 6 = 24$
Beth baked 24 cookies in all.

Write a multiplication story. Then find the product.

1.

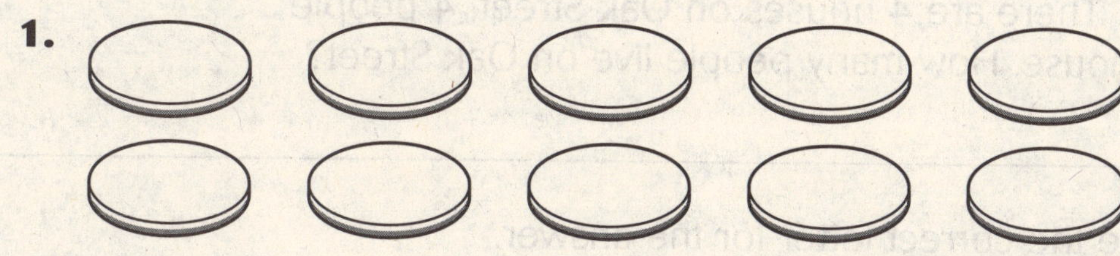

$2 \times 5 = $ ______

____

____

125

Writing Multiplication Stories (continued)

Write a multiplication story for each. Draw a picture to find each product.

2. $6 \times 6 =$ ___

____

____

3. $4 \times 5 =$ ___

____

____

4. Reasoning There are 4 houses on Oak Street. 4 people
live in each house. How many people live on Oak Street?

____

Test Prep Circle the correct letter for the answer.

5. Teresa filled a page in her stamp album with 5 rows of
8 stamps each. How many stamps does she have? Which
number sentence solves this story?

A $5 \times 9 = 45$ **B** $5 \times 8 = 40$ **C** $5 \times 7 = 35$ **D** $8 \times 6 = 48$

126

Name _______________________________________

Multiplying by 2

Example

Find 6×2.

You can skip count by 2's to help you find the product.

$2 + 2 + 2 + 2 + 2 + 2 = 12$

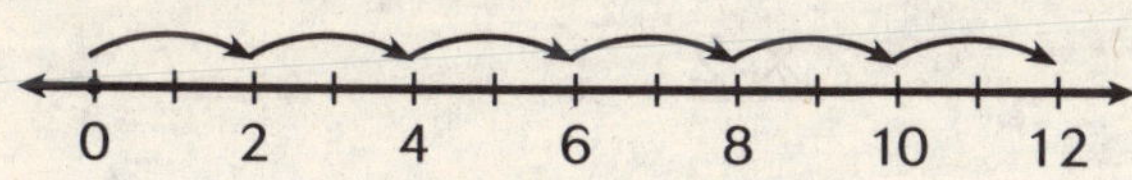

Count by 2's until you have said 6 numbers.

So, $6 \times 2 = 12$.

Use the number line to skip count by 2's and find the product.

1. $5 \times 2 =$ _____

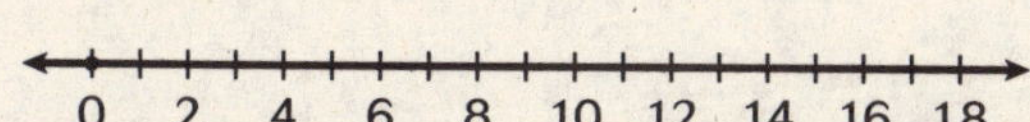

2. $3 \times 2 =$ _____

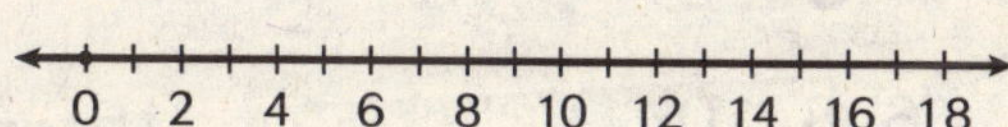

3. $4 \times 2 =$ _____

4. $9 \times 2 =$ _____

5. $2 \times 2 =$ _____

6. $8 \times 2 =$ _____

7. $7 \times 2 =$ _____

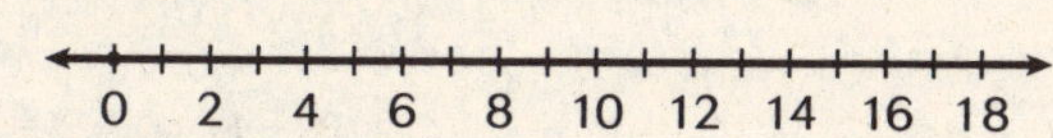

8. $6 \times 2 =$ _____

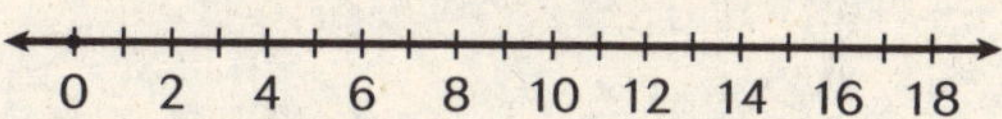

Name ____

Multiplying by 2 (continued)

9. $3 \times 2 =$ _____   **10.** $4 \times 2 =$ _____   **11.** $1 \times 2 =$ _____

12. $2 \times 9 =$ _____   **13.** $2 \times 5 =$ _____   **14.** $8 \times 2 =$ _____

15.
$$\begin{array}{r} 5 \\ \times\, 2 \\ \hline \end{array}$$
16.
$$\begin{array}{r} 2 \\ \times\, 3 \\ \hline \end{array}$$
17.
$$\begin{array}{r} 2 \\ \times\, 6 \\ \hline \end{array}$$
18.
$$\begin{array}{r} 2 \\ \times\, 2 \\ \hline \end{array}$$
19.
$$\begin{array}{r} 6 \\ \times\, 2 \\ \hline \end{array}$$

20.
$$\begin{array}{r} 2 \\ \times\, 1 \\ \hline \end{array}$$
21.
$$\begin{array}{r} 7 \\ \times\, 2 \\ \hline \end{array}$$
22.
$$\begin{array}{r} 2 \\ \times\, 7 \\ \hline \end{array}$$
23.
$$\begin{array}{r} 9 \\ \times\, 2 \\ \hline \end{array}$$
24.
$$\begin{array}{r} 2 \\ \times\, 4 \\ \hline \end{array}$$

25. Algebra Complete the pattern.

6, 8, 10, _____, _____, 16, _____

26. Will has 8 pairs of shoes in his closet. How many
shoes are in Will's closet? _____________________

Test Prep Circle the correct letter for the answer.

27. A package of candy is on sale for $2. Sarah wants to buy
4 packages and Bill wants to buy 3 packages. How much
money will Sarah need to buy her packages?

    A $12   **B** $6   **C** $8   **D** $14

28. Find 7×2.

    A 9   **B** 14   **C** 12   **D** 15

Name ______________________________

Multiplying by 5

Example

Find 3×5.

You can skip count by 5's to help you find the product.

$5 + 5 + 5 = 15$

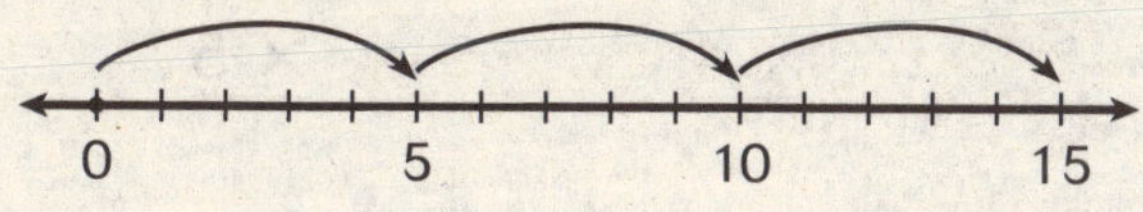

Count by 5's until you have said 3 numbers.

So, $3 \times 5 = 15$.

Use the number line to skip count by 5's and find the product.

1. $6 \times 5 =$ ______

2. $5 \times 5 =$ ______

3. $8 \times 5 =$ ______

4. $9 \times 5 =$ ______

5. $2 \times 5 =$ ______

6. $7 \times 5 =$ ______

7. $4 \times 5 =$ ______

8. $3 \times 5 =$ ______

Multiplying by 5 (continued)

9. $4 \times 5 =$ _____ **10.** $3 \times 5 =$ _____ **11.** $5 \times 5 =$ _____

12. $6 \times 5 =$ _____ **13.** $5 \times 7 =$ _____ **14.** $5 \times 8 =$ _____

15. $\begin{array}{r} 7 \\ \times\,5 \\ \hline \end{array}$	**16.** $\begin{array}{r} 5 \\ \times\,3 \\ \hline \end{array}$	**17.** $\begin{array}{r} 8 \\ \times\,5 \\ \hline \end{array}$	**18.** $\begin{array}{r} 5 \\ \times\,4 \\ \hline \end{array}$	**19.** $\begin{array}{r} 1 \\ \times\,5 \\ \hline \end{array}$
20. $\begin{array}{r} 2 \\ \times\,5 \\ \hline \end{array}$	**21.** $\begin{array}{r} 5 \\ \times\,6 \\ \hline \end{array}$	**22.** $\begin{array}{r} 9 \\ \times\,5 \\ \hline \end{array}$	**23.** $\begin{array}{r} 5 \\ \times\,1 \\ \hline \end{array}$	**24.** $\begin{array}{r} 5 \\ \times\,2 \\ \hline \end{array}$

25. Mental Math If $9 \times 5 = 45$, then $5 \times 9 =$ _____.

26. Jean reads 5 pages in a book before bedtime each
night. Bedtime is at 9:00 P.M. How many pages does
she read in 4 nights?   _______________

27. Movie tickets are on sale for $5 each. Ross, Emily and
John want to see the movie. Is $18 enough for
their tickets?

____

Test Prep Circle the correct letter for the answer.

28. Find 8×5.

    A 50 **B** 13 **C** 35 **D** 40

29. Each student in Mrs. Anderson's class brings 5 cans
to class for the food drive. There are 9 students in
Mrs. Anderson's class. How many cans were collected?

    A 40 cans **B** 14 cans **C** 45 cans **D** 46 cans

Name _______________________________

Multiplying by 10

Example

Find 5×10.

You can skip count by 10's to help you find the product.

$10 + 10 + 10 + 10 + 10 = 50$

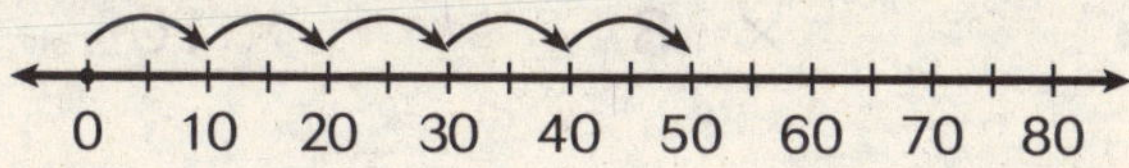

Count by 10's until you
have said 5 numbers.

So, $5 \times 10 = 50$.

---

1. $3 \times 10 = $ _____

2. $4 \times 10 = $ _____

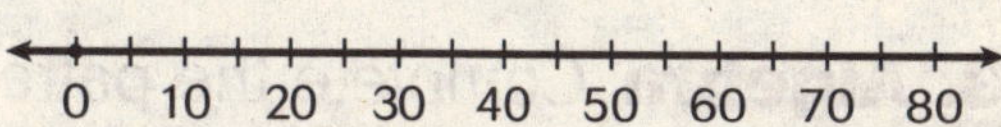

3. $6 \times 10 = $ _____

4. $8 \times 10 = $ _____

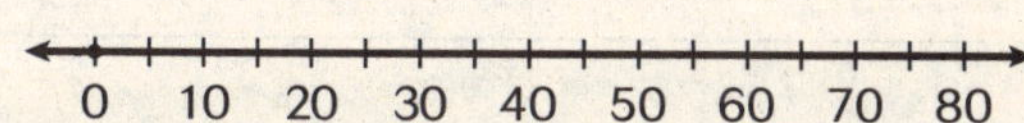

5. $2 \times 10 = $ _____

6. $7 \times 10 = $ _____

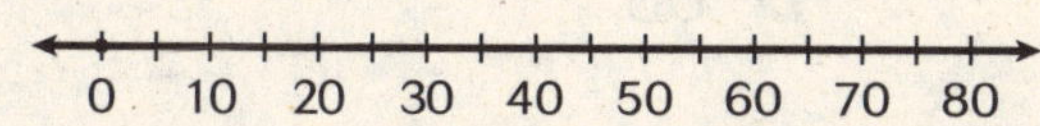

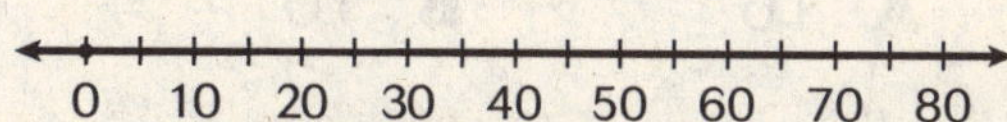

Name _______________________________________

Multiplying by 10 (continued)

7. $2 \times 10 =$ _____   **8.** $4 \times 10 =$ _____   **9.** $6 \times 10 =$ _____

10. $10 \times 6 =$ _____   **11.** $10 \times 2 =$ _____   **12.** $10 \times 5 =$ _____

13.   3   **14.**   10   **15.**   8   **16.**   10   **17.**   9
$\times 10$ $\times\ 9$ $\times 10$ $\times\ 8$ $\times 10$

18.   5   **19.**   10   **20.**   10   **21.**   1   **22.**   7
$\times 10$ $\times\ 3$ $\times\ 1$ $\times 10$ $\times 10$

23. Algebra Complete the pattern. 10, 20, _____, _____, 50, _____, 70

24. Seven friends get together to play a marble game. Sixty
marbles are needed to play this game. Each friend brings
ten marbles. Are there enough marbles to play the game?

____

____

Test Prep Circle the correct letter for the answer.

25. There are 10 dimes in each dollar. How many dimes are
there in $6?

   A 16   **B** 10   **C** 60   **D** 66

26. How many days are there in 10 weeks?

   A 50   **B** 30   **C** 70   **D** 75

Name _______________________________

Multiplying by 1 or 0

Example 1

Find 5×1.

When you multiply any number by 1, the product is that number.

So, $5 \times 1 = 5$.

Example 2

Find 7×0.

When you multiply any number by 0, the product is 0.

So, $7 \times 0 = 0$.

---

1. $3 \times 1 =$ _____   **2.** $4 \times 0 =$ _____   **3.** $7 \times 1 =$ _____

4. $6 \times 1 =$ _____   **5.** $8 \times 0 =$ _____   **6.** $3 \times 0 =$ _____

7. $2 \times 0 =$ _____   **8.** $2 \times 1 =$ _____   **9.** $5 \times 0 =$ _____

10. $9 \times 0 =$ _____   **11.** $4 \times 1 =$ _____   **12.** $5 \times 1 =$ _____

Multiplying by 1 or 10 (continued)

13. $2 \times 1 =$ _____   **14.** $4 \times 0 =$ _____   **15.** $6 \times 1 =$ _____

16. $1 \times 9 =$ _____   **17.** $1 \times 2 =$ _____   **18.** $4 \times 1 =$ _____

19. 3   **20.** 0   **21.** 8   **22.** 1   **23.** 9
      $\times 0$ $\times 9$ $\times 1$ $\times 8$ $\times 1$

24. 5   **25.** 5   **26.** 1   **27.** 1   **28.** 7
      $\times 1$ $\times 0$ $\times 1$ $\times 0$ $\times 1$

29. Writing in Math Explain why $1 \times 0 = 0$.

____

____

____

____

30. Five students in Mr. Brown's class take turns reading pages from a book. Each student reads one page, starting on page 6. How many pages do the students read? _______________

Test Prep Circle the correct letter for the answer.

31. Find 9×0.

  A 9   **B** 0   **C** 1   **D** 90

32. You order a chicken sandwich and no french fries. Each sandwich costs $2 and french fries cost $1. How much money do you spend on french fries?

  A $2   **B** $0   **C** $1   **D** $3

Multiplying by 9

Example

Find 4×9.

You can find the product by changing the order
of the factors: $4 \times 9 = 9 \times 4$.

You have learned how to multiply by 4's.

If you know $9 \times 4 = 36$, then you know $4 \times 9 = 36$.

So, $4 \times 9 = 36$.

---

1. 2   9
     ×9   ×2

2. 5   9
     ×9   ×5

3. 1   9
     ×9   ×1

4. 8   9
     ×9   ×8

5. 3   9
     ×9   ×3

6. 6   9
     ×9   ×6

7. 7   9
     ×9   ×7

8. 4   9
     ×9   ×4

Name _______________________________________

Multiplying by 9 (continued)

For Exercises 9–11, use the first fact to help you
multiply the second fact.

9. $\begin{array}{r} 3 \\ \times 9 \\ \hline \end{array}$ $\begin{array}{r} 9 \\ \times 3 \\ \hline \end{array}$ **10.** $\begin{array}{r} 6 \\ \times 9 \\ \hline \end{array}$ $\begin{array}{r} 9 \\ \times 6 \\ \hline \end{array}$ **11.** $\begin{array}{r} 5 \\ \times 9 \\ \hline \end{array}$ $\begin{array}{r} 9 \\ \times 5 \\ \hline \end{array}$

12. $\begin{array}{r} 1 \\ \times 9 \\ \hline \end{array}$ **13.** $\begin{array}{r} 9 \\ \times 2 \\ \hline \end{array}$ **14.** $\begin{array}{r} 9 \\ \times 4 \\ \hline \end{array}$ **15.** $\begin{array}{r} 9 \\ \times 0 \\ \hline \end{array}$

Algebra Find the rule, then complete the table.

16. Rule: Multiply by _____   **17.** Rule: Multiply by _____   **18.** Rule: Multiply by _____

Input	Output
2	18
1	_____
5	_____
4	_____

Input	Output
3	15
4	_____
6	_____
9	_____

Input	Output
5	10
7	_____
8	_____
9	_____

19. Reasoning Joshua and his sister have each saved $9.
They wish to buy a new game that costs $20. If they put
their savings together, do they have enough money to buy
the game?

Test Prep Circle the correct letter for the answer.

20. There are four quarters in a dollar. How many quarters are
there in 9 dollars?

A 36   **B** 90   **C** 27   **D** 4

Practicing Multiplication Facts

Use multiplication strategies to help remember multiplication facts.

Example 1

Use addition doubles to find the answer.

There are 2 rows with 7 chairs in each row. How many chairs are there?

2×7 is the same as 2 groups of 7 or $7 + 7$.
$7 + 7 = 14$
So, $2 \times 7 = 14$.

Example 2

Skip count to find the answer.

There are 7 houses. Each house has 5 windows. How many windows altogether?

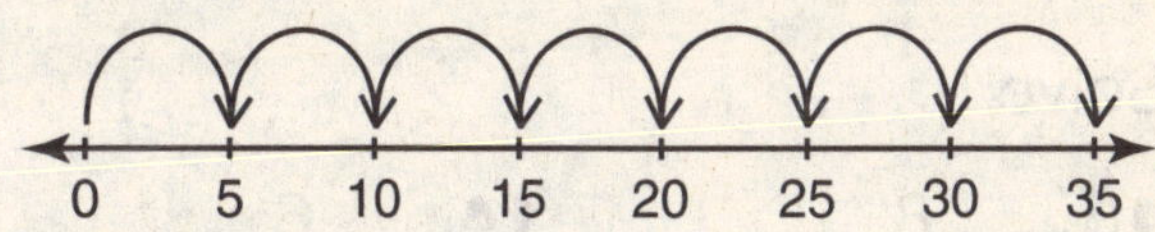

$5 + 5 + 5 + 5 + 5 + 5 + 5 = 35$
So, $7 \times 5 = 35$.

Example 3

Use a 9s pattern to solve 3×9.

The tens digit of the product is one less than the first factor.
$3 - 1 = $ **2**

The digits of the product must add to 9.
$2 + $ **7** $ = 9$.

So, $3 \times 9 = $ **27.**

Use a multiplication strategy to solve. Tell which strategy you used.

1. $2 \times 10 = $ _______

2. $4 \times 8 = $ _______

3. $6 \times 9 = $ _______

_______________   _______________   _______________

Practicing Multiplication Facts (continued)

Use addition doubles to find the product.

4. $2 \times 6 =$ _____   **5.** $2 \times 8 =$ _____   **6.** $2 \times 4 =$ _____

Use skip counting to find the product.

7. $8 \times 10 =$ _____   **8.** $6 \times 3 =$ _____   **9.** $5 \times 4 =$ _____

Use a 9s pattern to find the product.

10. $4 \times 9 =$ _____   **11.** $5 \times 9 =$ _____   **12.** $7 \times 9 =$ _____

Solve.

13.	**14.**	**15.**	**16.**
8	6	7	4
$\times 3$	$\times 5$	$\times 1$	$\times 0$

17. Reasoning A theater holds 70 people.
There are 10 rows of seats. If the same number
of seats are in each row, how many seats are
there in a row?   _______________

Test Prep Circle the correct letter for the answer.

18. $8 \times 5 =$

   A 37   **B** 48   **C** 32   **D** 40

19. 10
  $\times 0$

   A 10   **B** 0   **C** 11   **D** 1

Name ______________________________

Multiplying by 3

Example

Find 3×3.

You can skip count by 3's to help you find the product.

$3 + 3 + 3 = 9$

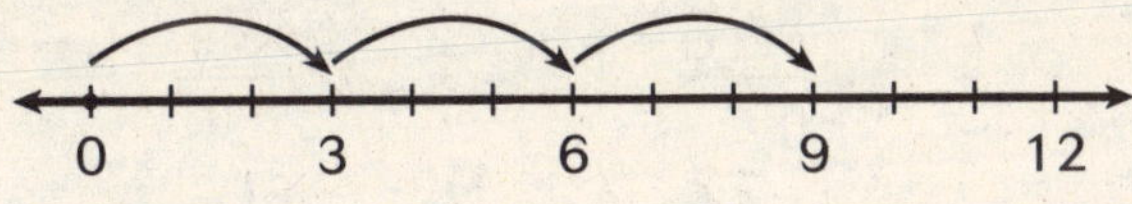

Count by 3's until you
have said 3 numbers.

So, $3 \times 3 = 9$.

Use the number line to skip count by 3's and find the product.

1. $2 \times 3 =$ _____

2. $4 \times 3 =$ _____

3. $8 \times 3 =$ _____

4. $9 \times 3 =$ _____

5. $7 \times 3 =$ _____

6. $3 \times 3 =$ _____

7. $5 \times 3 =$ _____

8. $6 \times 3 =$ _____

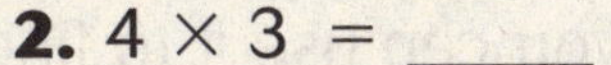

Name ____

Multiplying by 3 (continued)

9. $2 \times 3 =$ _____   **10.** $1 \times 3 =$ _____   **11.** $7 \times 3 =$ _____

12. $3 \times 4 =$ _____   **13.** $3 \times 6 =$ _____   **14.** $3 \times 7 =$ _____

15. $\begin{array}{r} 5 \\ \times\,3 \\ \hline \end{array}$ **16.** $\begin{array}{r} 8 \\ \times\,3 \\ \hline \end{array}$ **17.** $\begin{array}{r} 3 \\ \times\,8 \\ \hline \end{array}$ **18.** $\begin{array}{r} 3 \\ \times\,6 \\ \hline \end{array}$ **19.** $\begin{array}{r} 3 \\ \times\,1 \\ \hline \end{array}$

20. $\begin{array}{r} 3 \\ \times\,2 \\ \hline \end{array}$ **21.** $\begin{array}{r} 3 \\ \times\,3 \\ \hline \end{array}$ **22.** $\begin{array}{r} 4 \\ \times\,3 \\ \hline \end{array}$ **23.** $\begin{array}{r} 3 \\ \times\,5 \\ \hline \end{array}$ **24.** $\begin{array}{r} 9 \\ \times\,3 \\ \hline \end{array}$

25. Writing in Math If you know the product of 6×3,
explain how you can use it to find 7×3.

____

____

____

26. The weatherman says the temperature is rising
3 degrees every hour. How much hotter is it
when 2 hours pass? ___________________

Test Prep Circle the correct letter for the answer.

27. Mrs. Hernandez's class is raising money by selling boxes of
cookies for $3 each. Alex sold 4 boxes to her mother and
2 more to her neighbor. How much money did Alex raise?

  A $12   **B** $6   **C** $9   **D** $18

28. Which multiplication sentence can be represented by the
number line shown?

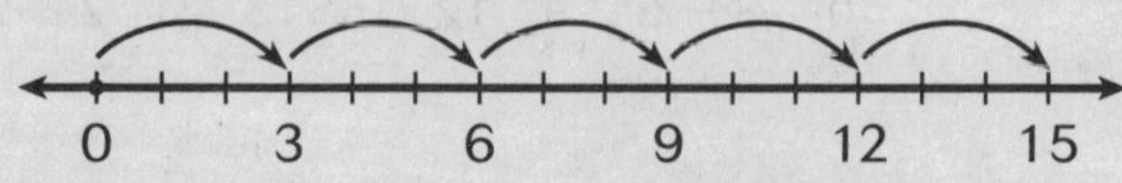

  A $5 \times 3 = 15$ **B** $6 \times 3 = 18$ **C** $3 \times 6 = 18$ **D** $4 \times 3 = 12$

140

Name _______________________________________

Multiplying by 4

Example

Find 7×4.

You can skip count by 4's to help you find the product.

$4 + 4 + 4 + 4 + 4 + 4 + 4 = 28$

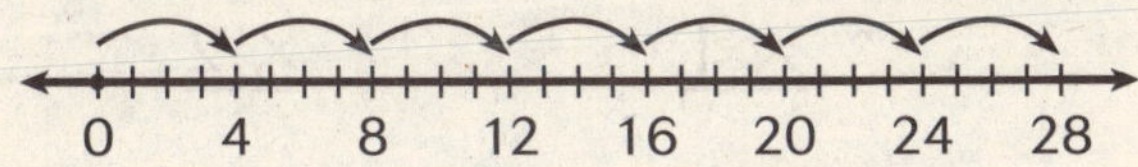

Count by 4's until you have said 7 numbers.

So, $7 \times 4 = 28$.

Use the number line to skip count by 4's and find the product.

1. $3 \times 4 = $ _____

2. $5 \times 4 = $ _____

3. $1 \times 4 = $ _____

4. $8 \times 4 = $ _____

5. $6 \times 4 = $ _____

6. $2 \times 4 = $ _____

7. $4 \times 4 = $ _____

8. $7 \times 4 = $ _____

Name _______________________________________

Multiplying by 4 (continued)

9. $8 \times 4 =$ _____   **10.** $3 \times 4 =$ _____   **11.** $1 \times 4 =$ _____

12. $4 \times 4 =$ _____   **13.** $4 \times 8 =$ _____   **14.** $9 \times 4 =$ _____

15.	**16.**	**17.**	**18.**	**19.**
7 $\times 4$	6 $\times 4$	4 $\times 6$	4 $\times 1$	4 $\times 2$

20.	**21.**	**22.**	**23.**	**24.**
4 $\times 5$	5 $\times 4$	4 $\times 7$	2 $\times 4$	4 $\times 3$

25. Algebra If $9 \times 4 = 36$, then $4 \times$ _____ $= 36$.

26. Helen is planting a garden. She buys 3 trays of
tomato plants. Each tray has 4 plants and costs
$2. How many tomato plants did Helen buy?   _______________

Test Prep Circle the correct letter for the answer.

27. Find 8×4.

   A 12   **B** 48   **C** 23   **D** 32

28. Which of the following is true?

   A $3 \times 4 = 3 + 3 + 3$ **C** $3 \times 4 = 4 + 4 + 4$

   B $3 \times 4 = 4 + 4 + 4 + 4$ **D** $3 \times 4 = 3 + 4$

Name ____

Multiplying by 6 or 7

Example

Find 7×6.

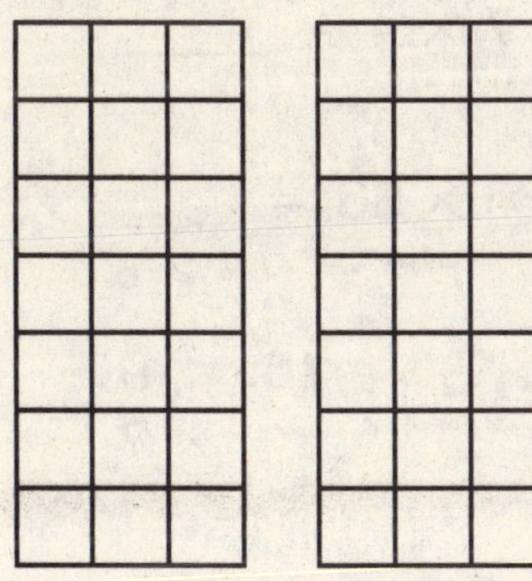

7 × 3 = 21   7 × 3 = 21

Think: $7 \times 3 = 21$

Double 21: $21 + 21 = 42$

So, $7 \times 6 = 42$.

---

1. $5 \times 6 =$ _______

2. $7 \times 4 =$ _______

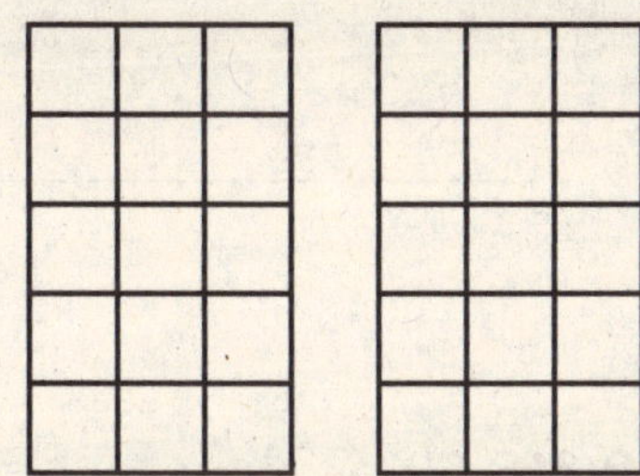

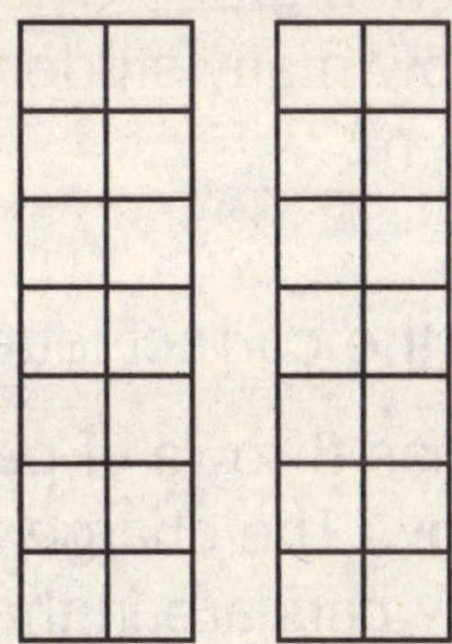

Use the first fact to help you find the second fact.

3. $6 \times 3 =$ _______

$6 \times 6 =$ _______

4. $2 \times 8 =$ _______

$4 \times 8 =$ _______

5. $8 \times 3 =$ _______

$8 \times 6 =$ _______

6. $7 \times 4 =$ _______

$7 \times 8 =$ _______

7. $9 \times 3 =$ _______

$9 \times 6 =$ _______

8. $7 \times 3 =$ _______

$7 \times 6 =$ _______

Name _______________________________________

Multiplying by 6 or 7 (continued)

In Exercises 9–11, use the first fact to help you find the second fact.

9. $3 \times 3 =$ _____   **10.** $7 \times 3 =$ _____   **11.** $7 \times 2 =$ _____

   $3 \times 6 =$ _____ $7 \times 6 =$ _____ $7 \times 4 =$ _____

12. $6 \times 1 =$ _____   **13.** $7 \times 8 =$ _____   **14.** $6 \times \$6 =$ _____

15.   1   **16.**   6   **17.**   6   **18.**   9
      $\times 7$ $\times 3$ $\times 8$ $\times 7$

19. Algebra Complete the pattern. 6, 12, 18, _____, 30, _____

20. Students in a classroom are in groups with
7 students in each group. There are 5 groups
of students. How many students are there
in the classroom?   _______________________

Test Prep Circle the correct letter for the answer.

21. A parking lot has 8 rows of parking spaces. There are six
cars in each row. The charge to park in this lot is $2 each
day. How many cars are in the parking lot?

   A 48   **B** 16   **C** 12   **D** 14

22. Which array represents the multiplication sentence $8 \times 7 = 56$?

A 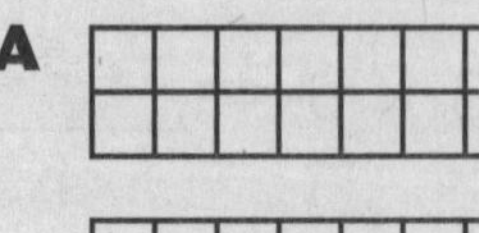   **B**    **C** 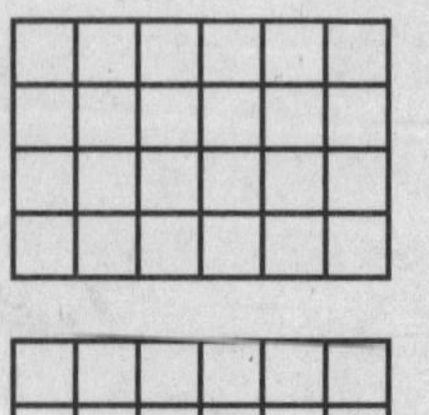   **D** 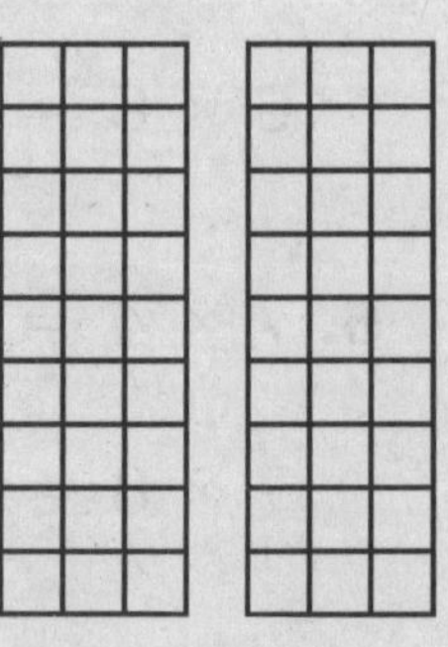

144

Name ____

Multiplying by 8

Example

Find 7×8.

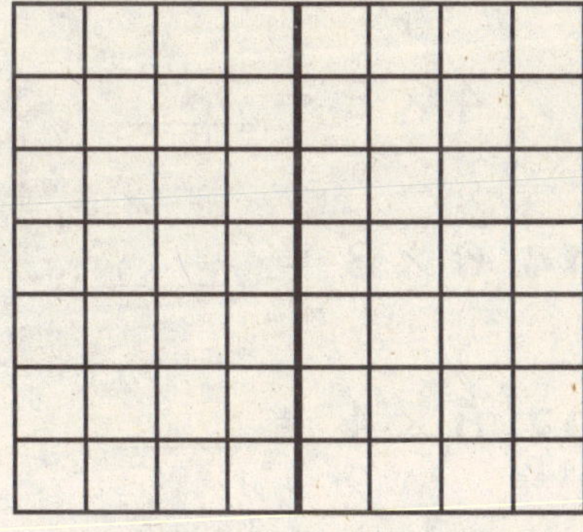

$7 \times 4 = 28$ $7 \times 4 = 28$

Think: $7 \times 4 = 28$

Double 28: $28 + 28 = 56$

So, $7 \times 8 = 56$.

---

1. $8 \times 8 =$ _______

2. $6 \times 8 =$ _______

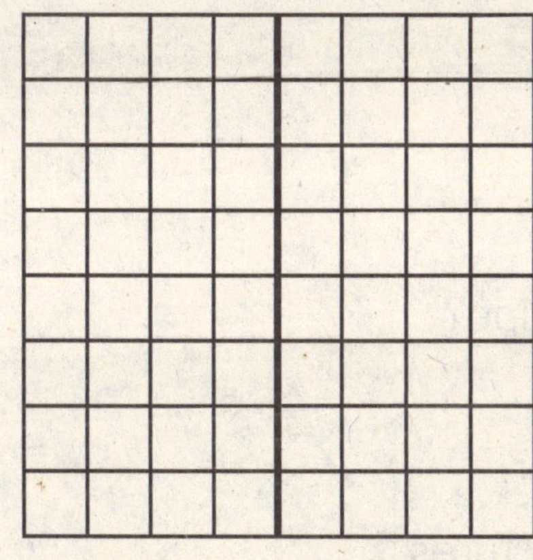

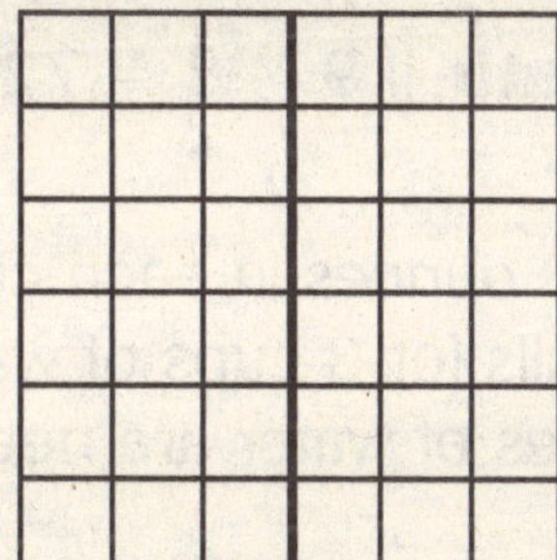

Use the first fact to help you find the second fact.

3. $6 \times 4 =$ _______

$6 \times 8 =$ _______

4. $5 \times 4 =$ _______

$5 \times 8 =$ _______

5. $2 \times 4 =$ _______

$2 \times 8 =$ _______

6. $3 \times 4 =$ _______

$3 \times 8 =$ _______

7. $4 \times 4 =$ _______

$4 \times 8 =$ _______

8. $9 \times 4 =$ _______

$9 \times 8 =$ _______

Multiplying by 8 (continued)

In Exercises 9–11, use the first fact to help you find
the second fact.

9. $3 \times 4 =$ _____   **10.** $7 \times 4 =$ _____   **11.** $4 \times 4 =$ _____

   $3 \times 8 =$ _____ $7 \times 8 =$ _____ $4 \times 8 =$ _____

12. $8 \times 1 =$ _____   **13.** $2 \times 8 =$ _____   **14.** $6 \times 8 =$ _____

15. $0 \times 8 =$ _____   **16.** $8 \times 2 =$ _____   **17.** $8 \times 4 =$ _____

18.   1   **19.**   8   **20.**   8   **21.**   9
       $\times\,8$ $\times\,3$ $\times\,6$ $\times\,8$

22. Mental Math If $9 \times 8 = 72$, then $8 \times 9 =$ _____.

23. There are 8 ounces in each cup of water.
     A recipe calls for 3 cups of water. How
     many ounces of water are needed for the recipe?   _______________

Test Prep Circle the correct letter for the answer.

24. Each chapter in a book has 8 pages and 3 pictures.
     There are 6 chapters in the book. How many pages
     are there in the book?

   A 24 pages   **B** 48 pages   **C** 18 pages   **D** 17 pages

25. Each student in Mrs. Williams's class checked out 8 books.
     How many books have 2 students checked out?

   A 10   **B** 24   **C** 16   **D** 8

Name _________________________________

Practicing Multiplication Facts

Find 6 × 7.

You can use more than one fact strategy to find the same multiplication fact.

Example 1

Change the order of the factors to find facts that you do not know.

6 × 7 is the same as 7 × 6.

If you know that 7 × 6 = 42, then you know that 6 × 7 = 42.

So, 6 × 7 = 42.

Example 2

Use doubles to find facts that you do not know.

3s facts can be doubled to find 6s facts.

3 × 7 = 21

21 doubled is 42.

So, 6 × 7 = 42

Example 3

Facts can be added together to find facts that you do not know.

Use 2s facts and 4s facts to multiply with 6.

2 × 7 = 14

4 × 7 = 28

14 + 28 = 42

So, 6 × 7 = 42.

1. Find 8 × 5. Tell which strategy you used.

____

____

Practicing Multiplication Facts (continued)

Find the product.

2. $6 \times 8 =$ _______   **3.** $3 \times 9 =$ _______   **4.** $0 \times 5 =$ _______

5. $7 \times 7 =$ _______   **6.** $4 \times 8 =$ _______   **7.** $8 \times 2 =$ _______

8. $9 \times 6 =$ _______   **9.** $6 \times 5 =$ _______   **10.** $3 \times 4 =$ _______

11. 7 $\underline{\times\,1}$	**12.** 9 $\underline{\times\,9}$	**13.** 4 $\underline{\times\,6}$	**14.** 8 $\underline{\times\,7}$
15. 2 $\underline{\times\,9}$	**16.** 8 $\underline{\times\,8}$	**17.** 5 $\underline{\times\,5}$	**18.** 9 $\underline{\times\,7}$

19. Writing in Math Will the answer to 496×2 be an even number or an odd number? Explain.

____

____

____

Test Prep Circle the correct letter for each answer.

20. Which has the same product as 6×9?

  A 6×6 **B** 7×9 **C** 6×7 **D** 9×6

21. If Pam uses a double to solve 4×9, what fact should be doubled?

  A 1×9 **B** 2×9 **C** 3×9 **D** 2×4

Name ____

Using Multiplication to Compare

Example

The word **times** in a word problem means multiplication.

Hiroko has 3 stickers. Ted has 2 times as many stickers as
Hiroko. How many stickers does Ted have?

Use cubes to represent the stickers.

3

3

2 times as many is 6

3   3

$2 \times 3 = 6$

Ted has 6 stickers.

5

Alicia's stickers
Wayne's stickers

5   5   5

1. Wayne has 3 times as many stickers as Alicia. Alicia has 5 stickers. How
many stickers does Wayne have?

2. Janos has 3 stickers. Lucy has twice as many stickers as Janos. How
many stickers does Lucy have?

Name _______________________

Using Multiplication to Compare (continued)

Solve.

3. Rob has 4 model airplanes. Julio has 3 times as many model airplanes as Rob. How many model airplanes does Julio have?

____

4. Mr. King has 5 apples left in his store. Ruth needs twice as many apples to bake apple pies. How many apples does Ruth need?

____

Use the recipe to answer Questions 5–8.

5. The recipe serves 5 people. Joan wants to make the recipe for 15 people. How many times more is this?

____

6. How many bananas will she need to make the recipe for 15 people?

____

7. How many cups of strawberries will Joan need?

____

> **Fruit Smoothie**
>
> 3 large bananas
> 2 cups strawberries
> 1 cup orange juice
> 1 cup cranberry juice
> 1 cup ice cubes
>
> Blend until smooth.
> Makes 5 servings.

8. Reasoning If Joan wants to make twice as much as the recipe in the chart, what will she need to do to all of the ingredients?

____

Test Prep Circle the correct letter for each answer.

9. Mico has 7 times as many pencils as Tina. Tina has 6 pencils. How many pencils does Mico have?

A 35   **B** 42   **C** 48   **D** 13

Name ____

Patterns on a Multiplication Table

Example 1

You can use the fact table to find 6×9.

Step 1   Find the 6s column across the top.
Step 2   Find the 9s row along the side.
Step 3   Follow the 6s column down and the
          9s row across until they meet at 54.

So, $6 \times 9 = 54$.

	0	1	2	3	4	5	6	7	8	9	10	11	12
0	0	0	0	0	0	0	0	0	0	0	0	0	0
1	0	1	2	3	4	5	6	7	8	9	10	11	12
2	0	2	4	6	8	10	12	14	16	18	20	22	24
3	0	3	6	9	12	15	18	21	24	27	30	33	36
4	0	4	8	12	16	20	24	28	32	36	40	44	48
5	0	5	10	15	20	25	30	35	40	45	50	55	60
6	0	6	12	18	24	30	36	42	48	54	60	66	72
7	0	7	14	21	28	35	42	49	56	63	70	77	84
8	0	8	16	24	32	40	48	56	64	72	80	88	96
9	0	9	18	27	36	45	54	63	72	81	90	99	108
10	0	10	20	30	40	50	60	70	80	90	100	110	120
11	0	11	22	33	44	55	66	77	88	99	110	121	132
12	0	12	24	36	48	60	72	84	96	108	120	132	144

Example 2

You can use patterns in the fact table to help you find products.

Find the row and column for the 2s facts.
Think: Each product increases by 2.
So, I can skip count by 2s to get answers to the 2s facts.

Find the row and column for the 4s facts.
Think: Each product is an even number.

Find the row and column for the 12s facts.
Think: The ones digits of multiples of 12 follow a pattern: 0, 2, 4, 6, 8.

Use patterns in the multiplication fact table to help you answer Questions 1–3.

1. Find the 11s row from 11 to 99. What pattern do you see?

____

____

2. What is the pattern in the 0s row and column?

____

____

3. Look at the 5s row. Explain why 76 cannot be in the 5s row.

____

Name _______________________________

Patterns on a Multiplication Table (continued)

Multiply.

4. $8 \times 3 =$ _____

5. $12 \times 2 =$ _____

6. $9 \times 8 =$ _____

7. $6 \times 6 =$ _____

8. $11 \times 5 =$ _____

9. $10 \times 0 =$ _____

10. $8 \times 8 =$ _____

11. $4 \times 5 =$ _____

12. $\begin{array}{r} 8 \\ \times\ 7 \\ \hline \end{array}$

13. $\begin{array}{r} 11 \\ \times\ 10 \\ \hline \end{array}$

14. The 2s factor has products that all end in even numbers. Which other factors also have products that end in even numbers?

____

15. Writing in Math Jerrolyn knows that $6 \times 12 = 72$. How can she use that fact to find 7×12?

____

____

16. Reasoning At a restaurant, Diane and her friends order 2 pizzas. Diane cuts each pizza into 8 slices. More friends join the group, so she orders 2 more pizzas and cuts them into 6 slices each. How many total pizza slices do Diane and her friends have?

____

Test Prep Circle the correct letter for the answer.

17. Which number sentence uses the fact $8 \times 6 = 48$ to help you find the answer to 9×6?

A $48 + 1 = 49$

C $48 + 8 = 56$

B $48 + 6 = 54$

D $48 + 9 = 57$

Name _______________________________

Multiplying Three Numbers

Find $5 \times 2 \times 3$.

Example 1

You can change the grouping of factors, and the product will be
the same.

Group the first 2 numbers together.
$(5 \times 2) \times 3$
$= 10 \times 3$
$= 30$

Group the second 2 numbers together.
$5 \times (2 \times 3)$
$= 5 \times 6$
$= 30$

The answer is 30 in both cases.

Example 2

Solve without using grouping symbols.

If there are no grouping symbols, you can choose any two factors
to multiply first.

$2 \times 3 \times 5$
Try 2×5 first.
$10 \times 3 = 30$

---

1. $(1 \times 3) \times 6 =$ _____

$1 \times (3 \times 6) =$ _____

2. $(5 \times 2) \times 4 =$ _____

$5 \times (2 \times 4) =$ _____

3. $(2 \times 4) \times 1 =$ _____

$2 \times (4 \times 1) =$ _____

4. $(2 \times 2) \times 5 =$ _____

$2 \times (2 \times 5) =$ _____

5. $2 \times 4 \times 3 =$ _____

6. $7 \times 1 \times 3 =$ _____

7. $3 \times 3 \times 2 =$ _____

8. $3 \times 2 \times 6 =$ _____

9. $(4 \times 2) \times 2 =$ _____

10. $3 \times (0 \times 7) =$ _____

Multiplying Three Numbers (continued)

11. $1 \times 7 \times 9 =$ _____ **12.** $8 \times (2 \times 3) =$ _____ **13.** $(2 \times 5) \times 6 =$ _____

14. $9 \times 0 \times 3 =$ _____ **15.** $4 \times 5 \times 1 =$ _____ **16.** $(3 \times 6) \times 1 =$ _____

17. Reasoning When multiplying 3 numbers, if one
of the factors is zero, what will the answer be? _______________________

18. A classroom of students is getting ready to take
a test. There are 5 rows of desks in the room and
4 students are in each row. Ten desks in the
room are empty. Each student is required to
have 2 pencils. How many pencils are needed? _______________________

Test Prep Choose the correct letter for each answer.

19. Find $5 \times 3 \times 3$.

   A 30   **B** 45   **C** 20   **D** 15

20. Gloves are on sale for $2 per pair. A family of four buys 2 pairs
each. How much is the total cost?

   A $16   **B** $8   **C** $6   **D** $4

Input/Output Tables

Example 1

Complete the table.
Rule: Subtract 3.

Input	Output
5	
7	4
9	
11	8

$5 - 3 = 2$

$9 - 3 = 6$

The missing outputs are 2 and 6.

Example 2

Write the rule.
Then complete the table.

Input	Output
5	25
4	20
3	
2	

The rule is multiply by 5.

$3 \times 5 = 15$

$2 \times 5 = 10$

The missing outputs are 15 and 10.

Complete each table.

1. Rule: Add 7.

Input	Output
18	25
15	
12	19
9	

2. Rule: Multiply by 4.

Input	Output
3	
5	20
	28
9	

3. Rule: Multiply by 2.

Input	Output
6	
	6
	2
0	0

Write the rule. Then complete the table.

4. Rule: _______________

Input	Output
4	
7	6
	8
12	11

5. Rule: _______________

Input	Output
0	
	19
15	24
20	29

6. Rule: _______________

Input	Output
3	18
4	24
7	
8	

Input/Output Tables (continued)

Complete each table.

7. Rule: Add 5.

Input	Output
6	
8	
	14
12	

8. Rule: Multiply by 8.

Input	Output
1	
3	
	40
7	

9. Rule: Add 12.

Input	Output
6	
14	
22	
35	

Write the rule. Then complete the table.

10. Rule: _______________

____

Input	Output
8	4
	12
21	
26	22
31	

11. Rule: _______________

____

Input	Output
2	6
4	12
6	18
7	
9	

12. Rule: _______________

____

Input	Output
20	13
17	10
14	
	4
7	

13. The rule for a table is multiply by 1. If an input is 9, what is the output? _______________

Test Prep Circle the correct letter for the answer.

14. Which number completes the table?

Input	Output
3	27
5	45
6	
8	72

A 63

B 36

C 54

D 58

15. What is the rule for the table?

Input	Output
3	12
7	16
11	20
16	25

A Subtract 9.

B Multiply by 3.

C Add 9.

D Add 8.

156

Name _______________________________

Division as Sharing

Make equal groups to solve.

Example

Ann, Ed, and Joe have 9 pickles. If they share the pickles equally, how many pickles should each get?

Ann, Ed, and Joe should each get 3 pickles.

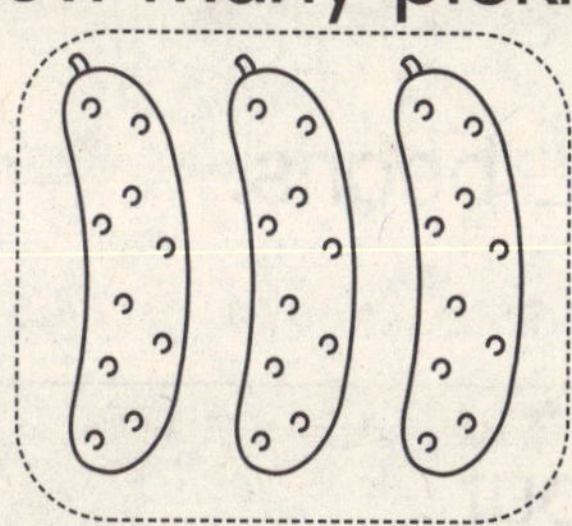 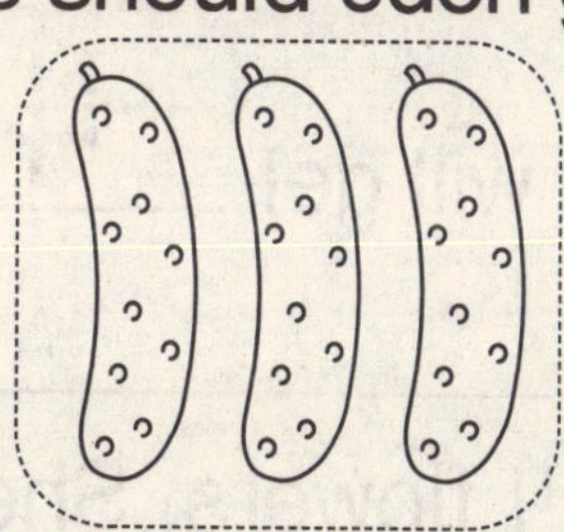 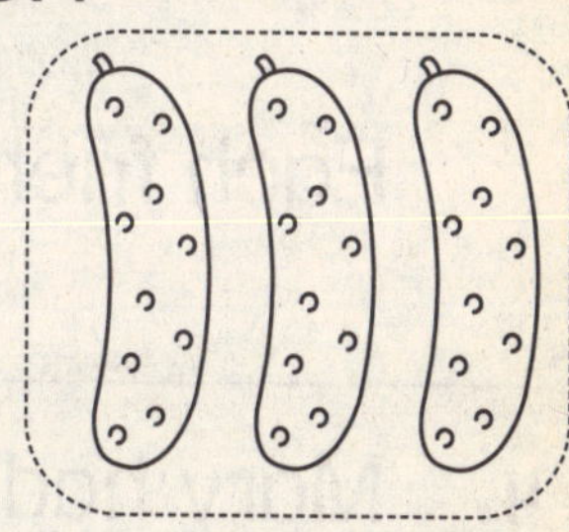

1. Lisa has 6 eggs. She places an equal number of eggs in 2 baskets. How many eggs are in each basket?

There are _______ eggs in each basket.

2. Dave shared 10 cherries with Zack. If they each got the same number of cherries, how many did each boy get?

They each got _______ cherries.

Name ___________________________

Division as Sharing (continued)

Use counters. Make equal groups to solve.

3. Sam has 12 beans to give to
    3 friends. If he shares the beans
    equally, how many beans will
    each friend get?

    Each friend will get __4__ beans.

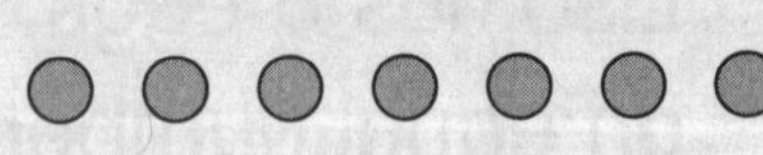

4. Mary had 14 flowers. She put
    the same number of flowers in
    2 vases. How many flowers
    did she put in each vase?

    She put ________ flowers in
    each vase.

5. Jeff had 16 pencils. If he put
    an equal number of pencils in
    4 boxes, how many pencils
    would he put in each box?

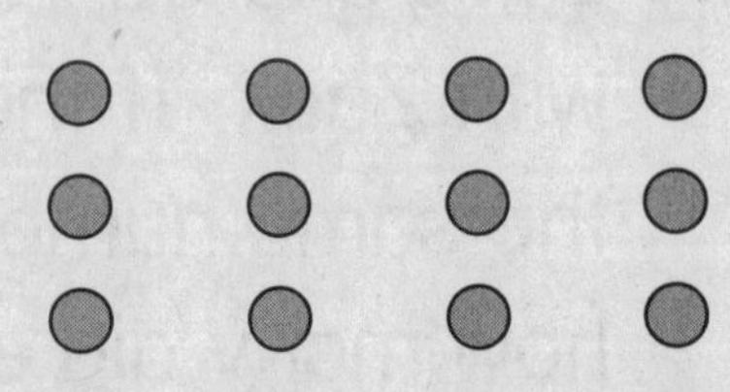

    He would put ________ pencils
    in each box.

Name ___________________________

Division as Repeated Subtraction

Example

Subtract equal groups to solve.

Rob has $10. Each day, he buys lunch at school
for $2. How many days can he keep buying lunch
at school?

Day 1	Day 2	Day 3	Day 4	Day 5
$10-2=8$	$8-2=6$	$6-2=4$	$4-2=2$	$2-2=0$

Rob can buy lunch at school for <u>5</u> days.

Subtract equal groups to solve.

1. Sally has 12 tickets for rides at
   the park. Each ride costs 4 tickets.
   How many rides can Sally go on?

  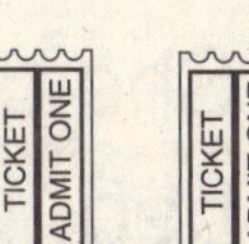

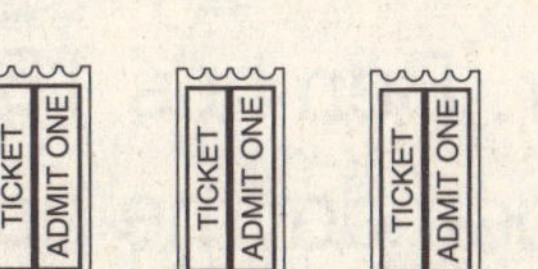

   Sally can go on _____ rides.

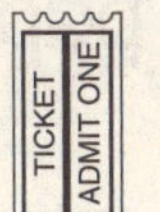  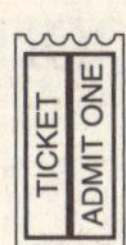 

159

Name _______________________________

Division as Repeated Subtraction (continued)

Subtract equal groups to solve.

2. 18 children are going to ride the
    train. 6 children will fit in each car.
    How many train cars will they need?

    They will need _____ train cars.

Use counters. Subtract equal groups to solve.
Draw to show what you did.

3. Mrs. Smith has 20 pillows. She
    has 5 beds and wants to place
    the same number of pillows on
    each bed. How many pillows will
    she place on each bed?

    She can place _________ pillows on each
    bed.

---

4. Mr. Ben has 15 sheets of paper.
    Each day he hands out 5 sheets
    of paper. How many days can
    he hand out paper?

    He can hand out paper for _________ days.

Name _______________________

Writing Division Stories

Example 1

You can write a division story for a number sentence.

Write a division story for $18 \div 3 = n$. Then solve it.

Look: Look at the division sentence.

Think: When might a greater number like 18 be divided by a lesser number? You might think of 18 peanuts divided between 3 friends.

Write: Write the division story.

Sandy invited 3 friends to her house after school. She has 18 peanuts that she wants to share equally with each of her 3 friends. How many peanuts will each friend get?

$18 \div 3 = 6$
Each friend gets 6 peanuts.

Example 2

Write a division story for the number sentence. Then solve it. Use the picture to help.

$15 \div 3 = x$

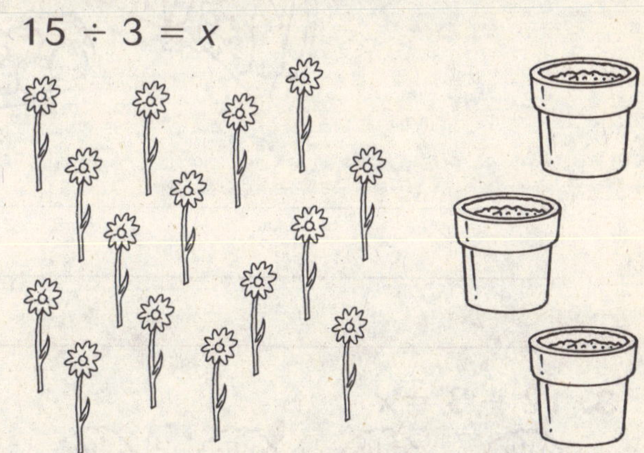

Ming picked 15 flowers from her garden. She has 3 flower pots. If she wants to plant the same number of flowers in each pot, how many flowers will she put in each?

$15 \div 3 = 5$
Ming will put 5 flowers in each flower pot.

---

1. Write a division story for the number sentence $10 \div 2 = n$. Use the picture to help.

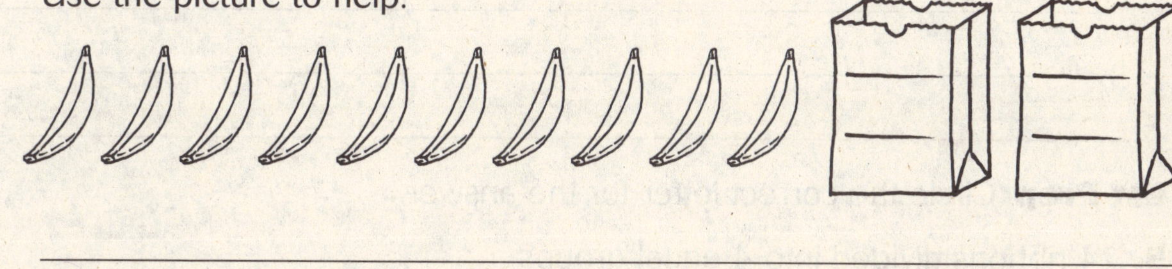

____

____

____

161

Name _______________________________________

Writing Division Stories (continued)

Write a division story for each number sentence below. Use the pictures to
help. Then use counters or draw a picture to solve.

2. $15 \div 5 = n$

____

____

____

3. $12 \div 3 = x$

____

____

____

Write a division story. Then use counters or draw a picture to solve.

4. $14 \div 2 = n$

____

____

____

Test Prep Circle the correct letter for the answer.

5. 24 ribbons divided into 4 equal groups

  A 4 ribbons in each group   **B** 12 ribbons in each group

  C 2 ribbons in each group   **D** 6 ribbons in each group

Name ________________________

Relating Multiplication and Division

Example

Use the array to complete each sentence.

$14 \div 7 = \underline{?}$

7 times what number equals 14?

$$7 \times \underline{2} = 14$$

So, $14 \div 7 = 2$.

Use the array to complete each sentence.

1.

$4 \times \underline{} = 20$

$20 \div 4 = \underline{}$

2.

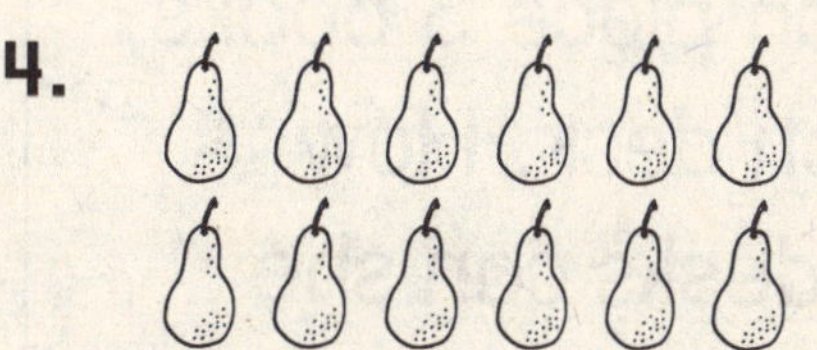

$3 \times \underline{} = 18$

$18 \div 3 = \underline{}$

3.

$3 \times \underline{} = 9$

$9 \div 3 = \underline{}$

4.

$6 \times \underline{} = 12$

$12 \div 6 = \underline{}$

Name ______________________________________

Relating Multiplication and Division (continued)

Solve each problem. Use counters if you wish.

5.

$6 \times \underline{\hspace{2cm}} = 6$

$6 \div 6 = \underline{\hspace{2cm}}$

6.

$5 \times \underline{\hspace{2cm}} = 15$

$15 \div 5 = \underline{\hspace{2cm}}$

7.

$4 \times \underline{\hspace{2cm}} = 12$

$12 \div 4 = \underline{\hspace{2cm}}$

8.

$7 \times \underline{\hspace{2cm}} = 14$

$14 \div 7 = \underline{\hspace{2cm}}$

9.

$4 \times \underline{\hspace{2cm}} = 16$

$16 \div 4 = \underline{\hspace{2cm}}$

10.

$8 \times \underline{\hspace{2cm}} = 16$

$16 \div 8 = \underline{\hspace{2cm}}$

Reasoning Solve. Write the number sentences.

11. Anna has 20 books. She can place 5 books on each desk. How many desks can she place books on?

____

12. Look back at 11. Write the multiplication sentence you could use to help solve the problem.

____

Dividing by 2 and 5

Example 1

Find 14 ÷ 2.

Think: $2 \times$ ____ $= 14$

$\qquad 2 \times 7 = 14$

So, 14 ÷ 2 = 7.

dividend   divisor   quotient

Example 2

Find 30 ÷ 5.

Think: $5 \times$ ____ $= 30$

$\qquad 5 \times 6 = 30$

So, 30 ÷ 5 = 6.

dividend   divisor   quotient

Use the multiplication fact to find each quotient.

1. $2 \times 4 = 8$

$8 \div 2 =$ ______

2. $2 \times 5 = 10$

$10 \div 2 =$ ______

3. $5 \times 1 = 5$

$5 \div 5 =$ ______

4. $2 \times 7 = 14$

$14 \div 2 =$ ______

5. $5 \times 4 = 20$

$20 \div 5 =$ ______

6. $2 \times$ ____ $= 12$

$12 \div 2 =$ ______

7. $5 \times$ ____ $= 45$

$45 \div 5 =$ ______

8. $2 \times$ ____ $= 16$

$16 \div 2 =$ ______

9. $5 \times$ ____ $= 40$

$40 \div 5 =$ ______

10. What multiplication fact can you use to find 20 ÷ 2?

____

Name ____

Dividing by 2 and 5 (continued)

Use the multiplication fact to find each quotient.

11. $2 \times 2 = 4$

$4 \div 2 = $ _____

12. $2 \times 5 = 10$

$10 \div 2 = $ _____

13. $5 \times 3 = 15$

$15 \div 5 = $ _____

14. $5 \times$ _____ $= 35$

$35 \div 5 = $ _____

15. $2 \times$ _____ $= 12$

$12 \div 2 = $ _____

16. $5 \times$ _____ $= 30$

$30 \div 5 = $ _____

Find each quotient.

17. $16 \div 2 = $ _____

18. $10 \div 2 = $ _____

19. $40 \div 5 = $ _____

20. $10 \div 5 = $ _____

21. $2 \div 2 = $ _____

22. $20 \div 5 = $ _____

23. $12 \div 2 = $ _____

24. $25 \div 5 = $ _____

25. $14 \div 2 = $ _____

26. Algebra Complete the pattern. 45, 40, 35, _____, _____, 20, _____

27. There are 10 cars in 2 lanes of traffic waiting
at a stop light. Each lane has the same number
of cars. Three of the cars are blue. How many
cars are in each lane of traffic? ______________________

Test Prep Circle the correct letter for the answer.

28. There are 18 boys and girls in a room. Half of them are
boys and half are girls. How many girls are in the room?

A 9   **B** 2   **C** 8   **D** 36

29. Beth spends $15 on five books. Each book costs the same
amount. How much did each book cost?

A $2   **B** $3   **C** $5   **D** $15

Name _______________________________

Dividing by 3 and 4

Example 1

Find 15 ÷ 3.

Think: $3 \times$ ___ $= 15$

$\qquad 3 \times 5 = 15$

So, $15 \div 3 = 5$.

Example 2

Find 20 ÷ 4.

Think: $4 \times$ ___ $= 20$

$\qquad 4 \times 5 = 20$

So, $20 \div 4 = 5$.

Use the multiplication fact to find each quotient.

1. $3 \times 4 = 12$

$12 \div 3 =$ _____

2. $3 \times 5 = 15$

$15 \div 3 =$ _____

3. $4 \times 1 = 4$

$4 \div 4 =$ _____

4. $3 \times 2 = 6$

$6 \div 3 =$ _____

5. $4 \times$ ___ $= 24$

$24 \div 4 =$ _____

6. $3 \times$ ___ $= 18$

$18 \div 3 =$ _____

7. $4 \times$ ___ $= 12$

$12 \div 4 =$ _____

8. $3 \times$ ___ $= 24$

$24 \div 3 =$ _____

9. $4 \times$ ___ $= 32$

$32 \div 4 =$ _____

10. What multiplication fact can you use to find $27 \div 3$?

____

Dividing by 3 and 4 (continued)

Use the multiplication fact to find each quotient.

11. $3 \times 2 = 6$ **12.** $4 \times 5 = 20$ **13.** $3 \times 5 = 15$

$6 \div 3 =$ _____ $20 \div 4 =$ _____ $15 \div 3 =$ _____

Find each quotient.

14. $28 \div 4 =$ _____   **15.** $12 \div 3 =$ _____   **16.** $8 \div 4 =$ _____

17. $18 \div 3 =$ _____   **18.** $3 \div 3 =$ _____   **19.** $16 \div 4 =$ _____

20. $27 \div 3 =$ _____   **21.** $24 \div 4 =$ _____   **22.** $21 \div 3 =$ _____

23. Number Sense If you know that $4 \times 11 = 44$,
then what is $44 \div 4$?   ___________________

24. Norio has 18 marbles in 3 different colors.
The number of red marbles is the same as
the number of green marbles and also the
same as the number of black marbles. How
many green marbles does Norio have?   ___________________

Test Prep Circle the correct letter for the answer.

25. There are 3 feet to every yard. There are 12 inches to
every foot. How many yards are equivalent to 12 feet?

A 1   **B** 4   **C** 36   **D** 24

26. Find a related division sentence for the multiplication
sentence $4 \times 9 = 36$.

A $24 \div 4 = 6$ **B** $9 \times 4 = 36$ **C** $36 \div 4 = 9$ **D** $12 \div 4 = 3$

Name _______________________________________

Dividing by 2 Through 5

Example

You can use multiplication facts to help you divide.

Find 24 ÷ 4.

Think: Four times what number
equals 24?

$4 \times 6 = 24$

Write: $24 \div 4 = 6$ **or** $\begin{array}{r} 6 \\ 4\overline{)24} \end{array}$

Find 45 ÷ 5.

Think: Five times what number
equals 45?

$5 \times 9 = 45$

Write: $45 \div 5 = 9$ **or** $\begin{array}{r} 9 \\ 5\overline{)45} \end{array}$

Use the multiplication fact to find each quotient.

1. $4 \times$ _____ $= 24$

$24 \div 4 =$ _____

2. $6 \times$ _____ $= 30$

$30 \div 6 =$ _____

3. $2 \times$ _____ $= 12$

$12 \div 2 =$ _____

4. $5 \times$ _____ $= 25$

$25 \div 5 =$ _____

5. $3 \times$ _____ $= 27$

$27 \div 3 =$ _____

6. $4 \times$ _____ $= 28$

$28 \div 4 =$ _____

7. Mario has 15 eggs. He wants to share them equally with 3 friends. How
many eggs will each friend get?

Think: $3 \times 5 = 15$. So, $15 \div 3 =$ _____ eggs.

Dividing by 2 Through 5 (continued)

Find each quotient.

8. 24 ÷ 3 = _____   **9.** 16 ÷ 4 = _____   **10.** 18 ÷ 2 = _____

11. 40 ÷ 5 = _____   **12.** 27 ÷ 3 = _____   **13.** 28 ÷ 4 = _____

14. 25 ÷ 5 = _____   **15.** 20 ÷ 4 = _____   **16.** 12 ÷ 3 = _____

17. 5$\overline{)35}$ **18.** 4$\overline{)36}$ **19.** 3$\overline{)21}$

20. Reasoning The store sells flowers for $3 a bunch. How many bunches
of flowers can Jill buy with $12?

____

21. Todd has 40 whistles. He wants to divide them evenly between his 5
friends. How many whistles will each friend get?

____

Test Prep Circle the correct letter for the answer.

22. 20 ÷ 5 =

　A 3　　　　**B** 4　　　　**C** 6　　　　**D** 8

23. There are 24 students in the class. If 4 students are to sit at each table,
how many tables are needed?

　A 9 tables　　**B** 6 tables　　**C** 7 tables　　**D** 8 tables

170

Name ____

Dividing by 6 and 7

Example 1

Find 12 ÷ 6.

Think: 6 × ____ = 12

      6 × 2 = 12

So, 12 ÷ 6 = 2.

Example 2

Find 21 ÷ 7.

Think: 7 × ____ = 21

      7 × 3 = 21

So, 21 ÷ 7 = 3.

Use the multiplication fact to find each quotient.

1. 6 × 5 = 30

  30 ÷ 6 = ______

2. 7 × 2 = 14

  14 ÷ 7 = ______

3. 6 × 1 = 6

  6 ÷ 6 = ______

4. 7 × 5 = 35

  35 ÷ 7 = ______

5. 6 × ______ = 36

  36 ÷ 6 = ______

6. 7 × ______ = 56

  56 ÷ 7 = ______

7. 6 × ______ = 24

  24 ÷ 6 = ______

8. 7 × 1 = 7

  7 ÷ 7 = ______

9. 6 × ______ = 60

  60 ÷ 6 = ______

10. 6 × 9 = 54

  54 ÷ 6 = ______

11. 7 × 9 = 63

  63 ÷ 7 = ______

12. 6 × 7 = 42

  42 ÷ 6 = ______

13. What multiplication fact can you use to find 63 ÷ 7?

____

Name ____

Dividing by 6 and 7 (continued)

Use the multiplication fact to find each quotient.

14. $7 \times 7 = 49$

$49 \div 7 =$ _____

15. $6 \times 8 = 48$

$48 \div 6 =$ _____

16. $7 \times 4 = 28$

$28 \div 7 =$ _____

Find each quotient.

17. $6\overline{)54}$

18. $7\overline{)42}$

19. $6\overline{)30}$

20. $7\overline{)7}$

21. $6\overline{)42}$

22. $7\overline{)70}$

23. Number Sense If you know that $6 \times 12 = 72$,
then what is $72 \div 6$? ___________________

24. Mrs. Carpenter's class is dividing into groups
for group work. There are 28 students in the
class and 35 desks. How many students will
be in each group if there are seven groups? ___________________

Test Prep Circle the correct letter for the answer.

25. Forty-eight cards are divided into groups of six.
How many cards are in each group?

    A 8   **B** 7   **C** 6   **D** 42

26. Which of the following is true?

    A $6 \div 6 = 6$ **B** $6 \div 1 = 1$ **C** $0 \div 6 = 6$ **D** $6 \div 6 = 1$

Name ____

Dividing by 8 and 9

Example 1

Find 24 ÷ 8.

Think: $8 \times \underline{\hspace{1cm}} = 24$

$8 \times 3 = 24$

So, 24 ÷ 8 = 3.

Example 2

Find 36 ÷ 9.

Think: $9 \times \underline{\hspace{1cm}} = 36$

$9 \times 4 = 36$

So, 36 ÷ 9 = 4.

Use the multiplication fact to find each quotient.

1. $8 \times 5 = 40$

40 ÷ 8 = _____

2. $9 \times 2 = 18$

18 ÷ 9 = _____

3. $8 \times 1 = 8$

8 ÷ 8 = _____

4. $9 \times 6 = 54$

54 ÷ 9 = _____

5. $8 \times \underline{\hspace{1cm}} = 32$

32 ÷ 8 = _____

6. $8 \times \underline{\hspace{1cm}} = 48$

48 ÷ 8 = _____

7. $9 \times \underline{\hspace{1cm}} = 27$

27 ÷ 9 = _____

8. $9 \times \underline{\hspace{1cm}} = 90$

90 ÷ 9 = _____

9. $8 \times \underline{\hspace{1cm}} = 72$

72 ÷ 8 = _____

10. What multiplication fact can you use to find 56 ÷ 8?

____

Dividing by 8 and 9 (continued)

Use the multiplication fact to find each quotient.

11. $8 \times 2 = 16$　　　　**12.** $9 \times 5 = 45$　　　　**13.** $8 \times 3 = 24$

$16 \div 8 =$ _____　　　　$45 \div 9 =$ _____　　　　$24 \div 8 =$ _____

Find each quotient.

14. $9\overline{)63}$　　　　**15.** $8\overline{)32}$　　　　**16.** $9\overline{)36}$

17. $8\overline{)64}$　　　　**18.** $9\overline{)81}$　　　　**19.** $8\overline{)16}$

20. Algebra Complete the pattern.

64, 56, _____, 40, _____, _____, 16

21. Nine friends go to lunch and split the $54 ticket evenly. How much does each friend pay for lunch?　___________________

Test Prep Circle the correct letter for the answer.

22. Eighteen apples are divided into 9 groups. How many apples are in each group?

A 8　　　　**B** 2　　　　**C** 6　　　　**D** 3

23. Jack has 48 minutes to finish a test. Sixteen other students are taking the test at the same time. There are 8 questions on the test. How long does Jack have to spend on each question?

A 6 minutes　　**B** 40 minutes　　**C** 2 minutes　　**D** 3 minutes

Name ______________________________

Dividing by 6 Through 9

Example

You can use multiplication facts to help you divide by 6, 7, 8, and 9.

Find $36 \div 9$.

Think: Nine times what number equals 36?

$$9 \times 4 = 36$$

Write: $36 \div 9 = 4$ **or** $9\overline{)36}$ with quotient 4

Find $49 \div 7$.

Think: Seven times what number equals 49?

$$7 \times 7 = 49$$

Write: $49 \div 7 = 7$ **or** $7\overline{)49}$ with quotient 7

Use the multiplication fact to help you find each quotient.

1. $6 \times$ _____ $= 30$

$30 \div 6 =$ _____

2. $8 \times$ _____ $= 48$

$48 \div 8 =$ _____

3. $9 \times$ _____ $= 36$

$36 \div 9 =$ _____

4. $7 \times$ _____ $= 56$

$56 \div 7 =$ _____

5. $6 \times$ _____ $= 24$

$24 \div 6 =$ _____

6. $9 \times$ _____ $= 63$

$63 \div 9 =$ _____

7. A box can hold 8 books. How many boxes are needed for 32 books?

Think: $8 \times 4 = 32$ So, $32 \div 8 =$ _____ boxes.

Name _______________________________

Dividing by 6 Through 9 (continued)

Find each quotient.

8. $36 \div 6 =$ _______ **9.** $64 \div 8 =$ _______ **10.** $72 \div 9 =$ _______

11. $48 \div 6 =$ _______ **12.** $63 \div 7 =$ _______ **13.** $24 \div 8 =$ _______

14. $21 \div 7 =$ _______ **15.** $54 \div 9 =$ _______ **16.** $28 \div 7 =$ _______

17. $7\overline{)49}$ **18.** $6\overline{)18}$ **19.** $9\overline{)27}$

20. Reasoning Luis has 30 dog treats. He wants to divide them evenly between his 6 dogs. How many treats will each dog get?

____

21. Reasoning The grocery store sells potatoes for $7 a bag. How many bags of potatoes could you buy with $42?

____

Test Prep Circle the correct letter for the answer.

22. $40 \div 8 =$

A 8 **B** 5 **C** 6 **D** 3

23. There are 28 students in the class. If 4 students sit at each table, how many tables are there?

A 9 tables **B** 8 tables **C** 7 tables **D** 6 tables

0 and 1 in Division

Example 1

Find $5 \div 1$.

Any number divided by 1 equals that number.

So, $5 \div 1 = 5$.

Check: $1 \times$ ____ $= 5$

$1 \times 5 = 5$

Example 2

Find $0 \div 7$.

Zero divided by any number (except 0) equals 0.

So, $0 \div 7 = 0$.

Check: $7 \times$ ____ $= 0$

$7 \times 0 = 0$

---

1. $7 \div 1 =$ ____

2. $0 \div 8 =$ ____

3. $6 \div 6 =$ ____

4. $0 \div 9 =$ ____

5. $5 \div 5 =$ ____

6. $3 \div 1 =$ ____

7. $4 \div 1 =$ ____

8. $2 \div 2 =$ ____

9. $0 \div 1 =$ ____

10. $0 \div 7 =$ ____

11. $5 \div 1 =$ ____

12. $0 \div 2 =$ ____

Name ____

0 and 1 in Division (continued)

13. $4 \div 1 =$ _____   **14.** $0 \div 5 =$ _____   **15.** $6 \div 6 =$ _____

16. $3\overline{)0}$ **17.** $9\overline{)9}$ **18.** $5\overline{)5}$

19. $1\overline{)6}$ **20.** $1\overline{)1}$ **21.** $8\overline{)0}$

22. Writing in Math Use the rule for division by 1 to find
247 ÷ 1. Explain.

____

____

23. Larry has 3 friends who would like some cookies but he has
no cookies to give them. How many cookies can Larry give
each friend?

____

Test Prep Circle the correct letter for the answer.

24. Five friends gather for lunch at one friend's house. This
friend has five sandwiches and 6 glasses of milk.
How many sandwiches will each friend get?

   A 5   **B** 11   **C** 2   **D** 1

25. In math class, 9 students each need one desk. How many
desks are needed?

   A 10   **B** 1   **C** 0   **D** 9

Name _________________________________

Dividing with Remainders

Example 1

Find $10 \div 3$.

Step 1 Use counters to make 10.

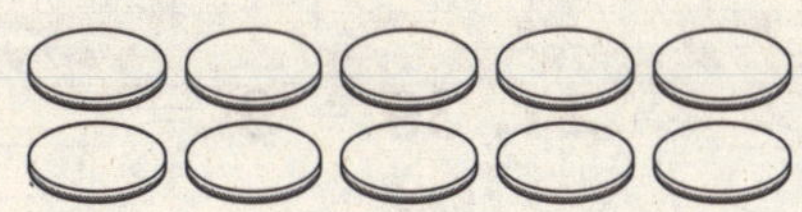

Step 2 Make groups of 3.

So, $10 \div 3 = 3$ R1.

Example 2

Find $24 \div 5$.

Step 1 Use counters to make 24.

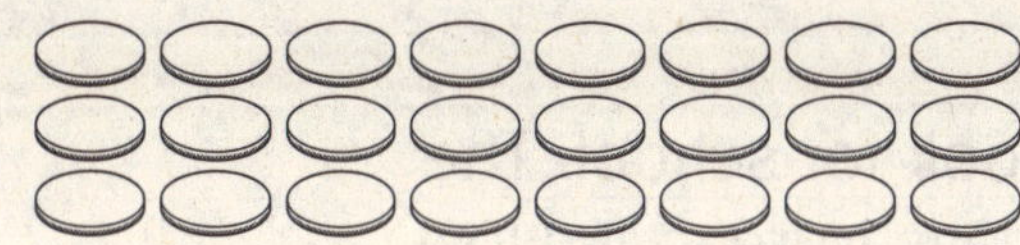

Step 2 Make groups of 5.

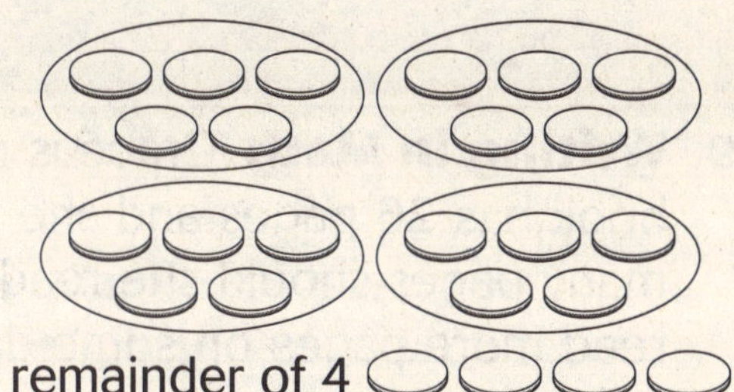

So, $24 \div 5 = 4$ R4.

Use counters or draw a picture to find each quotient and remainder.

1. $8 \div 3 = $ _______   **2.** $17 \div 3 = $ _______   **3.** $14 \div 3 = $ _______

4. $11 \div 4 = $ _______   **5.** $22 \div 4 = $ _______   **6.** $34 \div 4 = $ _______

7. $13 \div 5 = $ _______   **8.** $27 \div 5 = $ _______   **9.** $46 \div 5 = $ _______

10. $14 \div 6 = $ _______   **11.** $26 \div 6 = $ _______   **12.** $38 \div 6 = $ _______

Name ____

Dividing with Remainders (continued)

13. $17 \div 7 =$ _______   **14.** $27 \div 7 =$ _______   **15.** $45 \div 7 =$ _______

16. $18 \div 8 =$ _______   **17.** $28 \div 8 =$ _______   **18.** $37 \div 8 =$ _______

19. $14 \div 9 =$ _______   **20.** $28 \div 9 =$ _______   **21.** $39 \div 9 =$ _______

22. $12 \div 8 =$ _______   **23.** $68 \div 7 =$ _______   **24.** $59 \div 8 =$ _______

25. $9 \div 4 =$ _______   **26.** $26 \div 5 =$ _______   **27.** $34 \div 6 =$ _______

28. Algebra What number(s) could you divide 15
by and have 3 left over?   _______________

29. Writing in Math Grace is reading a book for school. The
book has 26 pages and she is given 3 days to read it. How
many pages should she read each day? Will she have to
read more pages on some days than on others? Explain.

____

____

Test Prep Circle the correct letter for the answer.

30. Find $44 \div 7$.

   A 6　　　　**B** 7　　　　**C** 5 R9　　　　**D** 6 R2

31. Crackers are selling at $3 a box. How many boxes can
Yao buy for $10 and how much change will he get?

   A 1 box, $3 change　　　**C** 3 boxes, no change

   B 4 boxes, no change　　　**D** 3 boxes, $1 change

180

Name ____

Division Patterns with 10, 11, and 12

Example

Look for patterns in the multiplication table
to help you divide by 10, 11, and 12.

×	0	1	2	3	4	5	6	7	8	9	10	11	12
0	0	0	0	0	0	0	0	0	0	0	0	0	0
1	0	1	2	3	4	5	6	7	8	9	10	11	12
2	0	2	4	6	8	10	12	14	16	18	20	22	24
3	0	3	6	9	12	15	18	21	24	27	30	33	36
4	0	4	8	12	16	20	24	28	32	36	40	44	48
5	0	5	10	15	20	25	30	35	40	45	50	55	60
6	0	6	12	18	24	30	36	42	48	54	60	66	72
7	0	7	14	21	28	35	42	49	56	63	70	77	84
8	0	8	16	24	32	40	48	56	64	72	80	88	96
9	0	9	18	27	36	45	54	63	72	81	90	99	108
10	0	10	20	30	40	50	60	70	80	90	100	110	120
11	0	11	22	33	44	55	66	77	88	99	110	121	132
12	0	12	24	36	48	60	72	84	96	108	120	132	144

When you divide a
number and the remainder
is 0, the number is **evenly
divisible.** You can also say
the number is a **multiple**
of the divisor.

Color the 10s column green.
Look for a pattern: The numbers 0 through 120 are all multiples of 10.

Each of these numbers is evenly divisible by 10.
For example,
$40 \div 10 = 4$

Color the 11s column yellow.
Look for a pattern: The numbers 0 through 132 are all multiples of 11.

Each of these numbers is evenly divisible by 11.
For example,
$77 \div 11 = 7$

Color the 12s column blue.
Look for a pattern: The numbers 0 through 144 are all multiples of 12.

Each of these numbers is evenly divisible by 12.
For example,
$96 \div 12 = 8$

Find each quotient. You may use the multiplication table or counters or draw a
picture to help.

1. $77 \div 11 =$ _______ **2.** $33 \div 11 =$ _______ **3.** $48 \div 12 =$ _______

Name ______________________________

Division Patterns with 10, 11, and 12 (continued)

Find each quotient. You may use the multiplication table
or counters or draw a picture to help.

4. $50 \div 10 =$ _____   **5.** $90 \div 10 =$ _____   **6.** $10 \div 10 =$ _____

7. $66 \div 11 =$ _____   **8.** $121 \div 11 =$ _____   **9.** $88 \div 11 =$ _____

10. $12\overline{)60}$ **11.** $12\overline{)84}$ **12.** $12\overline{)144}$

13. What multiplication fact can you use to make sure that the
quotients are correct? In the table below, fill in the quotient from
the questions above, and then write the related multiplication fact.

Check	Multiplication Fact
$40 \div 10 = 4$	$4 \times 10 = 40$
$66 \div 11 =$	
$88 \div 11 =$	
$84 \div 12 =$	

14. Reasoning You have 60 eggs. You have egg cartons that each
hold 12 eggs. How many egg cartons can you completely fill?

____

Test Prep Circle the correct letter for the answer.

15. $11 \div 11 =$

   A 0   **B** 1   **C** 22   **D** 121

16. $81 \div 9 =$

   A 10   **B** 9   **C** 8   **D** 7

182

Name _______________________________

Readiness for Addition and Subtraction

Fill in the ○ with the correct answer.

I. Which tells about the picture?

- ○ 2 frogs and 2 frogs
- ○ 4 frogs and 5 frogs
- ○ I frog and 2 frogs
- ○ 2 frogs and 4 frogs

2. Which tells about the picture?

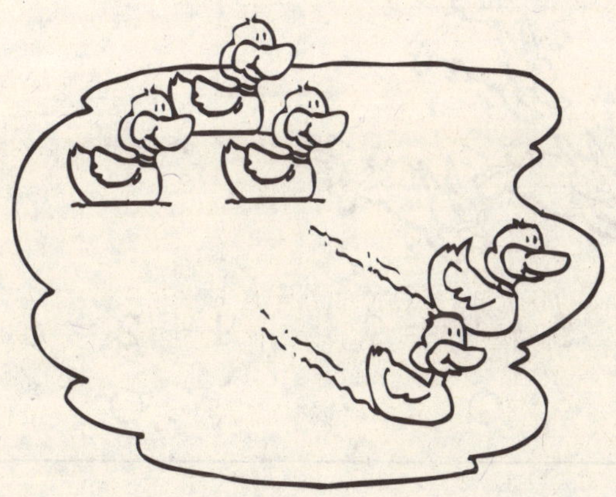

- ○ 5 ducks in all.
  2 ducks swim away.
- ○ 5 ducks in all.
  4 ducks swim away.
- ○ 5 ducks in all.
  I duck swims away.
- ○ 5 ducks in all.
  5 ducks swim away.

Understanding Addition

Fill in the ○ for the correct answer.

1. How can you put five bones into two dishes?

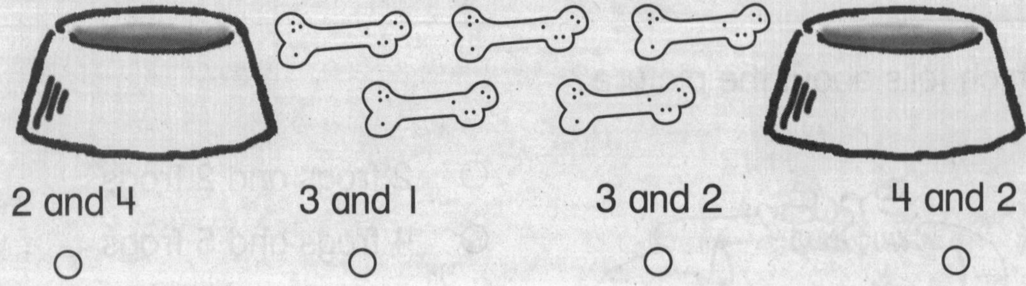

| 2 and 4 | 3 and 1 | 3 and 2 | 4 and 2 |
| ○ | ○ | ○ | ○ |

2. Which is a way to make 6?

| 1 and 4 | 4 and 2 | 0 and 4 | 4 and 3 |
| ○ | ○ | ○ | ○ |

3. Which number sentence shows the addition story in the picture?

| $4 + 3 = 7$ | $4 + 4 = 8$ | $5 + 4 = 9$ | $4 + 2 = 6$ |
| ○ | ○ | ○ | ○ |

4. Find the sum.

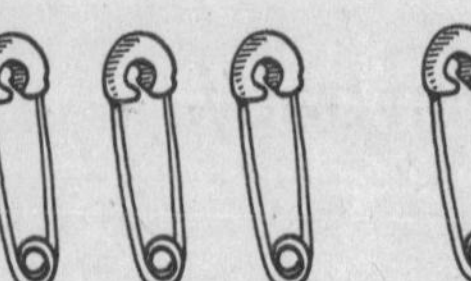

$3 + 1 =$ _______

| 3 | 4 | 5 | 6 |
| ○ | ○ | ○ | ○ |

Name _______________________________

Understanding Subtraction

Fill in the ○ for the correct answer.

I. How many girls and boys will fit on five swings?

I and 5	3 and 3	2 and 4	3 and 2
○	○	○	○

2. Which number sentence shows the subtraction story in the picture?

$5 - 2 = 3$	$6 - 3 = 3$	$6 - 2 = 4$	$5 - 3 = 2$
○	○	○	○

3. Find the difference.

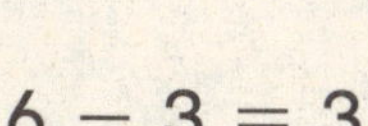 $4 - 1 =$ _______

3	4	5	2
○	○	○	○

Joining Stories

Fill in the ○ for the correct answer.

Tell how many there are in all.

1. 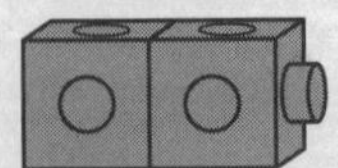 

1	2	3	4
○	○	○	○

2. 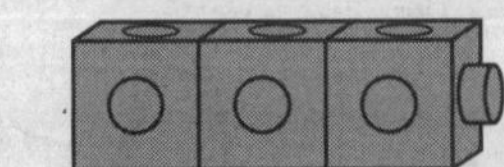 

9	5	8	6
○	○	○	○

3. 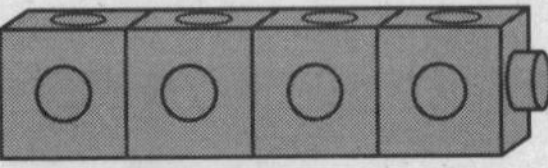 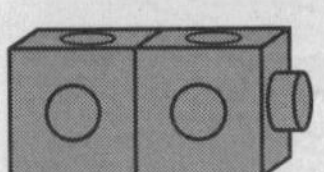

4	6	8	10
○	○	○	○

4. 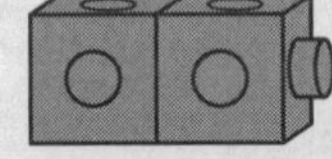 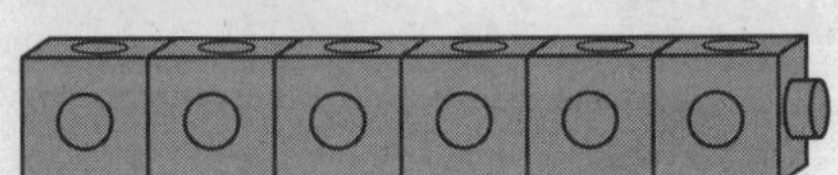

8	6	4	2
○	○	○	○

Using Pictures to Add

Fill in the ○ for the correct answer.

1. Which matches the picture?

- ○ 3 and 3
- ○ 3 and 2
- ○ 3 and 1
- ○ 2 and 1

2. Choose the addition story that matches the picture.

- ○ 1 and 1
- ○ 1 and 2
- ○ 2 and 2
- ○ 2 and 3

3. How many butterflies in all?

 and

- ○ 0
- ○ 1
- ○ 2
- ○ 3

4. Which matches the picture?

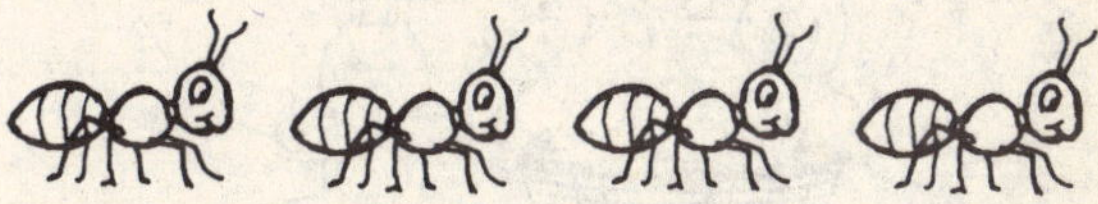

- ○ 4 and 0
- ○ 4 and 2
- ○ 1 and 4
- ○ 1 and 5

Name ______________________________

Using Symbols to Add

Fill in the ○ for the correct answer.

1. Choose the addition sentence for the picture.

- ○ $3 + 3 = 6$
- ○ $3 + 2 = 5$
- ○ $4 + 3 = 7$
- ○ $1 + 4 = 5$

2. Which picture shows one plus four equals five?

- ○ 
- ○ 
- ○ 
- ○ 

3. How many bunnies in all?

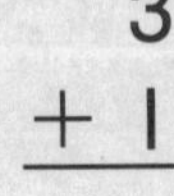

$$\begin{array}{r} 3 \\ +\,1 \\ \hline \end{array}$$

- ○ 2
- ○ 6
- ○ 3
- ○ 4

4. Choose the addition sentence for the picture.

- ○ $4 + 2 = 6$
- ○ $3 + 1 = 4$
- ○ $3 + 2 = 5$
- ○ $4 + 3 = 7$

Name ___________________

Ways to Add

Fill in the ○ for the correct answer.

1. 3 birds are on the branch. 2 more birds join them.
How many birds are there in all?

4	5	6	7
○	○	○	○

2. 4 dogs are playing. 3 more dogs join them.
How many dogs are there in all?

7	6	5	4
○	○	○	○

3. 5 cats are in a box. 3 more cats join them.
How many cats are there in all?

8	4	7	5
○	○	○	○

4. I duck is swimming in the pond. 5 more ducks join it.
How many ducks are there in all?

4	8	3	6
○	○	○	○

5. 6 pigs are in the mud. I more pig joins them.
How many pigs are there in all?

8	7	6	5
○	○	○	○

Name ___________________________

Adding with Zero

Fill in the ○ for the correct answer.

---

1. Choose the addition sentence for the picture.

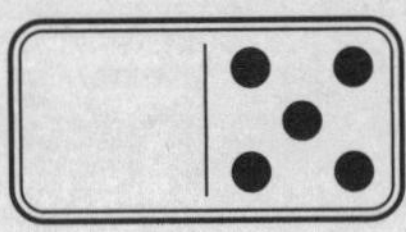

- ○ $2 + 5 = 7$
- ○ $3 + 3 = 6$
- ○ $5 + 0 = 5$
- ○ $3 + 5 = 8$

2. What is the sum of eight plus zero?

$$\begin{array}{r} 8 \\ + 0 \\ \hline \end{array}$$

- ○ 5
- ○ 6
- ○ 7
- ○ 8

---

3. Choose the addition sentence for the picture.

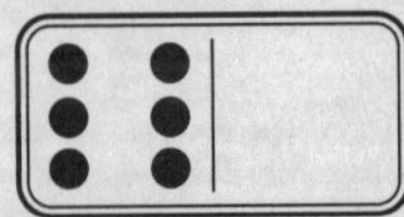

- ○ $0 + 7 = 7$
- ○ $0 + 8 = 8$
- ○ $0 + 6 = 6$
- ○ $0 + 5 = 5$

4. What is the sum of five plus two?

$$5 + 2 = \underline{\hspace{2cm}}$$

- ○ 6
- ○ 7
- ○ 5
- ○ 4

Name _______________________

Adding Across and Down

Fill in the ○ for the correct answer.

Which number sentence matches the picture?

1. 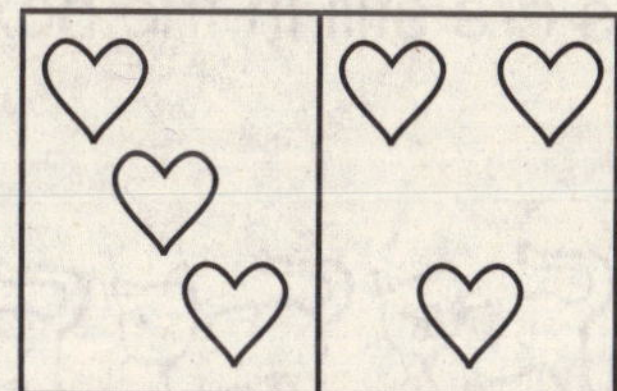

- ○ 3 + 3 = 6
- ○ 2 + 2 = 4
- ○ 5 + 2 = 7
- ○ 3 + 2 = 5

2. 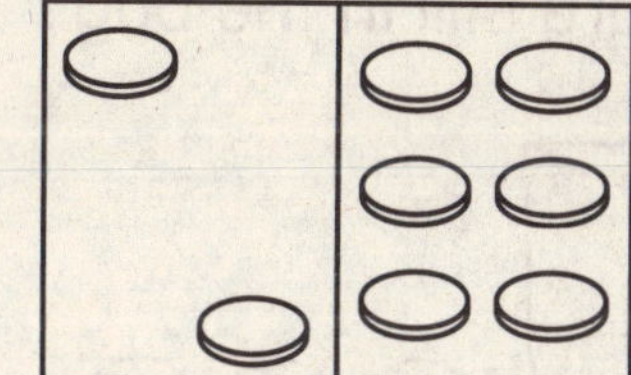

- ○ $\begin{array}{r} 1 \\ +4 \\ \hline 5 \end{array}$
- ○ $\begin{array}{r} 5 \\ +2 \\ \hline 7 \end{array}$
- ○ $\begin{array}{r} 3 \\ +3 \\ \hline 6 \end{array}$
- ○ $\begin{array}{r} 6 \\ +2 \\ \hline 8 \end{array}$

3. 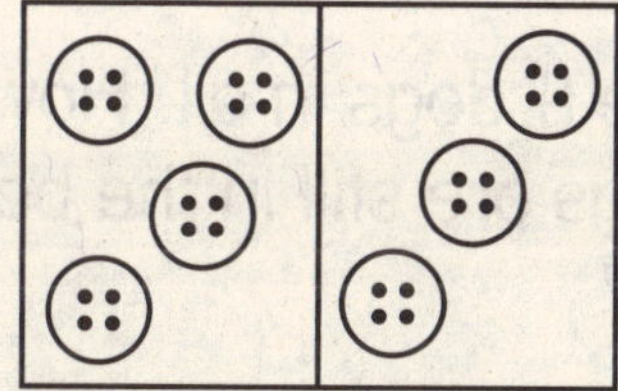

- ○ 2 + 4 = 6
- ○ 4 + 3 = 7
- ○ 4 + 4 = 8
- ○ 3 + 5 = 8

4. 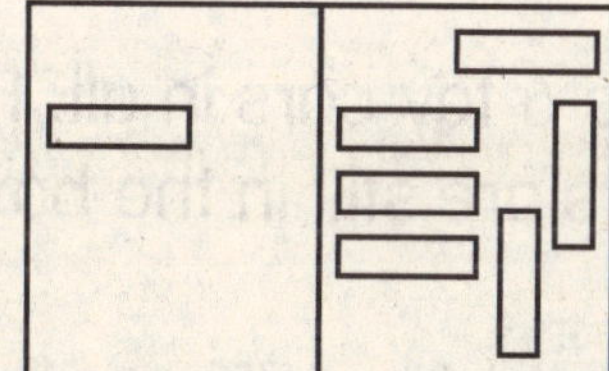

- ○ $\begin{array}{r} 5 \\ +3 \\ \hline 8 \end{array}$
- ○ $\begin{array}{r} 6 \\ +1 \\ \hline 7 \end{array}$
- ○ $\begin{array}{r} 3 \\ +2 \\ \hline 5 \end{array}$
- ○ $\begin{array}{r} 4 \\ +2 \\ \hline 6 \end{array}$

Name ___________________________________

Missing Parts

Fill in the ○ for the correct answer.

---

1. Sue has 8 oranges. How many oranges are still in the bag?

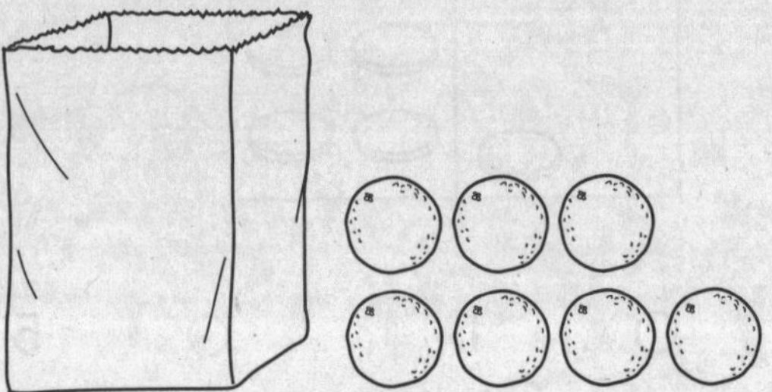

- ○ 0
- ○ 1
- ○ 2
- ○ 3

2. There are 5 cats in all. How many cats are still in the box sleeping?

- ○ 1
- ○ 2
- ○ 3
- ○ 4

3. Frank has 6 toy cars in all. How many cars are still in the box?

- ○ 2
- ○ 3
- ○ 4
- ○ 5

4. There are 4 dogs in all. How many dogs are still in the box sleeping?

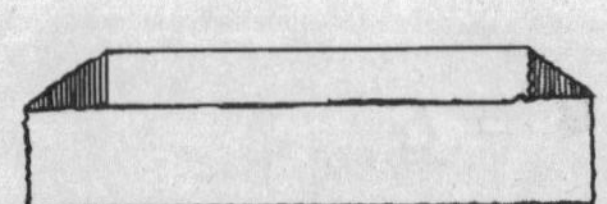

- ○ 0
- ○ 1
- ○ 2
- ○ 3

Name ______________________

Using Pictures to Subtract

Fill in the ◯ for the correct answer.

1. There are 5 dogs. 2 dogs go away. How many dogs are left?

◯ 3
◯ 4
◯ 5
◯ 6

2. There are 4 tigers. 2 tigers go away. How many tigers are left?

◯ 2
◯ 3
◯ 4
◯ 5

3. There are 4 butterflies. I butterfly goes away. How many butterflies are left?

◯ I
◯ 2
◯ 3
◯ 4

4. There are 6 turtles. I turtle goes away. How many turtles are left?

◯ 2
◯ 3
◯ 4
◯ 5

Name ___________________

Using Symbols to Subtract

Fill in the ○ for the correct answer.

Choose the subtraction sentence for the picture.

1. 

- ○ $5 - 1 = 4$
- ○ $5 - 4 = 1$
- ○ $6 - 1 = 5$
- ○ $4 - 2 = 2$

2. 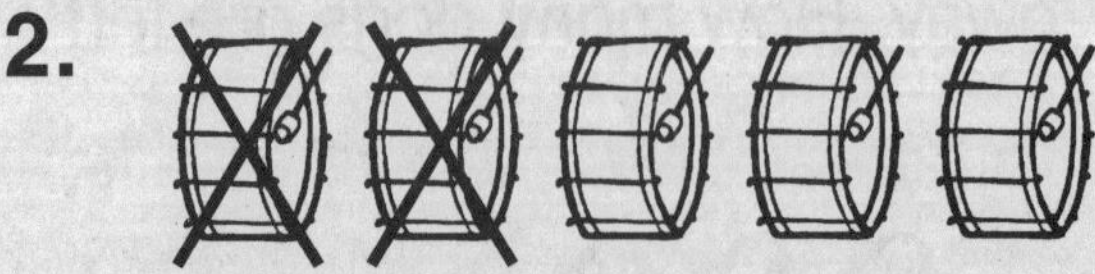

- ○ $3 - 2 = 1$
- ○ $6 - 2 = 4$
- ○ $2 - 1 = 1$
- ○ $5 - 2 = 3$

3. 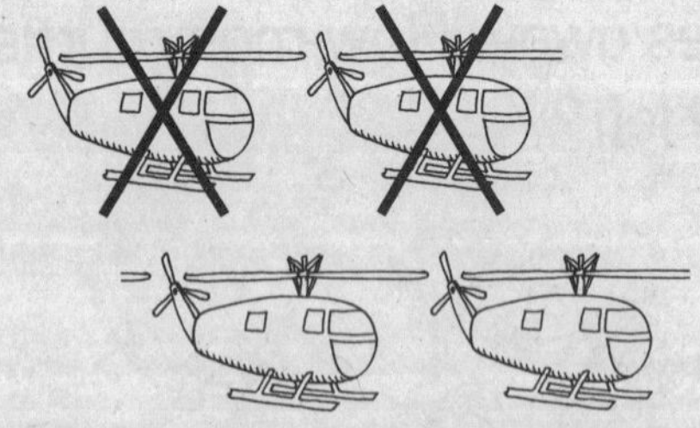

- ○ $6 - 2 = 4$
- ○ $4 - 2 = 2$
- ○ $5 - 4 = 1$
- ○ $3 - 2 = 1$

4. 

- ○ $5 - 3 = 2$
- ○ $3 - 2 = 1$
- ○ $4 - 3 = 1$
- ○ $6 - 3 = 3$

Name _______________________

Zero in Subtraction

Fill in the ○ for the correct answer.

Choose the subtraction sentence for the picture.

1. 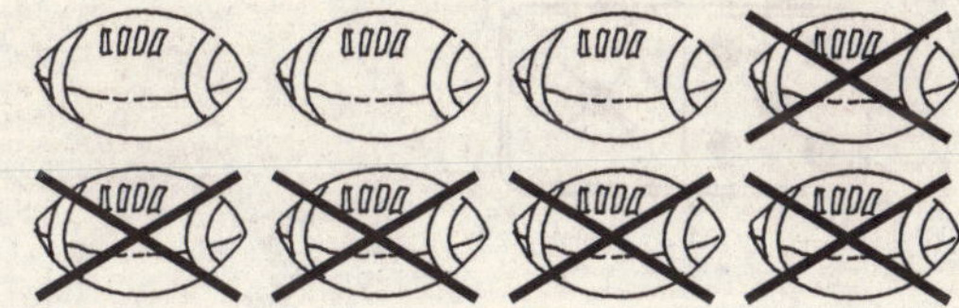

- ○ $8 - 8 = 0$
- ○ $8 - 5 = 3$
- ○ $7 - 5 = 2$
- ○ $8 - 7 = 1$

2. 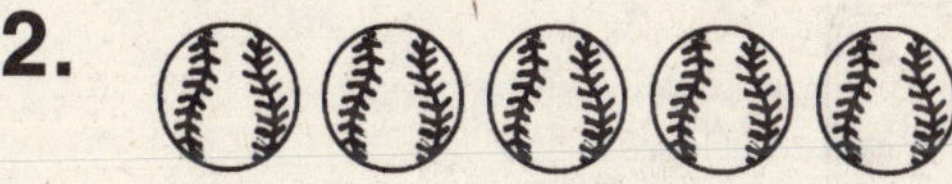

- ○ $6 - 6 = 0$
- ○ $5 - 1 = 4$
- ○ $5 - 0 = 5$
- ○ $4 - 1 = 3$

3. 

- ○ $8 - 7 = 1$
- ○ $7 - 5 = 2$
- ○ $7 - 6 = 1$
- ○ $7 - 7 = 0$

4. 

- ○ $8 - 6 = 2$
- ○ $6 - 6 = 0$
- ○ $4 - 0 = 4$
- ○ $6 - 1 = 5$

Name ______________________

Subtracting Across and Down

Fill in the ○ for the correct answer.

Choose the subtraction sentence for the picture.

1. 

○   7   ○   4
    − 4   − 2
      3   2

○   5   ○   8
    − 4   − 4
      1   4

2. 

○   8 − 5 = 3
○   6 − 1 = 5
○   5 − 4 = 1
○   7 − 3 = 4

3. 

7 − 2 = ______

○   2
○   3
○   5
○   6

4. 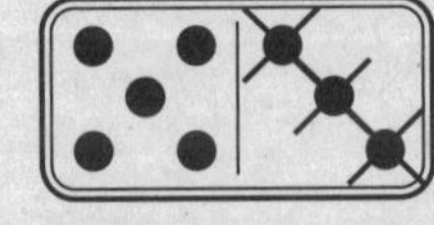

  8
− 3

○   5   ○   1
○   2   ○   3

Name ________________________

Subtracting to Find How Many More

Fill in the ○ for the correct answer.

How many more white cubes than gray cubes?

1. 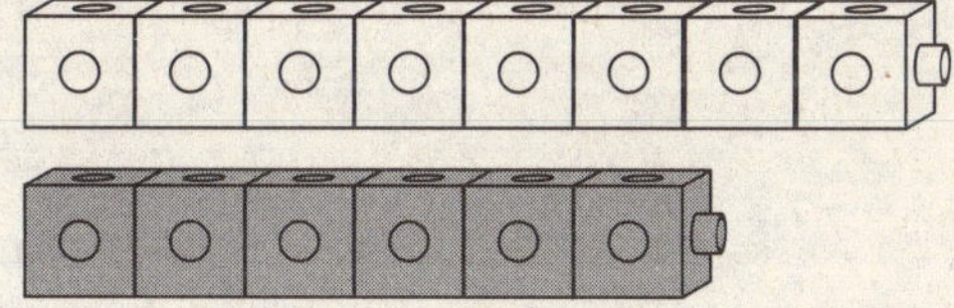

○ 0
○ 1
○ 2
○ 3

2. 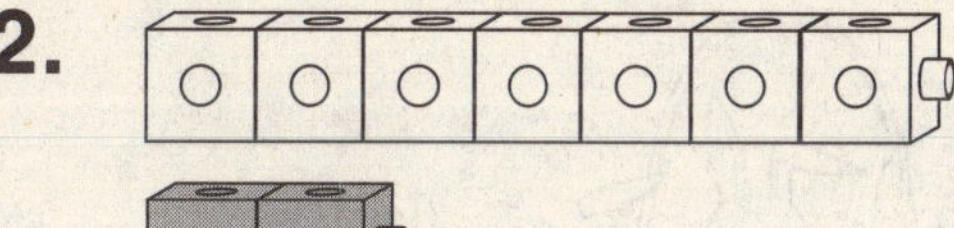

○ 4
○ 5
○ 6
○ 7

3. 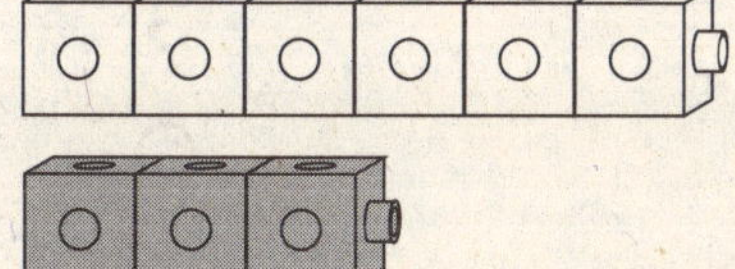

○ 2
○ 3
○ 4
○ 5

4. 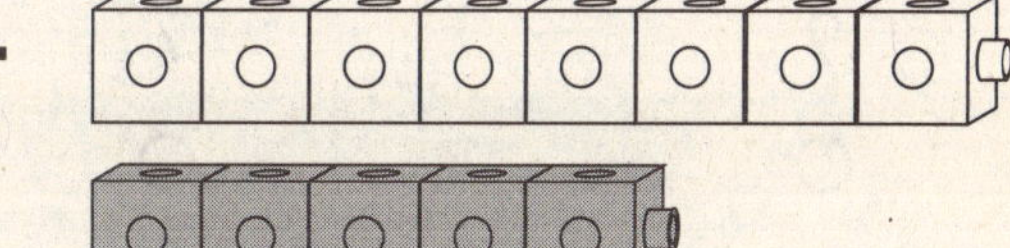

○ 3
○ 4
○ 5
○ 6

Counting On 1 and 2

Fill in the ○ for the correct answer.

Count on to add.

1.

$3 + 1 = $ _______

| 3 | 4 | 5 | 6 |
| ○ | ○ | ○ | ○ |

2.

0 1 2 3 4 5 6 7 8 9 10 11 12

$5 + 2 = $ _______

| 9 | 7 | 4 | 3 |
| ○ | ○ | ○ | ○ |

---

3. $4 + 1 = $ _______

| 5 | 6 | 7 | 4 |
| ○ | ○ | ○ | ○ |

---

4. $8 + 2 = $ _______

| 8 | 9 | 10 | 12 |
| ○ | ○ | ○ | ○ |

Name _______________________________

Counting On 1, 2, and 3

Fill in the ○ for the correct answer.

1. Count on to add.

$6 + 3 =$ _______

○ 6   ○ 9
○ 7   ○ 10

2. Count on to add.

8
+ 3

○ 11
○ 10
○ 9
○ 12

3. Count on to add.

8
+ 1

○ 1
○ 8
○ 9
○ 11

4. What number is missing in the table?

Count on 3	
1	4
3	6
5	8
7	

○ 9   ○ 11
○ 10   ○ 12

5. Count on to add. $4 + 3 =$ _______

6   8   7   9
○   ○   ○   ○

Name _______________________________

Adding in Any Order

Fill in the ○ for the correct answer.

1. Which number sentence has the same sum as $4 + 3$?

$6 + 2 = 8$ $3 + 4 = 7$ $4 + 0 = 4$ $2 + 3 = 5$

　　　○　　　　　　　○　　　　　　　○　　　　　　　○

2. Which number sentence has the same sum as $6 + 2$?

$1 + 5 = 6$ $2 + 5 = 7$ $5 + 0 = 5$ $2 + 6 = 8$

　　　○　　　　　　　○　　　　　　　○　　　　　　　○

3. Which number sentence has the same sum as $1 + 5$?

$5 + 1 = 6$ $6 + 2 = 8$ $0 + 7 = 7$ $3 + 4 = 7$

　　　○　　　　　　　○　　　　　　　○　　　　　　　○

4. Which number sentence has the same sum as $2 + 3$?

$5 + 1 = 6$ $0 + 8 = 8$ $3 + 2 = 5$ $6 + 1 = 7$

　　　○　　　　　　　○　　　　　　　○　　　　　　　○

5. Which number sentence has the same sum as $5 + 2$?

$1 + 4 = 5$ $3 + 3 = 6$ $1 + 7 = 8$ $2 + 5 = 7$

　　　○　　　　　　　○　　　　　　　○　　　　　　　○

Name ______________________________________

Adding 1, 2, or 3

Fill in the ○ for the correct answer.

Find the sum. Count on from the **greater** number.

1. 7 + 2 = _______

5	7	9	12
○	○	○	○

2. 9 + 3 = _______

9	10	11	12
○	○	○	○

3. 5 + 2 = _______

7	8	9	11
○	○	○	○

4. 8 + 3 = _______

8	10	11	15
○	○	○	○

5. 9 + 2 = _______

13	12	11	14
○	○	○	○

6. 6 + 2 = _______

8	7	10	9
○	○	○	○

Name ______________________________

Counting On from the Greater Number

Fill in the ○ for the correct answer.

Count on from the greater number to add.

1.

0 1 2 3 4 5 6 7 8 9 10 11 12

$1 + 7 =$ _______

| 6 | 7 | 8 | 9 |
| ○ | ○ | ○ | ○ |

2.

0 1 2 3 4 5 6 7 8 9 10 11 12

$\begin{array}{r} 3 \\ + 6 \\ \hline \end{array}$

| 8 | 9 | 10 | 11 |
| ○ | ○ | ○ | ○ |

3. $\begin{array}{r} 3 \\ + 9 \\ \hline \end{array}$

| 10 | 11 | 12 | 13 |
| ○ | ○ | ○ | ○ |

4. $2 + 8 =$ _______

| 10 | 11 | 12 | 8 |
| ○ | ○ | ○ | ○ |

Name ____

Adding Doubles

Fill in the ○ for the correct answer.

I. Which shows a doubles fact?

- ○ $5 + 5 = 10$
- ○ $0 + 10 = 10$
- ○ $2 + 4 = 6$
- ○ $5 + 6 = 11$

2. Which double makes four?

- ○ $1 + 1$
- ○ $2 + 2$
- ○ $3 + 3$
- ○ $4 + 4$

3. Add. $6 + 6 =$ ________

- ○ 9
- ○ 11
- ○ 10
- ○ 12

4. 3 children are playing. 3 more join them. Which number sentence shows how many children in all?

- ○ $3 + 2 = 5$
- ○ $3 + 3 = 6$
- ○ $4 + 3 = 7$
- ○ $6 + 6 = 12$

5. Add. $4 + 4 =$ ________

- ○ 0
- ○ 8
- ○ 4
- ○ 9

6. Which shows a doubles fact?

- ○ $5 + 3 = 8$
- ○ $1 + 1 = 2$
- ○ $2 + 9 = 11$
- ○ $1 + 2 = 3$

Name ______________________________

Using Doubles to Add

Fill in the ○ for the correct answer.

---

1. Which doubles fact can help
solve this doubles plus one fact?

$4 + 5 =$ _______

- ○ $2 + 4 = 6$
- ○ $4 + 4 = 8$
- ○ $9 + 0 = 9$
- ○ $3 + 3 = 6$

2. Find the sum.

$6 + 5 =$ _______

- ○ 9
- ○ 10
- ○ 11
- ○ 12

---

3. Which doubles fact can help
solve the doubles plus one fact?

$2 + 3 =$ _______

- ○ $1 + 1 = 2$
- ○ $2 + 2 = 4$
- ○ $4 + 4 = 8$
- ○ $5 + 5 = 10$

4. Which doubles fact can help
solve the doubles plus one fact?

$3 + 4 =$ _______

- ○ $1 + 1 = 2$
- ○ $2 + 2 = 4$
- ○ $3 + 3 = 6$
- ○ $5 + 5 = 10$

---

5. Find the sum.

$$\begin{array}{r} 5 \\ + 4 \\ \hline \end{array}$$

- ○ 6   ○ 9
- ○ 7   ○ 8

6. Find the sum.

$7 + 6 =$ _______

- ○ 13   ○ 11
- ○ 12   ○ 10

Name ____________________

Sums of 10

Fill in the O for the correct answer.

Find the missing numbers to find each sum of 10.

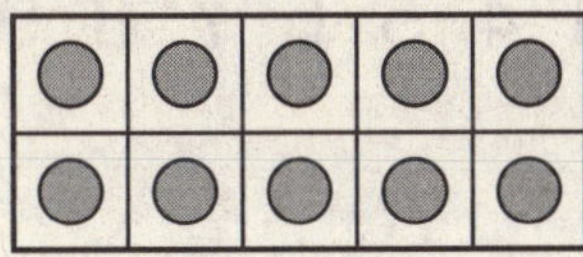

1. $7 + \underline{\hspace{2cm}} = 10$

3   4   7   10
○   ○   ○   ○

2. $8 + \underline{\hspace{2cm}} = 10$

1   2   3   4
○   ○   ○   ○

3.
$$\begin{array}{r} 9 \\ +\ \square \\ \hline 10 \end{array}$$

7   5   3   1
○   ○   ○   ○

4. $6 + \underline{\hspace{2cm}} = 10$

8   6   2   4
○   ○   ○   ○

5.
$$\begin{array}{r} 5 \\ +\ \square \\ \hline 10 \end{array}$$

0   3   5   7
○   ○   ○   ○

Name _______________________________

Counting Back 1, 2, and 3

Fill in the ○ for the correct answer.

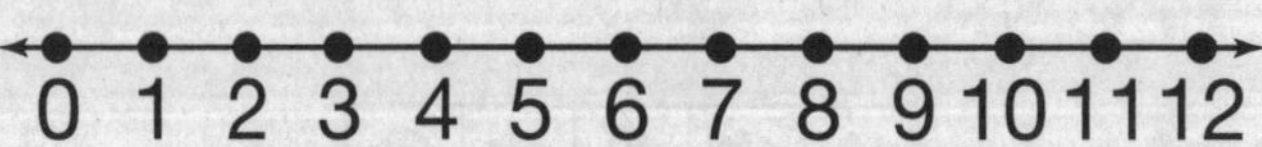

Count back to subtract.

1. 5 − 1 = _______

- ○ 5
- ○ 4
- ○ 3
- ○ 2

2. 10
   − 3

- ○ 9
- ○ 8
- ○ 7
- ○ 6

3. Juan uses the number line to subtract by counting back. What number should he write to complete the number sentence?

7 − 2 = _______

- ○ 5
- ○ 6
- ○ 7
- ○ 4

4. Count back to subtract.

6 − 3 = _______

- ○ 2
- ○ 3
- ○ 4
- ○ 5

Name ___________________________

Counting Back

Fill in the ○ for the correct answer.

Count back to subtract 1 or 2.

1.

$7 - 2 =$ _______

5	6	8	4
○	○	○	○

2. $5 - 1 =$ _______

5	4	3	6
○	○	○	○

3. $8 - 2 =$ _______

4	5	6	7
○	○	○	○

4.
$$\begin{array}{r} 10 \\ -\ 2 \\ \hline \end{array}$$

11	9	8	7
○	○	○	○

Using Doubles to Subtract

Fill in the ○ for the correct answer.

1. Which doubles fact can help you solve the subtraction problem?

   $10 - 5 =$ ________

   ○ $3 + 3 = 6$ ○ $4 + 4 = 8$
   ○ $5 + 5 = 10$ ○ $6 + 6 = 12$

2. Which doubles fact can help you solve the subtraction problem?

   $8 - 4 =$ ________

   ○ $1 + 1 = 2$ ○ $2 + 2 = 4$
   ○ $3 + 3 = 6$ ○ $4 + 4 = 8$

3. Use the doubles fact to subtract.

   $6 + 6 = 12$ so, $12 - 6 =$ ________

   3   5   6   8
   ○   ○   ○   ○

4. What addition fact can help Consuela solve this subtraction fact?

   $6 - 3 =$ ________

   ○ $6 + 3 = 9$ ○ $6 + 6 = 12$
   ○ $0 + 6 = 6$ ○ $3 + 3 = 6$

Name ___________________________________

Relating Addition and Subtraction

Fill in the ○ for the correct answer.

Complete the number sentence.

1.

$6 + 3 = 9$ $9 - \underline{} = 6$

○ 3
○ 4
○ 6
○ 9

2.

$1 + 8 = 9$ $9 - 8 = \underline{}$

○ 8
○ 7
○ 1
○ 2

3.

$2 + 5 = 7$ $\underline{} - 2 = 5$

○ 2
○ 5
○ 7
○ 8

4.

$4 + 6 = 10$ $10 - \underline{} = 4$

○ 5
○ 6
○ 7
○ 8

Fact Families

Fill in the ○ for the correct answer.

---

1. Which fact does Tonya need to complete the fact family?

2 + 8 = 10

10 − 2 = 8

10 − 8 = 2

○ 2 + 2 = 4

○ 8 + 2 = 10

○ 10 + 2 = 12

○ 8 + 6 = 14

2. Which fact does NOT belong in the fact family?

○ 7 − 2 = 5

○ 9 − 7 = 2

○ 9 − 2 = 7

○ 7 + 2 = 9

---

3. Which fact does Marcus need to complete the fact family?

7 + 2 = 9

9 − 2 = 7

9 − 7 = 2

○ 2 + 7 = 9

○ 7 − 2 = 5

○ 9 + 2 = 11

○ 11 − 9 = 2

4. Which fact does NOT belong in the fact family

○ 5 − 2 = 3

○ 7 − 2 = 5

○ 2 + 5 = 7

○ 7 − 5 = 2

---

5. Which fact does NOT belong in the fact family?

9 − 8 = 1   8 + 1 = 9   1 + 8 = 9   8 − 1 = 7

○   ○   ○   ○

210

Name _______________________________________

Using Addition to Subtract

Fill in the ○ for the correct answer.

1. Which addition fact can help Kito complete this subtraction sentence?

   $7 - 3 =$ _____

   | $7 + 3 = 10$ | $3 + 7 = 10$ | $5 + 2 = 7$ | $3 + 4 = 7$ |
   | ○ | ○ | ○ | ○ |

2. Which addition fact can help Amanda finish this subtraction sentence?

   $10 - 8 =$ _____

   | $8 + 8 = 16$ | $8 + 2 = 10$ | $10 + 2 = 12$ | $10 + 8 = 18$ |
   | ○ | ○ | ○ | ○ |

3. Which addition fact will help you subtract $11 - 6$?

   | $3 + 3 = 6$ | $4 + 7 = 11$ | $11 + 6 = 17$ | $6 + 5 = 11$ |
   | ○ | ○ | ○ | ○ |

4. Use the addition fact to help you subtract.

   $\begin{array}{r} 11 \\ -\ 9 \\ \hline 11 \end{array}$ $\qquad$ $\begin{array}{r} 9 \\ +\ 2 \\ \hline \end{array}$

   | 1 | 2 | 3 | 4 |
   | ○ | ○ | ○ | ○ |

5. Use the addition fact to help you subtract.

   $8 - 5 =$ _____ $5 +$ _____ $= 8$

   | 1 | 2 | 3 | 4 |
   | ○ | ○ | ○ | ○ |

Name ___________________________________

Doubles to 20

Fill in the ○ for the correct answer.

---

1. Ignacio lives 9 blocks away from school. Which number sentence can you use to find how many blocks he walks in all, going to school and then back home again?

○ $7 + 8 = 15$ ○ $8 + 9 = 17$

○ $9 + 9 = 18$ ○ $9 + 10 = 19$

---

2. 7 birds are in a tree. 7 more come.
How many birds are there in all?

$7 + 7 =$ ○ 12 birds

○ 14 birds

○ 15 birds

○ 16 birds

---

3. Add.

8	18	16	14	19
+ 8	○	○	○	○

---

4. Add.

$6 + 6 =$	8	10	12	13
	○	○	○	○

---

5. Which double makes 8?

8	$3 + 3$	$4 + 4$	$6 + 6$	$8 + 8$
	○	○	○	○

212

Name ___________________________

Using Doubles to Add

Fill in the ○ for the correct answer.

1. There are 8 chairs in the first row and 9 chairs in the second row. How many chairs are there in all?

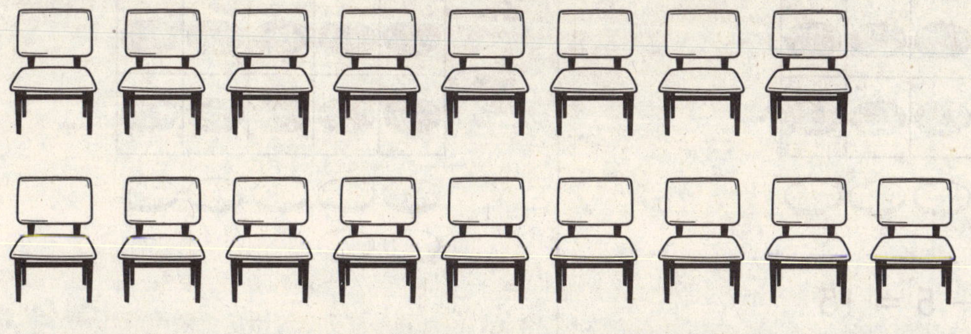

16 chairs	17 chairs	18 chairs	20 chairs
○	○	○	○

2. Which double can help you add 7 + 8?

7 + 8	3 + 3	6 + 6	7 + 7	8 + 8
	○	○	○	○

3. Add. 5 + 6 = _______

	7	9	10	11
	○	○	○	○

4. Add. 4 + 5 = _______

	10	9	8	7
	○	○	○	○

5. Nicole added 1 to 6 + 6 to help find the sum. Which sum did she find?

6 + 6

○ 5 + 5 = 10   ○ 6 + 6 = 12

○ 6 + 7 = 13   ○ 7 + 7 = 14

Name _______________________

Adding 10

Fill in the ○ for the correct answer.

Which addition sentence shows the sum for each ten-frame?

1.

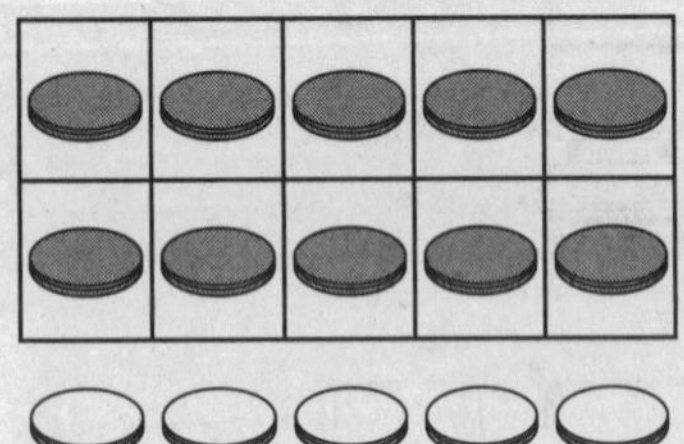

- ○ 10 + 5 = 15
- ○ 10 + 4 = 14
- ○ 10 + 6 = 16
- ○ 10 + 2 = 12

2.

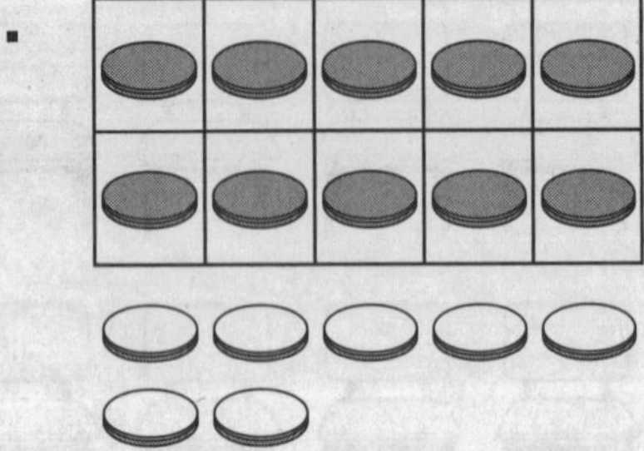

- ○ 10 + 4 = 14
- ○ 10 + 5 = 15
- ○ 10 + 7 = 17
- ○ 10 + 6 = 16

3.

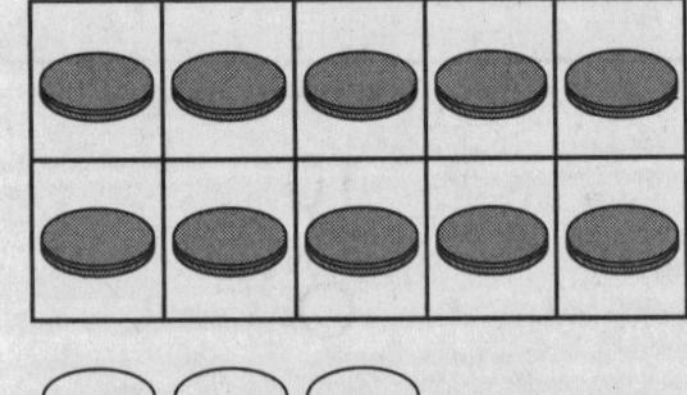

- ○ 10 + 2 = 12
- ○ 10 + 1 = 11
- ○ 10 + 3 = 13
- ○ 10 + 2 = 12

4.

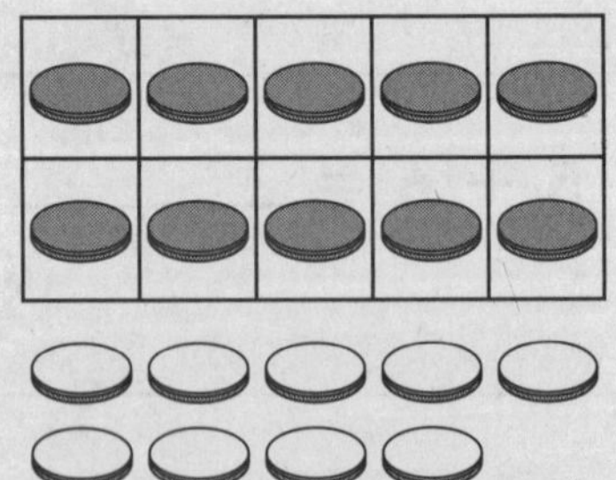

- ○ 10 + 2 = 12
- ○ 10 + 8 = 18
- ○ 10 + 6 = 16
- ○ 10 + 9 = 19

Name ___________________________

Making 10 to Add 7, 8, and 9

Fill in the ○ for the correct answer.

I. Find the sum.

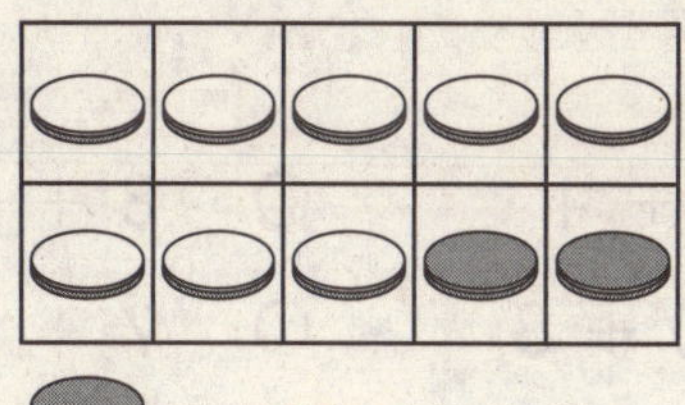

8 + 3 = _______

○ 10
○ 11
○ 12
○ 13

2. Which fact has the same sum as 8 + 5?

8 + 5 = _______

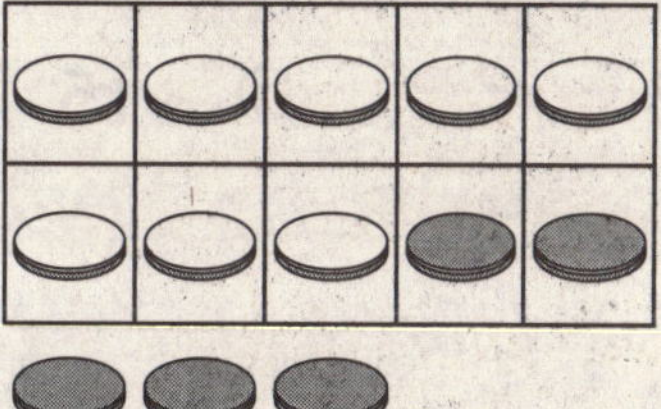

○ 10 + 1 = 11
○ 10 + 3 = 13
○ 10 + 2 = 12
○ 10 + 4 = 14

---

3. Find the sum.

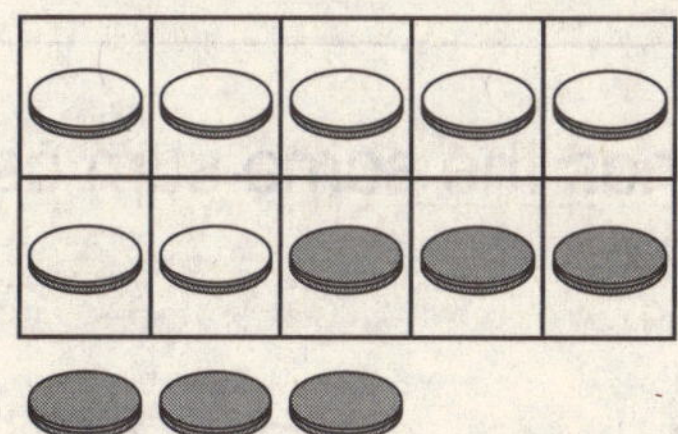

7 + 6 = _______

○ 13
○ 12
○ 11
○ 15

4. You have 9 toy drums. How many more drums do you need to have 15?

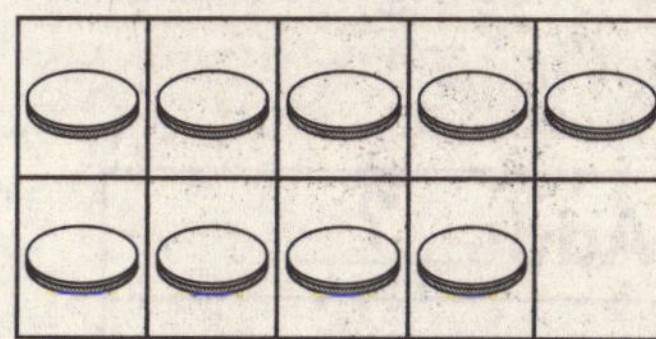

○ 8
○ 7
○ 6
○ 5

Using Addition Strategies

Fill in the ○ for the correct answer.

I. Find the sum.

$7 + 6 =$

○ 12   ○ 14
○ 13   ○ 15

2. Which has the same sum as
$9 + 4$?

○ $4 + 4$ ○ $8 + 4$
○ $10 + 3$ ○ $7 + 5$

3. Find the sum.

$9 + 7 =$

○ 15   ○ 17
○ 16   ○ 18

4. Which has the same sum as
$7 + 8$?

○ $14 + 1$ ○ $10 + 7$
○ $10 + 6$ ○ $16 + 1$

5. Find the missing number in
the rule.

Add ?	
3	9
5	11
1	7

○ 2   ○ 6
○ 4   ○ 7

6. Which has the same sum as
$8 + 6$?

○ $12 + 1$ ○ $10 + 3$
○ $16 + 1$ ○ $10 + 4$

Name _______________________

Adding Three Numbers

Fill in the ○ for the correct answer.

---

1. Find the sum.

$$\begin{array}{r} 3 \\ 3 \\ + 6 \\ \hline \end{array}$$

○ 6 ○ 12

○ 9 ○ 13

2. Which has the same sum?

$$\begin{array}{r} 4 \\ 4 \\ + 3 \\ \hline \end{array}$$

○ 5 + 7 ○ 8 + 4

○ 10 + 3 ○ 8 + 3

---

3. Find the sum.

9 + 1 + 7 = _______

○ 17

○ 16

○ 10

○ 20

4. Which has the same sum?

$$\begin{array}{r} 8 \\ 2 \\ + 4 \\ \hline \end{array}$$

○ 8 + 2 ○ 10 + 4

○ 10 + 2 ○ 8 + 4

---

5. Find the sum.

5 + 3 + 7 = _______

○ 12

○ 15

○ 16

○ 13

6. Find the sum.

6 + 4 + 4 = _______

○ 10

○ 14

○ 18

○ 12

Name ______________________

Relating Addition and Subtraction

Fill in the ○ for the correct answer.

---

1. Which addition fact can help you find the difference?

$$12 - 5$$

- ○ $2 + 5 = 7$
- ○ $5 + 5 = 10$
- ○ $5 + 6 = 11$
- ○ $5 + 7 = 12$

2. Use the addition fact to find the difference.

$$\begin{array}{cc} 8 & 14 \\ +6 & -8 \\ \hline 14 & ? \end{array}$$

- ○ 6   ○ 8
- ○ 7   ○ 9

---

3. Which addition fact can help you find the difference?

$$14 - 7$$

- ○ $6 + 6 = 12$
- ○ $7 + 7 = 14$
- ○ $8 + 8 = 16$
- ○ $9 + 9 = 18$

4. Find the missing number.

$$\begin{array}{cc} 13 & 7 \\ -7 & +? \\ \hline ? & 13 \end{array}$$

- ○ 8   ○ 6
- ○ 7   ○ 5

---

5. Use the addition fact to find the difference.

$$\begin{array}{cc} 5 & 11 \\ +6 & -6 \\ \hline 11 & ? \end{array}$$

- ○ 7   ○ 5
- ○ 6   ○ 4

6. Find the missing number.

$$\begin{array}{cc} 17 & 8 \\ -8 & +? \\ \hline ? & 17 \end{array}$$

- ○ 9   ○ 7
- ○ 8   ○ 6

Name _______________________________

Fact Families

Fill in the ○ for the correct answer.

I. Which fact does Juan need to complete this fact family?

> $5 + 6 = 11$ $11 - 5 = 6$
> $6 + 5 = 11$?

- ○ $11 - 6 = 5$
- ○ $10 - 4 = 6$
- ○ $11 - 4 = 7$
- ○ $3 + 8 = 11$

2. Which fact does Brittany need to complete this fact family?

> $8 + 9 = 17$
> $17 - 8 = 9$
> $17 - 9 = 8$
> ?

- ○ $9 - 8 = 1$
- ○ $9 + 8 = 17$
- ○ $9 + 17 = 26$
- ○ $17 + 8 = 25$

3. Which fact does Rachael need to complete this fact family?

> $9 + 6 = 15$
> $6 + 9 = 15$
> $15 - 9 = 6$
> ?

- ○ $15 + 6 = 21$
- ○ $9 - 6 = 3$
- ○ $15 - 3 = 21$
- ○ $15 - 6 = 9$

4. Which fact does not belong in the fact family?

> 4 8 12

- ○ $12 - 8 = 4$
- ○ $12 - 4 = 8$
- ○ $4 + 8 = 12$
- ○ $4 + 12 = 16$

Name _______________________________

Using Addition to Subtract

Fill in the ○ for the correct answer.

1. Which addition fact will help you subtract?

$14 - 8 =$ _______

○ $8 + 8 = 16$
○ $9 + 5 = 14$
○ $6 + 8 = 14$
○ $7 + 5 = 2$

2. $7 + 4 = 11$

$11 - 4 =$ _______

| 9 | 5 | 8 | 7 |
| ○ | ○ | ○ | ○ |

3. $9 + 3 = 12$

$12 - 3 =$ _______

| 3 | 8 | 9 | 11 |
| ○ | ○ | ○ | ○ |

4. Which addition fact will help you subtract?

$13 - 9 =$ _______

○ $8 + 9 = 17$
○ $4 + 9 = 13$
○ $6 + 8 = 14$
○ $7 + 6 = 13$

5. $9 + 6 = 15$

$15 - 6 =$ _______

| 11 | 10 | 9 | 7 |
| ○ | ○ | ○ | ○ |

6. $6 + 6 = 12$

$12 - 6 =$ _______

| 6 | 7 | 8 | 4 |
| ○ | ○ | ○ | ○ |

Name ___________________________

Using 10 to Subtract

Fill in the ○ for the correct answer.

I. Find the difference.

13
− 8

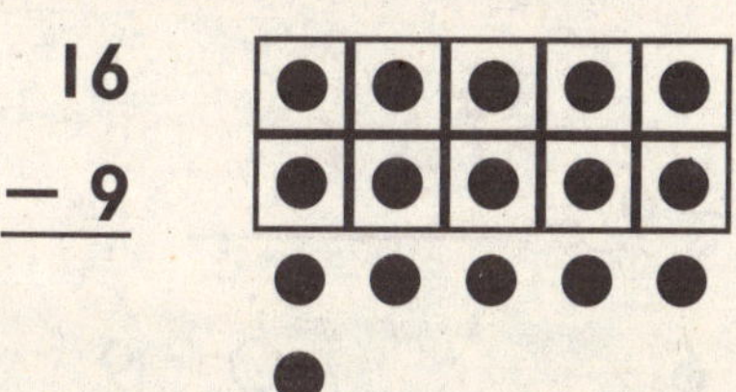

○ 4
○ 5
○ 6
○ 7

2. Which addition fact can help you solve 13 − 9?

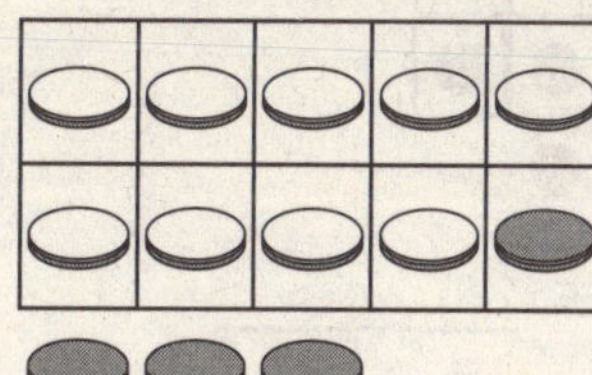

13 − 9 = _______

○ 2 + 4   ○ 2 + 3
○ 1 + 4   ○ 1 + 3

---

3. Find the difference.

16
− 9

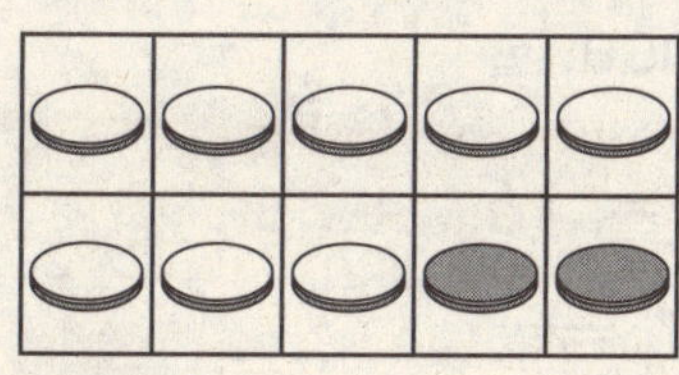

○ 5   ○ 7
○ 6   ○ 8

4. Find the difference.

17
− 8

○ 9   ○ 7
○ 8   ○ 6

---

5. Which addition fact can help you solve 11 − 8?

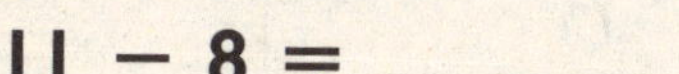

11 − 8 = _______

2 + 1   2 + 2   1 + 3   2 + 3
○   ○   ○   ○

221

Name ______________________________

Using Subtraction Strategies

Fill in the ○ for the correct answer.

---

1. Find the difference.

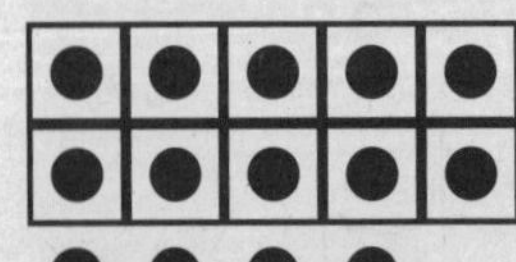

$14 - 8 =$ _______

○ 5   ○ 7
○ 6   ○ 8

2. Which addition fact can help you find the difference?

$17 - 8 =$ _______

○ $7 + 8 = 15$
○ $7 + 7 = 14$
○ $7 + 1 = 8$
○ $8 + 9 = 17$

---

3. Find the difference.

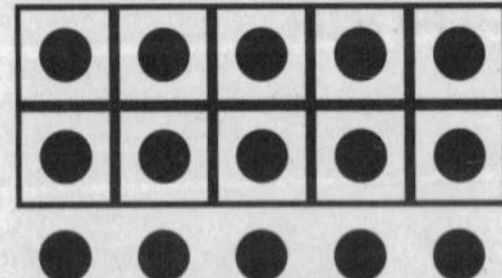

$15 - 7 =$ _______

○ 6   ○ 8
○ 7   ○ 9

4. Use the addition fact to find the difference.

$6 + 9 = 15$

$15 - 9 =$ _______

○ 6   ○ 9
○ 7   ○ 8

---

5. Count back to subtract. Find the difference.

$10 - 2 =$ _______

○ 9   ○ 7
○ 8   ○ 6

6. Use the addition fact to find the difference.

$9 + 7 = 16$

$16 - 7 =$ _______

○ 10   ○ 8
○ 9   ○ 7

Name ______________________________________

Joining Groups to Add

Fill in the ○ for the correct answer.

Count the number in each group. How many in all?

1. 

3 and 2 is __________ in all.

3	4	5	3
○	○	○	○

2. 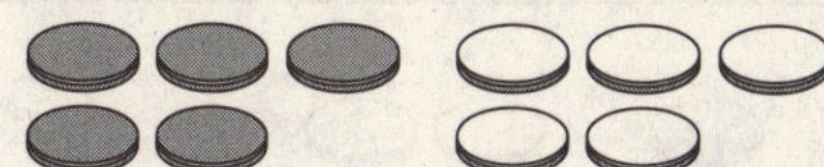

2 and 4 is __________ in all.

5	6	7	2
○	○	○	○

3.

6 and 2 is __________ in all.

8	7	6	10
○	○	○	○

4.

5 and 5 is __________ in all.

9	10	11	8
○	○	○	○

5. Which tells how many in all?

_____ and _____ is _____ in all.

○ 6 and 2 is 8 in all.

○ 4 and 2 is 6 in all.

○ 3 and 5 is 8 in all.

○ 6 and 3 is 9 in all.

6. Which tells how many in all?

_____ and _____ is _____ in all.

○ 9 and 1 is 10 in all.

○ 7 and 1 is 8 in all.

○ 8 and 1 is 9 in all.

○ 1 and 6 is 7 in all.

Name _______________________________

Writing Addition Sentences

Fill in the ○ for the correct answer.

Find how many there are in all.

1. 

$4 + 1 =$ _______

| 4 | 5 | 6 | 7 |
| ○ | ○ | ○ | ○ |

2. 

$2 + 4 =$ _______

| 6 | 5 | 7 | 4 |
| ○ | ○ | ○ | ○ |

3. 

$3 + 4 =$ _______

| 8 | 6 | 7 | 5 |
| ○ | ○ | ○ | ○ |

4. 

$2 + 8 =$ _______

| 9 | 10 | 11 | 8 |
| ○ | ○ | ○ | ○ |

5. Which tells how many there are in all?

- ○ $3 + 2 = 5$
- ○ $2 + 2 = 4$
- ○ $3 + 1 = 4$
- ○ $2 + 4 = 6$

6. Which tells how many there are in all?

- ○ $7 + 3 = 10$
- ○ $2 + 2 = 4$
- ○ $2 + 5 = 7$
- ○ $5 + 5 = 10$

Name ____

Taking Away to Subtract

Fill in the ○ for the correct answer.

Take away to subtract.

1.

6 take away 5 is _______

1	2	3	4
○	○	○	○

2.

7 take away 3 is _______.

3	4	5	2
○	○	○	○

3.

8 take away 4 is _______

6	2	4	5
○	○	○	○

4.

10 take away 4 is _______.

6	7	8	5
○	○	○	○

Which tells how many are left?

5.

- ○ 7 take away 2 is 5
- ○ 3 take away 2 is 1
- ○ 5 take away 3 is 2
- ○ 7 take away 5 is 2

6.

- ○ 7 take away 2 is 5
- ○ 6 take away 5 is 1
- ○ 5 take away 1 is 4
- ○ 7 take away 5 is 2

Name ______________________

Comparing to Find How Many More

Fill in the ○ for the correct answer.

1. 

How many more gray counters
are there?

2	3	4	6
○	○	○	○

2. 

How many more white counters
are there?

4	3	5	6
○	○	○	○

3. 

How many more gray counters
are there?

7	5	6	8
○	○	○	○

4. 

How many more white counters
are there?

6	4	5	7
○	○	○	○

5. 

How many more gray counters
are there?

4	5	6	7
○	○	○	○

6. 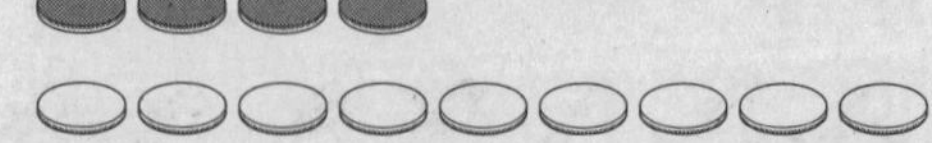

How many more white counters
are there?

6	4	8	5
○	○	○	○

Name ___________________________

Writing Subtraction Sentences

Fill in the ○ for the correct answer.

Choose the correct subtraction sentence.

1. 7 children were playing a game.
3 went home.
How many were left?

$7 - 2 = 5$	$7 - 3 = 4$	$7 - 1 = 6$	$7 - 4 = 3$
○	○	○	○

2. How many more baseballs are there?

$8 - 5 = 3$	$8 - 4 = 4$	$8 - 2 = 6$	$2 - 8 = 6$
○	○	○	○

3. There are 9 girls playing basketball.
There are 5 girls playing soccer.
How many more girls are playing basketball?

$9 - 5 = 4$	$9 - 3 = 6$	$9 - 2 = 7$	$9 - 4 = 5$
○	○	○	○

4. 10 children are playing at the park.
3 children go home.
How many children are left playing?

$10 - 5 = 5$	$10 - 6 = 4$	$10 - 3 = 7$	$10 - 7 = 3$
○	○	○	○

Name _______________________________

Ways to Make Ten

Fill in the ○ for the correct answer.

Complete each number sentence to make ten.

1. _______ $+ 7 = 10$

   2   3   4   5
   ○   ○   ○   ○

2. $6 +$ _______ $= 10$

   2   3   4   5
   ○   ○   ○   ○

3. $10 = 8 +$ _______

   2   3   4   1
   ○   ○   ○   ○

4. _______ $+ 5 = 10$

   3   4   5   6
   ○   ○   ○   ○

5. _______ $+ 10 = 10$

   0   1   2   3
   ○   ○   ○   ○

6. $10 = 1 +$ _______

   7   8   9   10
   ○   ○   ○   ○

7. $7 +$ _______ $= 10$

   1   2   3   4
   ○   ○   ○   ○

8. $10 = 2 +$ _______

   7   8   9   10
   ○   ○   ○   ○

Name _______________________

Missing Addends

Fill in the ○ for the correct answer.

Find the missing number that completes the number sentence.

1. ☐ + 9 = 14
- ○ 4
- ○ 5
- ○ 6
- ○ 7

2. 4 + ☐ = 13
- ○ 7
- ○ 8
- ○ 9
- ○ 12

3. 8 + ☐ = 16
- ○ 7
- ○ 8
- ○ 9
- ○ 11

4. 7 + ☐ = 10
- ○ 3
- ○ 4
- ○ 5
- ○ 2

5. 5 + ☐ = 12
- ○ 4
- ○ 5
- ○ 6
- ○ 7

6. 9 + ☐ = 17
- ○ 7
- ○ 8
- ○ 9
- ○ 6

Name _______________________________

Counting On

Fill in the ○ for the correct answer.

Count on to find each sum.

1. 6 + 2 = _______

   6   7   8   9
   ○   ○   ○   ○

2. 7 + 1 = _______

   9   10   8   7
   ○   ○   ○   ○

3.
$$\begin{array}{r} 5 \\ + \, 3 \\ \hline \end{array}$$

   8   9   10   11
   ○   ○   ○   ○

4. 9 + 3 = _______

   9   12   10   7
   ○   ○   ○   ○

5.
$$\begin{array}{r} 7 \\ + \, 3 \\ \hline \end{array}$$

   8   9   10   11
   ○   ○   ○   ○

6. Sandy had 5 pencils in her desk. She bought 2 more. How many pencils does she have in all?

   7   6   5   4
   ○   ○   ○   ○

7. Ari had 6 balloons. Jon gave him 3 more. How many balloons does Ari have in all?

   9   8   7   6
   ○   ○   ○   ○

Name ___________________________________

Making 10 to Add 9

Fill in the ○ for the correct answer.

1. Find the sum.

$10 + 4 = 14$, so

$9 + 5 =$ _______

- ○ 12
- ○ 14
- ○ 15
- ○ 17

2. Find the sum.

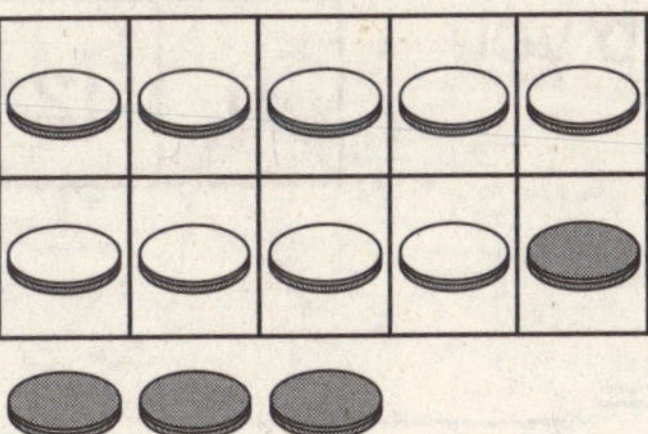

$9 + 4 =$ _______

- ○ 13
- ○ 14
- ○ 15
- ○ 16

3. Find the sum.

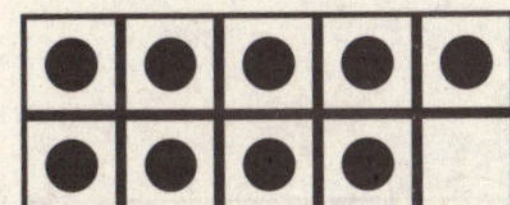

$10 + 7 = 17$, so

$9 + 8 =$ _______

- ○ 1
- ○ 16
- ○ 17
- ○ 15

4. Which fact has the same sum as $9 + 6$?

$9 + 6 =$ _______

- ○ $10 + 6$
- ○ $9 + 5$
- ○ $9 + 9$
- ○ $10 + 5$

Counting Back

Fill in the ○ for the correct answer.

Subtract.
Use the hundred
chart to help you.

1	2	3	4	5	6	7	8	9	10
11	12	13	14	15	16	17	18	19	20

1. $7 - 2 =$ _______

9	5	6	8
○	○	○	○

2. $18 - 1 =$ _______

19	15	18	17
○	○	○	○

3. $9 - 2 =$ _______

7	8	9	11
○	○	○	○

4. $13 - 2 =$ _______

9	10	11	12
○	○	○	○

5.
$$\begin{array}{r} 16 \\ -\ 2 \\ \hline \end{array}$$

18	16	12	14
○	○	○	○

6.
$$\begin{array}{r} 10 \\ -\ 1 \\ \hline \end{array}$$

11	10	9	6
○	○	○	○

Name ___________________________________

Addition Properties

Circle the correct letter for the answer.

1. Find the missing number.

$5 + 3 = 8$

$3 + 5 =$ _______

A 5   C 0

B 3   D 8

2. What is the missing number in

$6 +$ _______ $+ 3 = 17$?

A 3   C 6

B 8   D 4

3. John hit 5 home runs in the first game. Then he hit 3 more home runs in the second game and 2 more in the third game. How many home runs did he hit in all?

A 10   C 9

B 11   D 8

4. $95 + 0 =$ _______

A 0   C 95

B 14   D 96

5. Which will give you the same answer as $(8 + 5) + 4$?

A $(5 + 8) + 3$

B $8 + (5 + 4)$

C $(4 + 8) + 0$

D $(7 + 5) + 4$

6. Find the missing number in

_______ $+ 7 = 7 + 4$.

A 0   C 4

B 11   D 7

7. Find the missing number.

$456 +$ _______ $= 456$

A 4   C 0

B 6   D 5

8. Kimiko has 4 CDs. Mary gave her 3 more CDs, and Don gave her 1 more CD. Which shows how many CDs she has now?

A $(3 + 1) + 4$

B $(4 + 3) + 3$

C $(3 + 4) + 0$

D $(1 + 4) + 5$

Relating Addition and Subtraction

Circle the correct letter for the answer.

1. Find the related fact for
   $17 - 8 = 9$.
   - **A** $9 + 8 = 16$
   - **B** $9 + 7 = 16$
   - **C** $8 + 7 = 15$
   - **D** $8 + 9 = 17$

2. Eleven people are watching a
   soccer game. Six people leave.
   Which number sentence tells
   what happened?
   - **A** $5 + 6 = 11$
   - **B** $11 - 5 = 6$
   - **C** $11 - 6 = 5$
   - **D** $6 + 5 = 11$

3. Find the missing number.
   $$\underline{\hspace{2cm}} + 9 = 15.$$
   - **A** 9   **C** 15
   - **B** 7   **D** 6

4. Find the related fact for
   $6 + 6 = 12$.
   - **A** $6 + 5 = 11$
   - **B** $12 - 6 = 6$
   - **C** $12 - 12 = 6$
   - **D** $13 - 7 = 6$

5. There were 15 cows in the field.
   Seven cows left the field. Which
   number sentence tells what
   happened?
   - **A** $15 - 8 = 7$
   - **B** $7 + 8 = 15$
   - **C** $8 + 7 = 15$
   - **D** $15 - 7 = 8$

6. Find the missing number.
   $$\underline{\hspace{2cm}} - 5 = 8.$$
   - **A** 13   **C** 11
   - **B** 14   **D** 12

7. The sum of two numbers is 10.
   One of the numbers is 3. Which
   number sentence shows this
   problem?
   - **A** $10 - 3 = 7$
   - **B** $3 + 8 = 11$
   - **C** $7 + 3 = 10$
   - **D** $10 - 7 = 3$

8. Which fact does *not* belong in the
   fact family for $5 + 9 = 14$?
   - **A** $14 - 9 = 5$
   - **B** $9 + 5 = 14$
   - **C** $14 - 7 = 7$
   - **D** $14 - 5 = 9$

Name ____

Find a Rule

Circle the correct letter for the answer.

1. **What is the rule for the table?**

In	10	11	8	6
Out	5	6	3	1

A Add 5   **C** Add 4
B Subtract 6   **D** Subtract 5

2. **Tina uses the rule, add 4, for her table. If she puts in 8, what should she get out?**

A 12   **C** 11
B 13   **D** 4

3. **Wen puts 7 into his table and 14 comes out. What is his rule?**

A Add 6   **C** Add 7
B Subtract 7   **D** Subtract 5

4. **What is the missing number?**

In	15	12	10	13
Out	7	4	2	

A 3   **C** 6
B 5   **D** 7

5. **What is the rule for the table?**

In	6	12	5	8
Out	10	16	9	12

A Add 6   **C** Add 4
B Add 5   **D** Subtract 4

6. **Which number completes the table?**

In	9	10	13	12
Out	4	5	8	

A 7   **C** 4
B 8   **D** 5

7. **Kathy uses the rule, subtract 9, for her table. If she puts in 14, what should she get out?**

A 7   **C** 6
B 5   **D** 23

8. **What numbers complete the table?**

In	7	10	8	6	13
Out	11	14	12		

A 10, 16   **C** 10, 11
B 9, 17   **D** 10, 17

235

Skip Counting Equal Groups

Fill in the O for the correct answer.

Skip count to find how many there are in all.

1.

3	6	9	7
O	O	O	O

2. 2 groups, 4 in each group

5	6	7	8
O	O	O	O

3.

9	8	4	2
O	O	O	O

4. 4 groups, 3 in each group

6	8	10	12
O	O	O	O

5.

14	15	16	17
O	O	O	O

Name _______________________

Addition and Multiplication

Fill in the ○ for the correct answer.

1. Which shows another way to find $1 + 1 + 1 + 1$?

- ○ 4×1
- ○ 4×2
- ○ 4×4
- ○ 4×3

2. Which number sentence can you use to find the number of leaves?

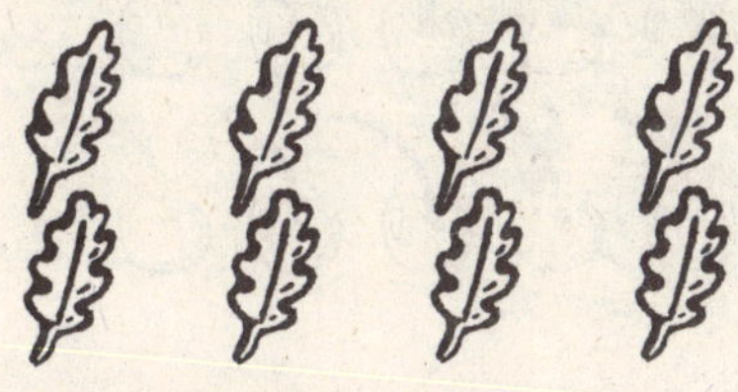

$4 \times 2 =$ _______

- ○ $2 + 4 = 6$
- ○ $1 + 8 = 9$
- ○ $2 + 2 + 2 + 2 = 8$
- ○ $6 + 1 = 7$

3. Which shows another way to find 3×2?

- ○ $3 + 3 + 3$
- ○ $1 + 1 + 1$
- ○ $2 + 2 + 2$
- ○ $2 + 2$

4. Which number sentence shows how many flowers altogether?

- ○ $5 + 5 + 5 = 15$
- ○ $2 \times 5 = 10$
- ○ $2 + 2 + 2 + 2 = 8$
- ○ $3 \times 4 = 12$

Using Arrays

Fill in the ○ for the correct answer.

1. Which number sentence shows how many cherries there are
in the 2 rows altogether?

○ $2 \times 6 = 12$ ○ $2 \times 5 = 10$

○ $1 \times 6 = 6$ ○ $3 \times 3 = 9$

2. Which number sentence shows how many beans there are
in the five rows altogether?

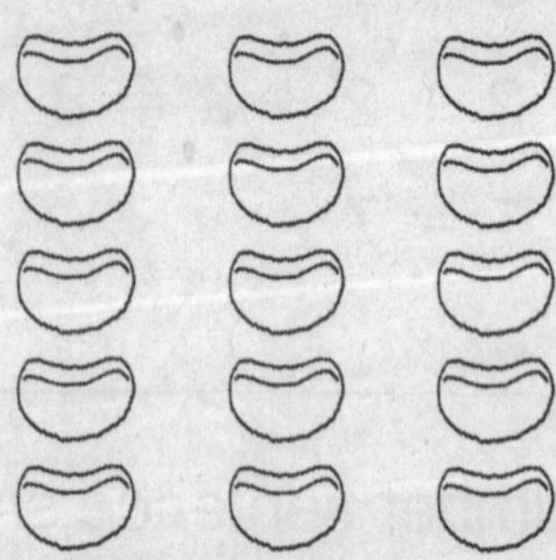

○ $3 \times 6 = 18$ ○ $5 \times 2 = 10$

○ $5 \times 3 = 15$ ○ $3 \times 4 = 12$

3. Which number sentence shows how many triangles there are
in the 2 rows altogether?

○ $2 \times 5 = 10$ ○ $2 \times 6 = 12$

○ $5 \times 5 = 25$ ○ $1 \times 5 = 5$

Name _______________________________

Multiplying in Any Order

Fill in the ○ for the correct answer.

1. Which of these has the same answer as 2×4?

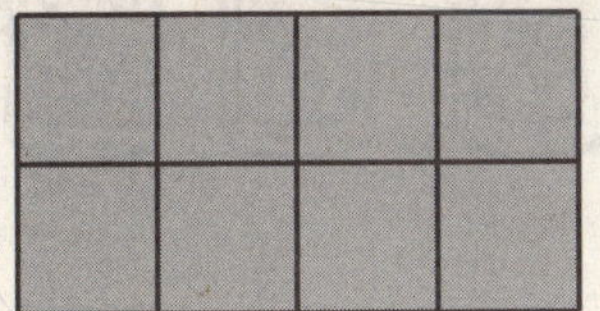

○ $2 + 2 =$ ○ $4 \times 2 =$

○ $2 \times 2 =$ ○ $4 - 2 =$

2. Which of these has the same answer as 3×5?

○ $3 + 5 =$ ○ $5 + 3 =$

○ $5 + 5 =$ ○ $5 \times 3 =$

3. Find the missing number.

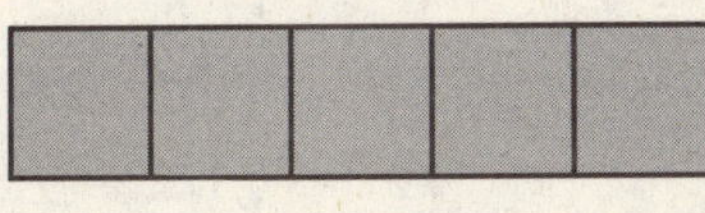

$5 \times 1 = \underline{\hspace{2cm}} \times 5$

1	3	4	5
○	○	○	○

4. Find the missing number.

$3 \times 2 = 2 \times \underline{\hspace{2cm}}$

1	2	3	4
○	○	○	○

Name _______________________________

Multiplying Across and Down

Fill in the ○ for the correct answer.

1. Which number sentence can you use
to find how many glue bottles in all?

1×4	2×4	4×3	4×4
○	○	○	○

2. Which number sentence can you *not* use to find
how many paste jars in all?

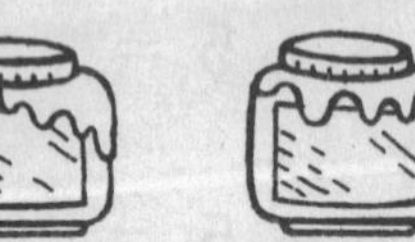

$3 + 3$	2×3	$\begin{array}{r} 3 \\ \times\, 2 \\ \hline \end{array}$	$\begin{array}{r} 3 \\ \times\, 1 \\ \hline \end{array}$
○	○	○	○

3. Which number sentence can you use to find how many balls in all?

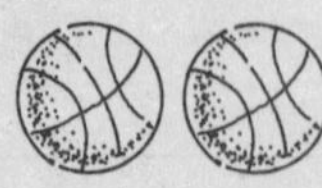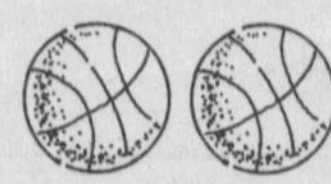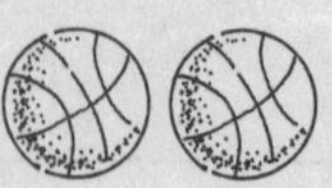

$\begin{array}{r} 3 \\ \times\, 2 \\ \hline 6 \end{array}$	$\begin{array}{r} 2 \\ \times\, 2 \\ \hline 4 \end{array}$	$\begin{array}{r} 6 \\ \times\, 2 \\ \hline 12 \end{array}$	$\begin{array}{r} 4 \\ \times\, 2 \\ \hline 8 \end{array}$
○	○	○	○

Name ______________________________

Modeling Division

Fill in the ○ for the correct answer.

Find the missing number.

1.

3 groups of ______

- ○ 2
- ○ 3
- ○ 4
- ○ 5

2.

2 groups of ______

- ○ 1
- ○ 2
- ○ 3
- ○ 4

3.

4 groups of ______

- ○ 1
- ○ 2
- ○ 3
- ○ 4

4.

5 groups of ______

- ○ 1
- ○ 2
- ○ 4
- ○ 5

Name ______________________________

Division with Remainders

Fill in the ○ for the correct answer.

1. Carly has 14 cotton balls. She uses 3 on each picture. She makes as many pictures as she can. How many cotton balls does Carly have left?

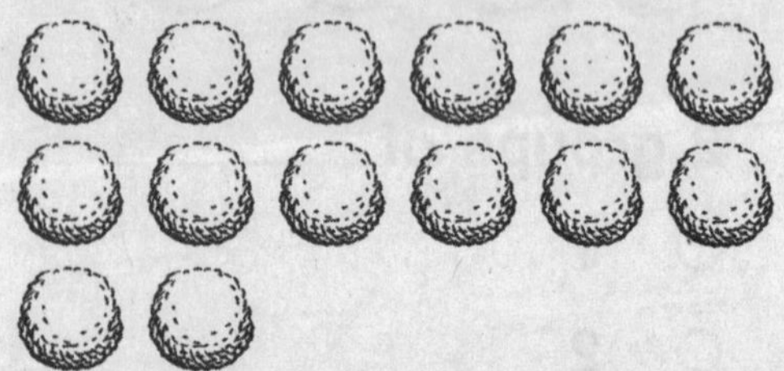

- ○ 1 cotton ball
- ○ 2 cotton balls
- ○ 3 cotton balls
- ○ 4 cotton balls

2. Sam picks 15 grapes. He puts 4 in each basket. How many baskets can he fill?

- ○ 4 baskets
- ○ 3 baskets
- ○ 2 baskets
- ○ 5 baskets

3. Joe picks 12 apples. He puts 7 in each basket. He fills as many baskets as he can. How many apples are left over?

- ○ 2 apples left over
- ○ 5 apples left over
- ○ 3 apples left over
- ○ 4 apples left over

4. Tina has 14 bananas. She puts 3 in each basket. How many baskets does she need?

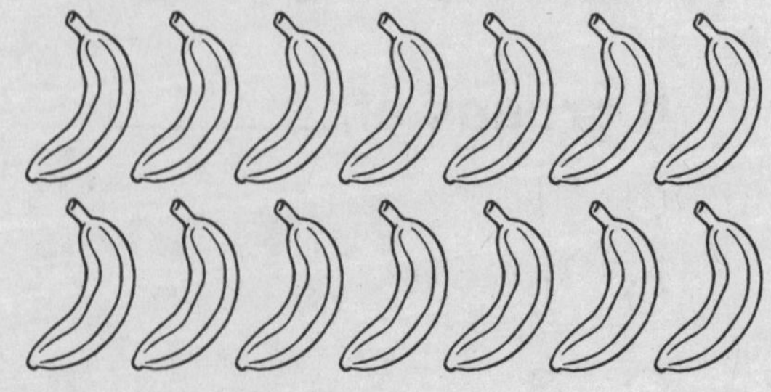

- ○ 2 baskets
- ○ 3 baskets
- ○ 4 baskets
- ○ 5 baskets

Name _______________________

Writing Division Sentences

Fill in the ○ for the correct answer.

Show the division sentence.

1.

○　$16 \div 4 = 4$

○　$12 \div 3 = 4$

○　$15 \div 3 = 5$

○　$12 \div 6 = 2$

2.

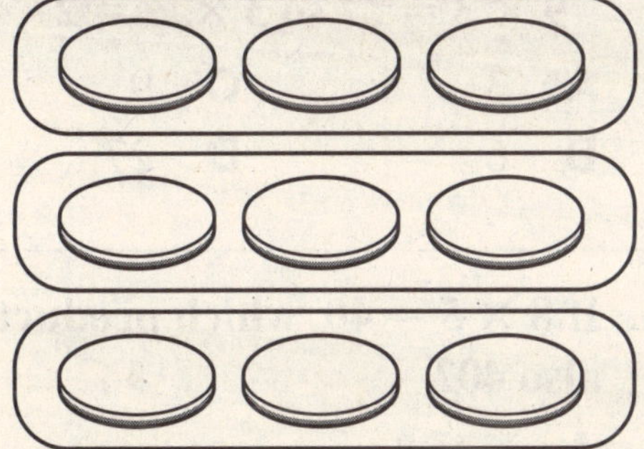

○　$9 \div 3 = 3$

○　$6 \div 2 = 3$

○　$18 \div 3 = 6$

○　$12 \div 3 = 4$

3.

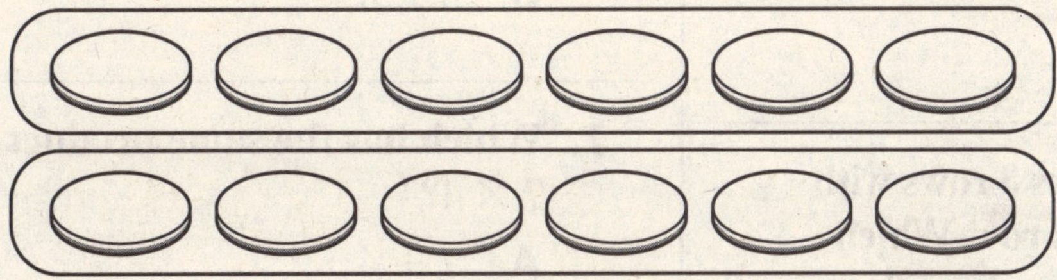

$12 \div 2 = 6$	$12 \div 4 = 3$	$6 \div 2 = 3$	$10 \div 2 = 5$
○	○	○	○

Name ___________________

Using Arrays

Circle the correct letter for the answer.

---

1. Which multiplication sentence
   describes the array?

   A $6 \times 4 = 24$
   B $6 \times 8 = 48$
   C $8 \times 3 = 24$
   D $8 \times 4 = 32$

---

2. There are 6 rows of students with
   5 students in each row. Which
   shows the number of students
   in all?

   A $6 + 5 = 11$
   B $6 \times 6 = 36$
   C $6 \times 5 = 30$
   D $5 \times 5 = 25$

---

3. A game board has 8 rows with
   8 squares in each row. Which
   shows the total number of squares?

   A $4 \times 8 = 32$
   B $8 \times 8 = 64$
   C $4 \times 4 = 16$
   D $2 \times 8 = 16$

---

4. Your garden has 2 rows of tomato
   plants and 2 rows of bean plants.
   There are 5 plants in each row.
   How many plants are in the
   garden?

   A 10 plants
   B 15 plants
   C 20 plants
   D 25 plants

---

5. What number is missing?

   $9 \times 3 = 27$ so $3 \times \blacksquare = 27$

   A 3   **C** 9
   B 6   **D** 27

---

6. If $8 \times 5 = 40$, which product is
   also 40?

   A 6×8
   B 5×8
   C 5×5
   D 8×8

---

7. Which has the same product as
   7×4?

   A $7 \div 4$
   B $4 \div 7$
   C $4 + 7$
   D 4×7

Name _______________________________________

Writing Multiplication Stories

Circle the correct letter for the answer.

Which number sentence solves the multiplication story?

1. Murray buys 3 boxes of pencils. There are 8 pencils in each box. How many pencils does he buy in all?

  A $8 \times 2 = 16$ **C** $4 \times 8 = 32$

  B $3 + 8 = 11$ **D** $3 \times 8 = 24$

---

2. There are 4 rows of desks in our classroom. If each row has 6 desks, how many desks are in our classroom?

  A $5 \times 6 = 30$ **C** $4 \times 5 = 20$

  B $4 \times 6 = 24$ **D** $6 \times 3 = 18$

---

3. Eight boys each carried 2 books. How many books did they carry altogether?

  A $8 + 2 = 10$ **C** $8 \times 2 = 16$

  B $2 \times 7 = 14$ **D** $8 + 2 = 10$

---

4. Eva drew an array of 5 rows of dots with 3 dots in each row. How many total dots did she draw?

  A $2 \times 5 = 10$ **C** $3 + 5 = 8$

  B $5 \times 4 = 20$ **D** $5 \times 3 = 15$

---

5. Corey has 3 dimes in his pocket. How many cents does he have?

  A $3 \times 10 = 30$ **C** $3 + 10 = 13$

  B $3 \times 5 = 15$ **D** $3 \times 9 = 27$

---

6. There are 27 children in the park. They are playing in groups of 3. How many children are in each group?

  A $3 \times 8 = 24$ **C** $3 + 27 = 30$

  B $3 \times 7 = 21$ **D** $3 \times 9 = 27$

---

7. If there are 25 bananas altogether, how many bananas are in each group of 5?

  A $5 + 25 = 30$ **C** $5 \times 5 = 25$

  B $5 + 3 = 8$ **D** $5 \times 4 = 20$

---

8. Jessie has 6 friends over after school. He gives each friend 10 raisins. How many raisins did Jessie give altogether?

  A $6 + 10 = 16$ **C** $6 \times 10 = 60$

  B $6 \times 5 = 30$ **D** $6 \times 4 = 20$

Name _______________________

Multiplying by 2

Circle the correct letter for the answer.

1. The seats in a minibus are arranged in rows. There are 5 rows with 2 seats in each row. How many seats are there altogether?

  A 8 seats

  B 10 seats

  C 12 seats

  D 14 seats

2. Which means the same as $2 + 2 + 2 + 2$?

  A 1×2 **C** 3×2

  B 2×2 **D** 4×2

3. $\begin{array}{r} 2 \\ \times\, 8 \\ \hline \end{array}$

  A 10   **C** 14

  B 12   **D** 16

4. Makena bought 6 packages of erasers. Each package had 2 erasers. How many erasers did Makena buy?

  A 12 erasers   **C** 16 erasers

  B 14 erasers   **D** 18 erasers

5. The solution to Denny's problem is 18. Which problem did he NOT solve?

  A 9×2 **C** 9×9

  B $9 + 9$ **D** 2×9

6. $2 \times 6 =$

  A 10   **C** 14

  B 12   **D** 16

7. Each of 7 friends is wearing 2 rings. How many rings do the friends have altogether?

  A 7 rings   **C** 12 rings

  B 10 rings   **D** 14 rings

8. $\begin{array}{r} 2 \\ \times\, 3 \\ \hline \end{array}$

  A 5

  B 6

  C 7

  D 8

Name ___________________________

Multiplying by 5

Circle the correct letter for the answer.

1. $6 \times 5 =$
   - **A** 1
   - **B** 30
   - **C** 25
   - **D** 35

2. Which has the same product as 9×5?
   - **A** $9 \div 5$
   - **B** $5 \div 9$
   - **C** $5 + 9$
   - **D** 5×9

3. Jen has 5 pennies. Tara has 3 times as many pennies as Jen. How much money does Tara have?
   - **A** 3¢
   - **B** 8¢
   - **C** 15¢
   - **D** 53¢

4.   5
   $\times$ 5
   - **A** 20
   - **B** 25
   - **C** 30
   - **D** 35

5. Jeremy has 7 nickels, 2 dimes, and 8 pennies. How much money does Jeremy have in nickels?
   - **A** 10¢
   - **B** 15¢
   - **C** 20¢
   - **D** 35¢

6. $5 \times 8 =$
   - **A** 30
   - **B** 35
   - **C** 40
   - **D** 45

7. Mr. Hanson's class has 4 tables. Each table has 5 students. How many students are in Mr. Hanson's class?
   - **A** 9 students
   - **B** 15 students
   - **C** 20 students
   - **D** 25 students

8. Liza has 4 dolls. Each doll has 5 outfits. How many doll outfits does Liza have?
   - **A** 20 outfits
   - **B** 25 outfits
   - **C** 30 outfits
   - **D** 35 outfits

Name ___________________________

Multiplying by 10

Circle the correct letter for the answer.

1. 10
   × 9

   A 9   **C** 99
   B 90   **D** 900

2. There are 6 tables in the cafeteria. There are 10 students sitting at each table. How many students are sitting at the tables in all?

   A 6 students
   B 16 students
   C 60 students
   D 66 students

3. Rollo cooked 3 packages of hot dogs. There were 10 hot dogs in each package. How many hot dogs did Rollo cook?

   A 3 hot dogs
   B 13 hot dogs
   C 30 hot dogs
   D 33 hot dogs

4. $1 \times 10 =$

   A 1
   B 10
   C 11
   D 100

5. Which means the same as 2×10?

   A $2 + 10$ **C** 10×10
   B $10 \div 2$ **D** $10 + 10$

6. There are 10 turquoise stones in one bracelet. How many turquoise stones are in 8 bracelets?

   A 16 stones   **C** 80 stones
   B 18 stones   **D** 800 stones

7. Lou has 5 dimes. How much money does Lou have?

   A 5¢   **C** 25¢
   B 15¢   **D** 50¢

8. The parking lot has 10 rows. Each row has 10 spaces. How many cars can park in the parking lot?

   A 20 cars
   B 100 cars
   C 110 cars
   D 1,000 cars

Name ___________________________

Multiplying by 1 or 0

Circle the correct letter for the answer.

1. A set of tools has 7 screwdrivers.
Moesha bought 1 tool set. How
many screwdrivers did she buy?

A 1 screwdriver

B 7 screwdrivers

C 8 screwdrivers

D 70 screwdrivers

2. $6 \times 0 =$

A 6   **C** 1

B 5   **D** 0

3. Yoko saw 5 birds' nests. Each nest
had 0 eggs. How many eggs did
Yoko see in the nests?

A 0 eggs   **C** 6 eggs

B 5 eggs   **D** 50 eggs

4. 8
  $\times 1$

A 0   **C** 8

B 1   **D** 9

5. Megan bought 3 notebooks. Each
notebook cost $1. How much
money did Megan spend on
notebooks?

A $3   **C** $8

B $5   **D** $15

6. $9 \times 0 =$

A 0   **C** 9

B 1   **D** 90

7. A package of bubble gum comes
with 4 sports cards. Jason bought
1 package of bubble gum. How
many sports cards did he get?

A 1 sports card

B 2 sports cards

C 3 sports cards

D 4 sports cards

8. $1 \times 0 =$

A 0   **C** 9

B 1   **D** 10

Name ____

Multiplying by 9

Circle the correct letter for the answer.

1. 9
 $\times 8$

  A 45

  B 54

  C 63

  D 72

2. Anne picked 7 boxes of lemons. She put 9 lemons in each box. How many lemons did Anne pick?

  A 45 lemons   **C** 56 lemons

  B 54 lemons   **D** 63 lemons

3. A train stops 9 times during a run. The train makes 9 of these runs each day. How many stops does the train make each day?

  A 99 stops   **C** 72 stops

  B 18 stops   **D** 81 stops

4. $5 \times 9 =$

  A 14

  B 45

  C 48

  D 59

5. Kathy's brother has 3 pennies. Kathy has 9 times as many pennies as her brother. How much money does Kathy have?

  A 27¢

  B 20¢

  C 18¢

  D 9¢

6. There are 4 lines at the bank. There are 9 people in each line. How many people are waiting in the lines?

  A 6 people   **C** 36 people

  B 28 people   **D** 45 people

7. $2 \times 9 =$

  A 18   **C** 24

  B 21   **D** 27

8. What number belongs in the box to make this number sentence true?

$0 \times 9 = \square$

  A 0   **C** 9

  B 1   **D** 90

Practicing Multiplication Facts

Circle the correct letter for the answer.

1. $5 \times 9 =$

  A 40   **C** 50

  B 45   **D** 54

2.   7
  $\times\,4$

  A 35   **C** 28

  B 32   **D** 21

3. $6 \times 8 =$

  A 48   **C** 42

  B 40   **D** 56

4.   5
  $\times\,2$

  A 5   **C** 11

  B 7   **D** 10

5. $3 \times 4 =$

  A 15   **C** 12

  B 20   **D** 10

6. Which number sentence is shown?

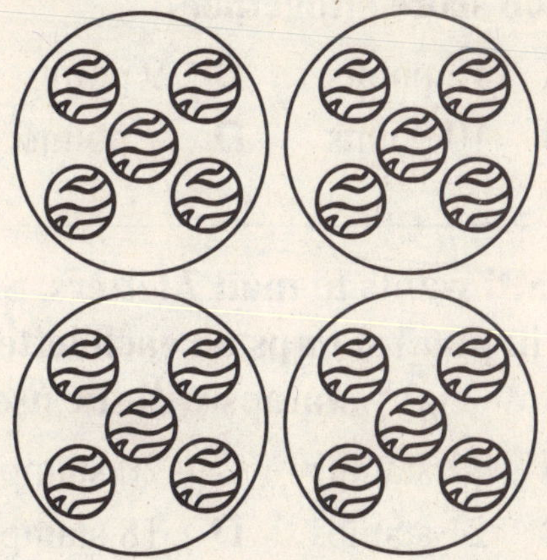

  A $5 \times 5 = 25$ **C** $4 \times 5 = 20$

  B $3 \times 5 = 15$ **D** $4 \times 4 = 16$

7. George has a rock collection. He arranges the rocks in rows of 9 with 7 rocks in each row. How many rocks does he have altogether?

  A 63   **C** 56

  B 54   **D** 60

8. Maria has a stamp collection. She puts 9 stamps on each page in her stamp album. The album has 10 pages. How many stamps can she put in the album altogether?

  A 72   **C** 80

  B 90   **D** 100

Multiplying by 3

Circle the correct letter for the answer.

1. Bob scored three points in each of four games. How many points did Bob score altogether?

A 12 points   **C** 9 points
B 10 points   **D** 7 points

2. Patti wants to mail 7 letters. She will put 3 stamps on each letter. How many stamps will she use?

A 22 stamps   **C** 20 stamps
B 21 stamps   **D** 18 stamps

3. $5 \times 3 =$

A 14   **C** 15
B 18   **D** 24

4. Which three numbers come next in the pattern?
9, 12, 15, ___, ___, ___

A 16, 17, 18
B 17, 19, 21
C 18, 21, 24
D 20, 25, 30

5.
$$\begin{array}{r} 3 \\ \times\,9 \\ \hline \end{array}$$

A 27   **C** 12
B 24   **D** 7

6. Which number sentence describes this picture?

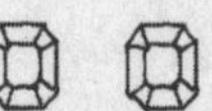 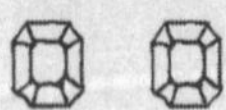 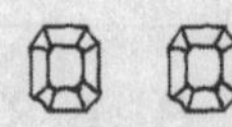 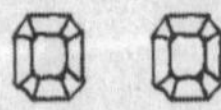

A $3 \times 2 = 6$
B $3 \times 6 = 18$
C $6 \times 6 = 36$
D $3 \times 3 = 9$

7. A playground has 3 sets of swings. There are 3 swings in each set. How many swings are there all together?

A 18 swings
B 15 swings
C 9 swings
D 6 swings

Name ____

Multiplying by 4

Circle the correct letter for the answer.

1. $\begin{array}{r} 4 \\ \times\, 9 \\ \hline \end{array}$

    A 36   **C** 24
    B 32   **D** 20

2. Groups of 4 students work together in math class. There are 5 groups. How many students are there in all?

    A 9 students
    B 16 students
    C 20 students
    D 45 students

3. $7 \times 4 =$

    A 16   **C** 20
    B 18   **D** 28

4. There are 4 people in the Smith family. Each person reads 4 books per month. How many books does the family read in one month?

    A 8 books
    B 16 books
    C 24 books
    D 30 books

5. Each table in the school library has space for 4 students. There are 8 tables in all. If all the tables are full, how many students are sitting at the tables?

    A 12 students
    B 28 students
    C 30 students
    D 32 students

6. Mary made 3 bracelets. She used 4 gold beads in each bracelet. Which number sentence tells how many gold beads Mary used in all?

    A $2 \times 4 = 8$
    B $3 \times 3 = 9$
    C $3 \times 4 = 12$
    D $4 \times 4 = 16$

7. $\begin{array}{r} 4 \\ \times\, 6 \\ \hline \end{array}$

    A 10   **C** 24
    B 18   **D** 30

253

Name ____

Multiplying by 6 or 7

Circle the correct letter for the answer.

1. Bree bought 7 boxes of granola bars for her class party. There were 6 bars in each box. Which number sentence tells how many granola bars Bree bought in all?

   A $7 + 6 = 13$

   B $6 \times 6 = 36$

   C $7 \times 6 = 42$

   D $56 \div 7 = 6$

2. $\begin{array}{r} 7 \\ \times\, 4 \\ \hline \end{array}$

   A 21   **C** 28

   B 20   **D** 24

3. $6 \times 6 =$

   A 12   **C** 42

   B 30   **D** 36

4. There are 7 markers in a package. How many markers are in 2 packages?

   A 6 markers   **C** 14 markers

   B 8 markers   **D** 16 markers

5. It costs $6 per night to camp in Guadalupe Mountains National Park. How much will it cost to camp for 5 nights?

   A $30   **C** $24

   B $35   **D** $40

6. Which means the same as $6 + 6 + 6$?

   A 1×6 **C** 3×6

   B 2×6 **D** 4×6

7. Tyrone has a rock collection. His rocks are arranged in 3 rows. There are 7 rocks in each row. How many rocks does Tyrone have?

   A 9 rocks   **C** 27 rocks

   B 21 rocks   **D** 18 rocks

8. $6 \times \$8 =$

   A $40   **C** $56

   B $42   **D** $48

Multiplying by 8

Circle the correct letter for the answer.

---

1. Each pair of roller skates has 8 wheels. How many wheels are there on 9 pairs of roller skates?

9 × 

A	36 wheels	**C**	72 wheels
B	54 wheels	**D**	81 wheels

---

2. 7 × 8 =

A	15	**C**	56
B	48	**D**	78

---

3. An octopus has 8 arms. How many arms do 4 octopuses have?

A	24 arms	**C**	36 arms
B	32 arms	**D**	48 arms

---

4. 0 × 8 =

A 0
B 1
C 8
D 80

---

5. Which has the same product as 6 × 8?

A	6 + 8	**C**	6 ÷ 8
B	8 × 6	**D**	8 ÷ 6

---

6. One table seats 8 people. How many people can sit at 3 tables?

A	24 people	**C**	36 people
B	28 people	**D**	83 people

---

7. 2
  × 8
  ―――

A	4	**C**	16
B	10	**D**	19

---

8. Craig filled 8 punch bowls with fruit punch. Each bowl holds 8 quarts. How many quarts of fruit punch does Craig have?

A 56 quarts
B 64 quarts
C 72 quarts
D 81 quarts

255

Practicing Multiplication Facts

Circle the correct letter for the answer.

1. $7 \times 7 =$

  A 42   **C** 56

  B 49   **D** 63

2.
$$\begin{array}{r} 6 \\ \times\,8 \\ \hline \end{array}$$

  A 56   **C** 24

  B 32   **D** 48

3. Which has the same product as 7×9?

  A 7×8

  B 9×7

  C 6×9

  D 9×6

4. Ramon has 5 spiders in a jar. Each spider has 8 legs. What is the total number of spider legs in the jar?

  A 40   **C** 50

  B 45   **D** 35

5. $9 \times 0 =$

  A 10   **C** 0

  B 1   **D** 9

6.
$$\begin{array}{r} 4 \\ \times\,8 \\ \hline \end{array}$$

  A 24   **C** 36

  B 40   **D** 32

7. Which fact do you double to solve 8×7?

  A 4×8

  B 3×7

  C 4×7

  D 8×3

8. Art uses 2s facts and 5s facts to find 7×6. If one of the facts he uses is 2×6, what is the other fact he should add to it?

  A 5×6

  B 5×7

  C 4×6

  D 2×6

Using Multiplication to Compare

Circle the correct letter for the answer.

---

1. Silvia has 5 times as many apples as Pepe. Pepe has 8 apples. Which number sentence shows how to find how many apples Silvia has?

A $5 \times 7 = 35$

B $5 + 8 = 13$

C $5 \times 8 = 40$

D $8 \times 4 = 32$

---

2. Rita has 4 times as many balloons as Robert. Robert has 9 balloons. How many balloons does Rita have?

A 32 balloons

B 13 balloons

C 27 balloons

D 36 balloons

---

3. Raul is 3 times older than his brother. If his brother is 7 years old, how old is Raul?

A 12 years old

B 10 years old

C 21 years old

D 18 years old

---

4. Which number is 9 times more than 5?

A 27   **C** 36

B 45   **D** 32

---

5. Ms. Brown wants to double her recipe for pizza. If the recipe says to use 3 cups of flour, how many cups should Ms. Brown use?

A 3 cups

B 9 cups

C 4 cups

D 6 cups

---

6. A baby has 4 teeth. Her sister has 3 times as many teeth. How many teeth does her sister have?

A 7 teeth

B 8 teeth

C 12 teeth

D 15 teeth

Patterns on a Multiplication Table

Circle the correct letter for the answer.

1. If you knew $4 \times 5 = 20$, which
   number sentence could you use to
   find the answer to 5×5?

   A $20 + 4 = 24$

   B $25 + 5 = 30$

   C $20 + 6 = 26$

   D $20 + 5 = 25$

2. $4 \times 12 =$

   A 44   **C** 40

   B 48   **D** 36

3. All the products for 5s end in one
   of these 2 numbers.

   A 5 and 6

   B 0 and 5

   C 4 and 5

   D 1 and 5

4.   5
   $\times\,7$

   A 35   **C** 28

   B 32   **D** 22

5. Jerry bought 3 bags of 7 apples.
   How many apples did he buy?

   A 18 apples

   B 21 apples

   C 28 apples

   D 33 apples

6. $8 \times$ _______ $= 40$

   A 4   **C** 8

   B 5   **D** 6

7. If you know that $4 \times 9 = 36$,
   which number sentence would
   help you to find the answer to
   5×9?

   A $36 + 4 = 40$

   B $36 + 9 = 45$

   C $36 + 8 = 44$

   D $36 + 9 = 44$

8. Catie bought 2 bags of 10 marbles
   for $0.35 each. How many
   marbles did she buy?

   A 20 marbles

   B 35 marbles

   C 30 marbles

   D 15 marbles

Name _______________________________________

Multiplying Three Numbers

Circle the correct letter for the answer.

1. $6 \times 0 \times 9$

A 0   C 54

B 15   D 90

2. What number belongs in the box to make this number sentence true?

$2 \times \square \times 2 = 16$

A 2   C 6

B 4   D 8

3. Mrs. Wong has 3 children. She gave each of them 2 sandwiches. On each sandwich, she put 2 slices of cheese. How many slices of cheese did Mrs. Wong use in all?

A 6 slices   C 12 slices

B 8 slices   D 16 slices

4. $(4 \times 2) \times 7$

A 8

B 14

C 42

D 56

5. It takes John 5 minutes to brush his teeth. He brushes twice every day. How many minutes does he brush his teeth in 4 days?

A 10 minutes

B 20 minutes

C 30 minutes

D 40 minutes

6. Which has the same product as 9×6?

A $3 \times 3 \times 6$

B $3 \times 2 \times 6$

C $3 \times 3 \times 3$

D $3 \times 4 \times 5$

7. Eight friends each have a pair of roller skates. Each skate has 4 wheels. How many wheels are there in all?

A 8 wheels

B 32 wheels

C 64 wheels

D 72 wheels

Input/Output Tables

Circle the correct letter for the answer.

1. Which number completes
this table?
Rule: Multiply by 4.

Input	Output
4	16
5	20
6	
7	28

A 21
B 22
C 24
D 25

2. The rule for a table is add 9. If an
input is 22, what is the output?

A 41
B 13
C 31
D 29

3. What is the rule for this table?

In	2	3	4	5	6
Out	6	9	12	15	18

A Add 4.
B Multiply by 4.
C Multiply by 3.
D Add 6.

4. Which number completes
this table?

In	20	16		10	5
Out	18	14	11	8	3

A 12
B 15
C 14
D 13

5. What is the rule for this table?

Input	Output
2	0
4	0
6	0
8	0
10	0

A Add 2.
B Subtract 2.
C Add 0.
D Multiply by 0.

6. The rule for a table is multiply
by 2. If an input is 2, what is
the output?

A 2
B 3
C 4
D 6

Name ___________________

Division as Sharing

Fill in the ○ for the correct answer.

I. Ed has 14 eggs. He puts an equal number of eggs in 2 baskets. How many eggs are in each basket?

  ○ 4   ○ 7
  ○ 6   ○ 8

2. Ann, Phil, and Jan have 12 apples. If they each get an equal number of apples, how many will each person get?

  ○ 3   ○ 5
  ○ 4   ○ 6

3. Four friends shared 16 cherries equally. How many cherries did each friend get?

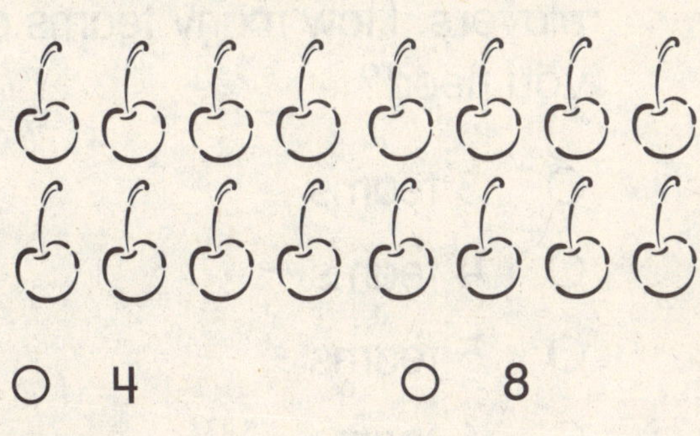

  ○ 4   ○ 8
  ○ 6   ○ 9

4. Five friends read 15 books. They each read the same number of books. How many books did each friend read?

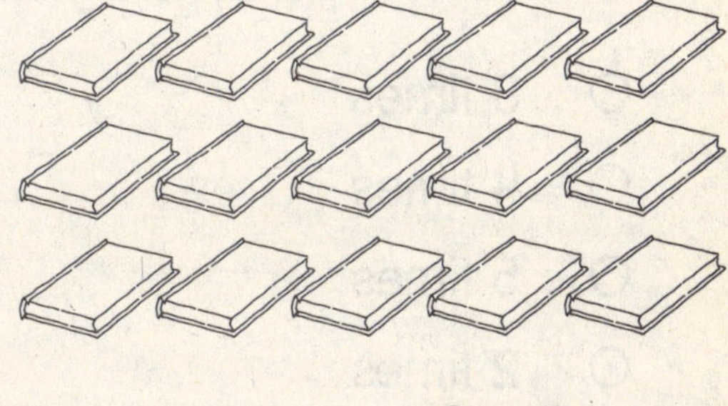

  ○ 1   ○ 3
  ○ 2   ○ 5

Name ________________________

Division as Repeated Subtraction

Fill in the ○ for the correct answer.

1. Gene has 6 apples. He put the same number of apples in each basket. He put 3 apples in each basket. How many baskets did he have?

○ 2 baskets

○ 3 baskets

○ 4 baskets

○ 5 baskets

2. Alan bought 9 tomatoes. Each bag has 3 tomatoes. How many bags of tomatoes did he buy?

○ 6 bags

○ 4 bags

○ 3 bags

○ 5 bags

3. Sara has 8 quarters to play a game. She needs 2 quarters for each game. How many times can she play the game?

○ 3 times

○ 4 times

○ 5 times

○ 2 times

4. Sixteen players are needed for a game. Each team has 4 players. How many teams do you need?

○ 3 teams

○ 4 teams

○ 5 teams

○ 6 teams

Name ____________________

Writing Division Stories

Circle the correct letter for the answer.

1. Marla has 40 beads. She shares them equally with her 8 friends. Which division sentence shows the story?

   A $40 \div 5 = 8$ **C** $40 \div 8 = 5$

   B $40 \div 8 = 8$ **D** $40 \times 8 = 320$

2. Which picture shows the story? Cleo has 15 granola bars. She shares them with 5 friends. How many granola bars will each friend get?

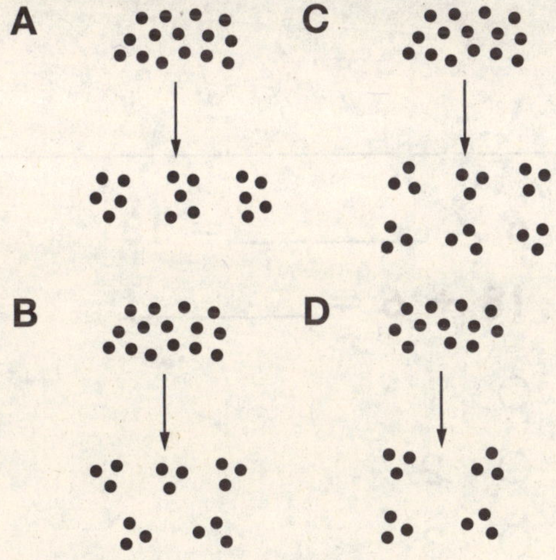

3. 48 eggs are put in boxes. 12 eggs are in each box. How many boxes are needed?

   A 12 boxes   **C** 3 boxes

   B 5 boxes   **D** 4 boxes

4. 45 flowers are picked. 5 flowers are put in each pot. How many pots are needed?

   A 9 pots   **C** 5 pots

   B 11 pots **D** 8 pots

5. $80 is divided among 10 people. How much money will each person get?

   A $10   **C** $8

   B $6   **D** $7

6. Leon has 55 books. He puts 5 books on each of his shelves. How many shelves will he need for all the books?

   A 11 shelves   **C** 10 shelves

   B 12 shelves   **D** 5 shelves

7. 24 ribbons are divided into 4 equal groups. How many ribbons are in each group?

   A 4 ribbons   **C** 2 ribbons

   B 12 ribbons   **D** 6 ribbons

Name _______________________

Relating Multiplication and Division

Fill in the ○ for the correct answer.

Find the missing number.

1. $4 \times$ _______ $= 12$

$12 \div 4 =$ _______

- ○ 3
- ○ 4
- ○ 5
- ○ 6

2. $5 \times$ _______ $= 10$

$10 \div 5 =$ _______

- ○ 1
- ○ 2
- ○ 5
- ○ 3

3. $3 \times$ _______ $= 9$

$9 \div 3 =$ _______

- ○ 2
- ○ 3
- ○ 4
- ○ 5

4. $6 \times$ _______ $= 18$

$18 \div 6 =$ _______

- ○ 1
- ○ 2
- ○ 3
- ○ 4

Name ___________________________

Dividing by 2 and 5

Circle the correct letter for the answer.

1. If $8 \times 2 = 16$, then what is $16 \div 2$?

A 14 **C** 10

B 2 **D** 8

2. The Sports Area sells tennis balls for $2 per can. How many cans of tennis balls will cost $18?

A 20 cans

B 16 cans

C 9 cans

D 5 cans

3. $10 \div 5 =$

A 5 **C** 3

B 2 **D** 10

4. There are 12 eggs. They are put into 2 baskets. How many eggs are in each basket?

A 5 eggs **C** 24 eggs

B 6 eggs **D** 14 eggs

5. $45 \div 5 =$

A 5 **C** 8

B 7 **D** 9

6. Rosa sold 15 garlic bagels. Each customer bought 3 garlic bagels. How many customers bought garlic bagels?

A 3 customers

B 6 customers

C 5 customers

D 30 customers

7. The 20 dancers lined up in rows. There were 5 dancers in each row. How many rows of dancers were there?

A 5 rows **C** 20 rows

B 4 rows **D** 10 rows

8. $4 \div 2 =$

A 2 **C** 8

B 4 **D** 6

Dividing by 3 and 4

Circle the correct letter for the answer.

1. $21 \div 3 =$

   A 5 C 8
   B 6 D 7

2. There were 20 pioneers. They rode west in 4 wagons. Each wagon had the same number of people. How many pioneers were in each wagon?

   A 4 pioneers C 10 pioneers
   B 5 pioneers D 8 pioneers

3. What number belongs in the box to make this number sentence true?

   $12 \div 3 = \square$

   A 3 C 9
   B 4 D 15

4. Tammy has 24 beads for necklaces. Each necklace uses 4 beads. How many necklaces can she make?

   A 4 necklaces C 6 necklaces
   B 12 necklaces D 3 necklaces

5. Juan has 18 stickers. He put 3 stickers on each of his notebooks. Which number sentence tells how many notebooks Juan has?

   A $18 + 3 = 21$
   B $18 \div 3 = 6$
   C $18 - 3 = 15$
   D $3 + 3 = 6$

6. An orchestra has 32 musicians. They are seated in 4 equal rows. How many musicians are in each row?

   A 6 musicians C 9 musicians
   B 7 musicians D 8 musicians

7. $16 \div 4 =$

   A 2 C 4
   B 6 D 3

8. Find the number that makes both number sentences true.

$3 \times \square = 15$	$15 \div 3 = \square$

   A 4 C 6
   B 5 D 7

Dividing by 2 Through 5

Circle the correct letter for the answer.

1. Lynette put 36 pennies into 9 equal stacks. How many pennies were in each stack?

   A 4 pennies   **C** 7 pennies
   B 6 pennies   **D** 9 pennies

2. $28 \div 4 =$

   A 4   **C** 7
   B 6   **D** 9

3. What multiplication fact will help you find $40 \div 8$?

   A $4 \times 8 = 32$ **C** $5 \times 8 = 40$
   B $4 \times 10 = 40$ **D** $1 \times 40 = 40$

4. Josh has 30 cards. He wants to make groups of 5 cards each. How many groups will he make?

   A 4 groups   **C** 6 groups
   B 5 groups   **D** 7 groups

5. There are 28 cans lined up in rows. If there are 4 cans in each row, how many rows of cans are there?

   A 8 rows   **C** 5 rows
   B 7 rows   **D** 4 rows

6. What multiplication fact will help you find $16 \div 4$?

   A $4 \times 4 = 16$ **C** $32 \div 2 = 16$
   B $7 \times 2 = 14$ **D** $2 \times 9 = 18$

7. Curt has 20 stamps. He wants to put 5 stamps on each page of his album. How many pages will it take?

   A 8 pages   **C** 6 pages
   B 7 pages   **D** 4 pages

8. $3\overline{)24}$

   A 7   **C** 8
   B 12   **D** 6

Dividing by 6 and 7

Circle the correct letter for the answer.

1. Kathy has 36 packages. On each trip to her car, she can carry 6 packages. How many trips to her car will she need to make to load all the packages?

    A 4 trips   **C** 9 trips
    B 6 trips   **D** 8 trips

2. $7\overline{)35}$

    A 6   **C** 9
    B 7   **D** 5

3. Mica needs 21 bags of microwave popcorn. There are 7 bags of popcorn in a box. How many boxes of popcorn does Mica need to buy?

    A 1 box   **C** 3 boxes
    B 7 boxes   **D** 14 boxes

4. Which of these belongs to the same fact family as $12 \div 6 = 2$?

    A $6 - 2 = 4$ **C** $6 + 2 = 8$
    B $2 \times 6 = 12$ **D** $6 \div 2 = 3$

5. Angelo's family spent $24 on admissions to the Natural Bridge Caverns. Admission costs $6 for each person. How many people are in Angelo's family?

    A 35 people   **C** 3 people
    B 5 people   **D** 4 people

6. There are 56 fish in a pet store. An equal number of fish are kept in each of the 7 aquariums. How many fish are in each aquarium?

    A 8 fish   **C** 9 fish
    B 7 fish   **D** 6 fish

7. $54 \div 6 =$

    A 5   **C** 8
    B 6   **D** 9

8. $7\overline{)49}$

    A 8   **C** 5
    B 7   **D** 6

Name ____

Dividing by 8 and 9

Circle the correct letter for the answer.

1. In a theater, there are 8 seats in each row. How many rows are needed to seat 40 children?

   A 4 rows   **C** 8 rows

   B 5 rows   **D** 6 rows

2. There are 36 different puppets in a show. Each puppeteer uses 9 different puppets. How many puppeteers are needed for the show?

   A 4 puppeteers

   B 6 puppeteers

   C 7 puppeteers

   D 8 puppeteers

3. $9\overline{)72}$

   A 6   **C** 9

   B 7   **D** 8

4. Carlos has 16 photos. He plans to put an equal number of photos into each of 8 frames. How many photos will he put in each frame?

   A 2 photos   **C** 8 photos

   B 4 photos   **D** 6 photos

5. Beatrix has 45 paintings to display at an art gallery. She puts an equal number of paintings on each of 9 walls. How many paintings are on each wall?

   A 2 paintings

   B 4 paintings

   C 5 paintings

   D 8 paintings

6. $64 \div 8 =$

   A 6   **C** 9

   B 7   **D** 8

7. $8\overline{)8}$

   A 1   **C** 64

   B 8   **D** 16

8. Mr. Cho bought 54 flowers in 9 different colors. He bought the same number of each color flower. Which number sentence tells how many red flowers he bought?

   A $54 + 9 = 63$

   B $54 \div 9 = 6$

   C $54 - 9 = 45$

   D $9 \times 6 = 54$

Dividing by 6 Through 9

Circle the correct letter for the answer.

1. There are 24 children at the beach. They are playing in 6 groups. If each group has the same number of children, how many are in each group?

   A 5 children   **C** 3 children
   B 4 children   **D** 2 children

2. $54 \div 9 =$

   A 4   **C** 7
   B 6   **D** 9

3. If $3 \times 9 = 27$, then what is $27 \div 9$?

   A 3   **C** 5
   B 4   **D** 9

4. There are 56 buttons in the jar. Akemi sorts the buttons into groups of 8. How many buttons are in each group?

   A 5 buttons   **C** 7 buttons
   B 6 buttons   **D** 9 buttons

5. There are 63 students in the marching band. They march in rows of 7. How many rows of students are there?

   A 5 rows   **C** 8 rows
   B 6 rows   **D** 9 rows

6. What multiplication fact could you use to find $48 \div 6$?

   A $6 \times 8 = 48$ **C** $5 \times 9 = 45$
   B $6 \times 7 = 42$ **D** $9 \times 6 = 54$

7. Greg scored 24 goals in 8 games. If he scored the same number of goals in each game, how many goals did he score in each game?

   A 2 goals   **C** 4 goals
   B 3 goals   **D** 6 goals

8. $9\overline{)81}$

   A 7   **C** 9
   B 8   **D** 11

Name ____

0 and 1 in Division

Circle the correct letter for the answer.

1. $9 \div 1 =$

  A 0   **C** 9

  B 8   **D** 10

2. Sandra eats 8 ounces of yogurt. She eats 0 grams of fat. Which number sentence tells how many grams of fat are in each ounce of yogurt?

  A $0 \div 8 = 0$

  B $8 \div 1 = 8$

  C $8 \div 8 = 1$

  D $8 \times 8 = 81$

3. $0 \div 4 =$

  A 0   **C** 4

  B 1   **D** 40

4. The Mule Ear Peaks trail in Big Bend National Park is 4 miles long. It takes about 4 hours to hike. If Ayo hikes at the same pace, about how many miles will he hike each hour?

  A 0 miles   **C** 4 miles

  B 1 mile   **D** 16 miles

5. Mrs. Orinda handed out 5 robes to the new singers in the choir. Each singer got 1 robe. How many new singers are in the choir?

  A 0 new singers

  B 1 new singer

  C 4 new singers

  D 5 new singers

6. $7 \overline{)7}$

  A 0   **C** 7

  B 1   **D** 49

7. Marissa has 4 subway tokens. She uses 1 token each time she rides the subway. How many times can Marissa ride the subway before she has to buy more tokens?

  A 0 times   **C** 4 times

  B 1 time   **D** 5 times

8. $1 \overline{)2}$

  A 0   **C** 2

  B 1   **D** 12

271

Dividing with Remainders

Circle the correct letter for the answer.

1. $15 \div 2 =$

  A 8 R2   **C** 6 R1

  B 7 R1   **D** 7 R5

2. $16 \div 3 =$

  A 5 R2   **C** 5 R1

  B 4 R2   **D** 7 R3

3. Fumiko baked 31 biscuits. She put 7 biscuits in each basket to serve to her guests. How many biscuits does she have left over?

  A 6 biscuits   **C** 7 biscuits

  B 4 biscuits   **D** 3 biscuits

4. $36 \div 8 =$

  A 4 R4   **C** 3 R6

  B 6 R4   **D** 4 R1

5. $34 \div 4 =$

  A 8 R3   **C** 6 R0

  B 8 R2   **D** 7 R5

6. Steve made 42 decorations. He put the same number of decorations into each of 5 bags. How many decorations did he put into each bag?

  A 5 decorations

  B 2 decorations

  C 8 decorations

  D 6 decorations

7. Jose's video games need 3 new batteries each. He bought 8 new batteries. How many video games can get new batteries?

  A 1 game   **C** 24 games

  B 2 games   **D** 3 games

8. Jamie has 31 shells. He puts them in 5 equal groups. How many shells does he have left over?

  A 1 shell   **C** 4 shells

  B 2 shells   **D** 3 shells

Division Patterns with 10, 11, and 12

Circle the correct letter for the answer.

1. Which of these numbers is a multiple of 10?

   A 36   **C** 20

   B 25   **D** 14

2. $36 \div 12 =$

   A 3   **C** 12

   B 4   **D** 0

3. $99 \div 11 =$

   A 10   **C** 8

   B 11   **D** 9

4. Jim needs 120 plates for a picnic. The plates are sold in packs of 12. How many packs are needed?

   A 4   **C** 12

   B 10   **D** 20

5. $10 \div 10 =$

   A 11   **C** 1

   B 10   **D** 0

6. Sam has 50 photos. He plans to put an equal number of photos onto each of 10 pages in his photo album. How many photos will he put on each page?

   A 5 photos   **C** 16 photos

   B 15 photos   **D** 20 photos

7. Which multiplication fact can you use to check $77 \div 11 = 7$?

   A $77 \times 1 = 77$ **C** $7 \times 11 = 77$

   B $11 \times 6 = 66$ **D** $7 \times 10 = 70$

8. Hidori has 96 marbles. He wants to put them into bags with 12 marbles in each bag. How many bags will he need?

   A 12 bags   **C** 11 bags

   B 9 bags   **D** 8 bags